CHRIST'S LORDSHIP AND RELIGIOUS PLURALISM

CHRIST'S LORDSHIP AND RELIGIOUS PLURALISM

*Edited by Gerald H. Anderson
and Thomas F. Stransky, C.S.P.*

ORBIS BOOKS
Maryknoll, New York 10545

Second Printing, November 1983

Library of Congress Cataloging in Publication Data
Main entry under title:

Christ's lordship and religious pluralism.

   Papers presented at a conference held at Union
Theological Seminary, Richmond, Va.
   Includes bibliographical references.
   1. Christianity and other religions—Congresses.
I. Anderson, Gerald H. II. Stransky, Thomas F.
BR127.C476   261.2   80-25406
ISBN 0-88344-088-1 (pbk.)

Contents

Foreword

In his concluding summary in this volume, Wilfred Cantwell Smith from Harvard University says that the conference that this volume represents "marks . . . a milestone in historical development. . . . Not long ago *this* sort of conference just would not have happened." Something is significantly new, not only about the reality and extent of religious pluralism in today's world, but also about the different ways by which Christians experience, interpret, and accept that fact.

Until recently it has not proven possible—at least in North America—to bring together representatives of the broad spectrum of present Christian thinking on the theme "Christ's Lordship and Religious Pluralism." Therefore this book pioneers, with both the strength and limitations of breaking new ground in company with colleagues who differ greatly about how the task should be done—while all attempt to be faithful to the Christ they profess as the ever active Lord. Here is a cross-section of Christian voices—theologians and church leaders, Roman Catholic, Orthodox, conservative evangelical and ecumenical Protestant, men and women, lay and ordained, with Third World representatives—who engage in open and candid discussion, "speaking the truth in love" (Eph. 4:15), about how God works both within and beyond explicit Christian communities. It is a book about mission, but also about dialogue, evangelism, service, and social justice in Christian witness. It deals with biblical perspectives, the history of Christian attitudes toward people of other faiths, and the development of theologies in the different contexts of religious pluralism. It is concerned with faithfulness to the whole gospel of Jesus Christ and to the whole church sent to proclaim that gospel to the whole world. Christians now at least agree that the relation of Christian faith to people of other faiths

vii

is an issue of such importance for the life and witness of the church that it must be addressed with fresh thinking and greater seriousness if the church is to be faithful to its task in the world. We see this discussion as part of a process—a moment of grace in that much longer and larger effort to understand and participate in what Krister Stendahl describes as "the mending of the Creation." But such discussion is only a moment, only a milestone, not a terminus. Neither participants nor readers will be fully satisfied with where we are in this pilgrimage. So it should be—yet press on we must.

Special appreciation is here expressed for the invitation and hospitality extended to this conference in October 1979 by Union Theological Seminary in Richmond, Virginia. From that faculty Donald G. Dawe and D. Cameron Murchison, Jr. gave able leadership in its planning and administration. At the seminary a very comprehensive bibliography was prepared for independent publication: *Christian Faith Amidst Religious Pluralism: An Introductory Bibliography,* edited by Martha B. Aycock, Donald G. Dawe, S. Eleanor Godfrey, and John B. Trotti.

In the opening session of this conference, the Roman Catholic Bishop of Richmond, Walter F. Sullivan, presided and set a tone of genuine Christian fraternity and fidelity for our discussion. This carried throughout the conference, to the closing panel discussion moderated by Philip Scharper, editor-in-chief of Orbis Books, and to Wilfred Cantwell Smith's summation. We trust that this tone is communicated in these pages as well, and that it will continue to mark our relationships as Christians, with the expectation "that we may be mutually encouraged by each other's faith" (Rom. 1:12).

Gerald H. Anderson
Thomas F. Stransky, C.S.P.

Introduction

Donald G. Dawe

One of the most difficult and crucial theological problems before the church today is understanding the Lordship of Jesus Christ over a world that is religiously plural. It is not simply that the Christian church is one religious community among others, with its own particular faith, cultus, and institutional forms. The problematic for the Christian is that he or she is committed to a very particular faith that claims universality for its vision of God and God's purposes in the world. This faith is summed up in that earliest and most universal of all Christian confessions: "Jesus Christ is Lord." The question that presses upon the Christian community is what faithfulness to that confession means in a world where the overwhelming majority of humankind lives by other faiths and ideologies.

As the confessional life of the church unfolded in the early centuries of its life, it became clear that Christians were not content simply to call Jesus their Lord, while leaving others to be the "lords" of different times and places. The kingdom of God, Christians believe, has broken into history through Jesus, so that his Lordship is coterminous with the Lordship of God himself. His Lordship demands the response of faith by all persons, so "that at the name of Jesus every knee should bow, in heaven and on earth and under the earth, and every tongue confess that Jesus Christ is Lord, to the glory of God the Father" (Phil. 2:10–11).

Born amid religious pluralism, the early church sought to actualize the Lordship of Christ by its missionary outreach to the ancient world of the Roman empire. Empowered by the Holy Spirit, missionaries preached the gospel of Jesus Christ, people were converted to faith in him as Savior and Lord, and in this faith they were baptized, leaving their ancestral faiths to embrace the life and teachings of the church. So great was the success of this mission that, by the fourth century, Christianity became the official religion of the empire. And by the ninth century, the tribes of northern and eastern Europe had been Christianized. A basic change had been made in the religious geography of humankind. The Western world had become Christian. No matter how spiritually and morally ambiguous, one fact predominates. The triumph of Christendom replaced the gods of Roman and European paganism with the worship of God, Father, Son and Holy Spirit. An indelible mark had been left on the mind of the Christian community. The Lordship of Christ had been made real by his triumph over the gods. The Lord (*kurios*) had become the Conqueror (*nike*), and with him the church had become triumphant over other religions. The triumph of Christianity was no longer thought to be purely eschatological. It had become an accomplished fact in human history.

During the Middle Ages, relatively little was known of other peoples and their religions. The Jews, the internal dissenters from the religious unity of Christendom, were ghettoized not only physically but spiritually. An anti-Semitic theology said that they could not even interpret their own Scriptures properly. Islam was perceived around the edges of Christian Europe as the enemy to be consigned to the sword not only as a political enemy but as the enemy of God. While there were brilliant exceptions in Raymond Lull, Nicholas of Cusa, and the early Dominican and Franciscan missionaries, a consensus dominated this time The full extent of Christian universality was believed to have been reached. The catholicity of the church, and with it the full extent of the Lordship of Christ, had become real because Christendom was now "co-terminous with the inhabited world" (*oikoumene*). Awareness of the religions of India, Africa, and China remained on the fringe of consciousness revealed by rare travelers' reports as only strange fantasies or crude superstitions.

With the beginning of the age of exploration and colonization in the sixteenth century, Christians came to a startling new awareness of the other religions of the world. First through trading relationships and then in the actual planting of colonies, Western Christians started to learn of Hinduism, Buddhism, Islam, Confucianism, and the tribal religions not merely as eccentricities, but as the ways in which millions of people shaped their lives and faith. By the end of the eighteenth century, Arabic, Sanskrit, and Chinese were being studied in European universities, and the riches of these cultures were being unfolded.

Religious pluralism was again on the agenda of the Christian community. This awareness of a vast world as yet untouched by Christian witness and faith came at a time when the life of Christendom was being renewed by pietism and repeated waves of revival. Out of this fruitful combination there emerged in the eighteenth century, the modern missionary movement. Its vision was that religious pluralism is temporary because Christianity will ultimately express its universality through the conversion of all people to its faith. The missionary call to conversion was to express the Lordship of Christ over religious pluralism.

By the middle of the nineteenth century, the vision of reaching the whole world for Christ by missionary outreach had developed its theological stance. By the preaching of the gospel and the spread of modern Western technology and education, the non-Christian religions would collapse by their own inner contradictions and be replaced by Christianity. Indeed, there was much evidence to support this view. In many places, Islam, Hinduism, and Buddhism were riddled by superstition and moral indifference. Their own reformers had long inveighed against them. The work of education, healing, and technological growth were to be a *preparatio evangelium* for the proclamation of Christ as Lord of all. The way was being opened, it was believed, to repeat the triumphalism of the early church. Christ was to be seen not simply as the Lord of the Western world but the whole world. Now we could sing that indeed "Jesus shall reign where-e'er the sun, doth its successive journeys run." The vision was bright, but its consummation eluded us.

In this latter part of the twentieth century, Christians are facing in a new way the continuing and seemingly incurable religious pluralism of the world. Pluralism is not temporary but a persistent part of the world. While the modern missionary movement planted churches throughout the world, other religions have not disappeared but have taken on new vitality and in some areas have expanded their influence. Ancient religions faced the challenge of Western Christianity and culture and have renewed themselves, not by rejecting but by reappropriating their own traditions. And in other places, secular ideologies and Marxism have reshaped whole nations. A renewed Hinduism, Buddhism, and Islam have started small but highly visible countermissionary movements. How are we to understand these facts in light of the Lordship of Christ?

There is a variety of responses to the religious situation of our time as Christians have sought to be faithful to Christ. For some Christians, this perception of religious pluralism has prompted the development of dialogue with other religious traditions. This dialogue not only aims at overcoming destructive animosities and social antagonism, but also seeks to penetrate to the spiritual center of other religions. In other cases, the work of conversion and the establishing of new churches has gone on apace. Awareness of the continuing vitality of other religions, for these Christians, marks out the vastness and difficulty of the task to which the church has been called. Still others have tried to work in terms of a Christian presence in society. They affirm that their faith calls them to share in the liberating transformation of the social, economic, and political situations of which they are part. Not only has no consensus been reached on these questions, but deep and keenly felt divisions have marked Christian thinking and action. Common commitment to Christ's Lordship calls us all to probe more deeply than we have done before the theological foundations and personal commitments that shape our responses to religious pluralism. Biblically stated, the task before the Christian community is to interpret Acts 4:12—"And there is salvation in no one else, for there is no other name under heaven given among men by which we must be saved"—in light of Acts 14:17—"yet he did not leave himself without witness. . . ."

For these reasons the Consultation on Christ's Lordship and Religious Pluralism was called for October 24–27, 1979, at Union Theological Seminary in Richmond, Virginia. In planning the consultation it was evident that a good deal of work had already been done on the Christian understanding of other religions. Of particular importance were those explorations of the universality and particularity of Christian faith made at a symposium held at Washington and Lee University in 1976. The results of this symposium were published in *Christian Faith in a Religiously Plural*

World, edited by Dawe and Carman (Maryknoll, N. Y.: Orbis Books, 1978), which has helped form the background of this consultation. The Washington and Lee meeting brought together a group of Christian scholars with their counterparts from Hindu, Buddhist, Muslim, and Jewish traditions. Out of this vigorous interchange one thing became evident. The diversity among Christians was so deep and central as to make continuing encounter with other religions unfruitful if not impossible. The priority concern for Christians was to face their own inner diversity before being able to deal adequately with the diversity of other faiths. To do this theologians and leaders of mainline Protestantism, Evangelicals, Orthodox, Catholics, and theologians from the Third World and the Black Church convened at Union Theological Seminary, Richmond, at the invitation of the Planning Committee for this consultation. Sponsorship for the consultation came from ten church and educational groups representing a wide spectrum of theological and scholarly commitments.*

The consultation was to provide for clear expression of the alternatives by their major interpreters and to give perspective on them by respondents representing different backgrounds. The invitation of the Planning Committee to take up this task was graciously accepted by *Stanley J. Samartha*, director of the Program on Dialogue with People of Living Faiths and Ideologies, World Council of Churches; *Waldron Scott*, general secretary of the World Evangelical Fellowship; *Pietro Rossano*, secretary of the Vatican Secretariat for Non-Christian Religions; and *Orlando E. Costas*, then director of the Latin American Evangelical Center for Pastoral Studies. *Krister Stendahl* undergirded the work of the consultation by his Bible studies, while *Wilfred Cantwell Smith* accepted the task of summation and reflection on what had transpired in these days together. Response was made to the major presentations by twelve theologians, historians of religion, mis-

*The consultation was cosponsored by: Center for the Study of World Religions, Harvard University; Diocese of Richmond, Roman Catholic Church; Maryknoll Center for Mission Studies; National Council of Churches, Division of Overseas Ministries; Overseas Ministries Study Center; Presbyterian Church in the U.S., Division of International Mission; Southern Baptist Home Mission Board, Department of Interfaith Witness; Union Theological Seminary in Virginia; and Washington Theological Union—in cooperation with the International Association for Mission Studies.

siologists, and biblical scholars. What has emerged from this consultation is a basic tool, in the form of this book, that will make possible a deeper and fuller exploration of what faithfulness to Christ means in face of the pluralism of the religions of humankind. What is hoped is that this may be a first step, in the power of the Spirit, toward that time when faith and understanding are at one and "God may be everything to every one" (1 Cor. 15:28).

I

Notes for Three Bible Studies

Krister Stendahl

A. A BIBLICAL VISION

Whatever question that I have to ponder as a reader of the Bible, it is important to consider it in the total setting of the biblical panorama. When we are to ponder together "Christ's Lordship and Religious Pluralism," the wider setting of a biblical vision may well be what we need first—the whole spectrum from the creation of the world to the redemption thereof.

Thus I begin with the obvious question—cast in simple language: What is it all about—from Genesis to Revelation? Let me sketch a biblical vision in the playfully poetic language of biblical theology.

God created the world—cosmos out of chaos. We do not know why God did so. We may humbly guess. God was lonely. Or, in other words, there is something in the very nature, the very heart of God that longs for communion, for company. In any case, God created the world. And as the crowning feature of that world it was God's dream that there be a type of creature that would serve God in perfect freedom, not out of nature's necessity. And human beings were made in God's image—male and female God created them.

There are many details here that are good to remember. First, these humans are obviously important, but lest they brag too much, or lest they come to think that I-Thou relationships and individual salvation are the only things that count (or lest they come to fear Charles Darwin), they do not have a day of their own in the scheme of creation, but share the sixth day with "cattle and creeping things and beasts of the earth."

Second, the whole story in Genesis 1:1–2:3 is told as if the most important lesson to be learned from it is that we keep the Sabbath. The Sabbath rest on the seventh day is part of the cosmic order, not an arbitrary convention. This, I guess, to protect the creation against the tendencies of overzealous efficiency of a greedy humanity.

Third, there is the delight of Adam in finally—after having named all the animals and found no equal—finding a true and absolute equal "at last bone of my bone and flesh of my flesh" (Gen. 2:23), although our male cultures made that saying a symbol for the derivativeness and subordination of woman, instead of a word of total identity and equality.

It was God's dream that humans would serve God freely. It was a beautiful dream—and risky. And it went sour already in chapter 3—Adam, of course, blaming it on Eve, as he has done through the ages (cf. 1 Tim. 2:13–15), initiating the well-known pattern of blaming the victim.

Since that day God has been at work toward the mending of the creation. Once he tried to flood the whole world, but that proved to be not so good an idea; and we have the rainbow as the sign of God's promise never to try that again—the only nonconditional promise in the Bible.

So God decided to set up a laboratory toward the redemption of the creation and concentrate the efforts, according to the wise and holy laws given to Israel on Sinai. And God sent prophets and prophetesses of judgment and of hope. And there were great achievements and sad setbacks, and a growing hope for the day when the Law would one day be written in hearts of people. That would be the mending of the creation, the redemption of the world.

In due time God took a bolder step, the new move in Jesus Christ. Through the ages Christians have reflected on the significance of that move of God's, and rich languages of confession and reflection have developed among us—"the Lordship of Christ" being one, and the one chosen for our consideration in this study.

But in the sweeping vision of God's total work, I think it is of importance to note that when Jesus came, he chose to express his mission and his message in terms of the kingdom (Mk. 1:14, par.). Of all the some hundred themes that he could have lifted up from the Jewish tradition (biblical and postbiblical), and of all the infinite number of themes available to him in his divine fullness, he chose this one: the kingdom. How come? Again, we may guess.

And my guess is that this very term expressed the continuity with the old and eternal dream of God's for a mended creation, for a redeemed world. Kingdom is more than a King and a Lordship, and Reign. The kingdom of God, the kingdom of heaven, stands for a mended creation, with people and things, a social, economic, ecological reality. Thus Jesus' miracles were not primarily signs of his power but acts of mending the creation, pushing back the frontier of Satan, healing minds and bodies, feeding, even counteracting the devastation of premature death of the young and needy. The kingdom with its justice is for the wronged and the oppressed, the little people who hunger and thirst for bread and for justice, the peacemakers who are so easily liquidated.

Such, it seems, was the mission and message of our Lord, the New Creator, one with the Father "before the foundation of the world." And we should be deeply grateful to the evangelists that they have preserved for us this vision of Jesus and the kingdom. That is quite remarkable, for the kingdom-language tends to be replaced by other languages in the life and teaching of the church. A glance in a concordance to the New Testament makes that clear. Its dominant and crucial role in the Synoptic Gospels stands in stark contrast to its relative absence in the other twenty-four writings of the New Testament (including Acts and John).

It is not difficult to guess how that happened. In blunt language we would say that the kingdom did not come—a fact as obvious to us when we look around in the world as it was to the early disciples. But the Redeemer, the Savior, the King, the Messiah *had* come (note, however, Acts 3:20, where the Christ is to come, not as a second coming, but as *the* coming). And so the focus shifts from the kingdom to the King, from the realm to the reign, from the redemption of the creation to the relation between the believer and the Lord. An outside observer might well interpret this development as "a solution out of embarrassment." For the church it was certainly not felt to be such. On the contrary, there was the enormous gratitude and joy over the gift of Jesus Christ.

But it remains a fact worth pondering that Jesus had preached the kingdom, while the church preached Jesus. And thus we are faced with a danger: we may so preach Jesus that we lose the vision of the kingdom, the mended creation.

Much has been made of various types of eschatologies: realized, anticipatory, future, otherworldly, transcended, and the like. As for the Jesus material, I wonder if his ministry is not best understood if we surmise that there were days when he was hopeful that God's dream could be realized within space and time, and there were days when he felt that the only possibility was the apocalyptic one, "a new heaven and a new earth." Scholarly and theological debates on this matter tend to overshadow the more important issue: be it here or there, the matter that matters is the kingdom—and we are called to be guinea pigs in God's new laboratory for the kingdom, the church.

In the final book of our Bible the old vision, the old and persistent dream of God's for a mended world, emerges in all its visionary splendor, out of the final spasmodic desperation of evil. It emerges as a New Creation with people and trees and cities, lest we forget the total vision.

Nor should we forget that *the* prayer of the Christian church, the Lord's Prayer, is an extended cry for the coming of the kingdom. In that prayer we cry out for the time when the whole creation recognizes God as God, when the kingdom comes, when the will of God is realized on earth as in heaven. We pray for a community gathered and fed by the messianic banquet, a community of mutually forgiven people who trust in God's power to rescue them from the powers of pain and evil—in short, for the victory of One who brings the kingdom and the power and the glory, finally and fully.

An observation about the Lucan setting of the Lord's Prayer may be helpful. Luke tells us that the prayer was given to the disciples in response to their request (11:1). John the Baptist had given his disciples a special prayer. Now Jesus' disciples wanted one also; a prayer that would be their "badge," their distinctive symbol. Jesus answers by giving a prayer that grows out of the themes familiar from Jewish prayers. Actually, there is nothing in the Lord's Prayer that could not be prayed wholeheartedly by a faithful Jew—then or now. (That does not mean that we should urge the Jews: "Let us say the Lord's Prayer together." Prayers gather unto themselves symbolic meanings, beyond the meaning of the words, and this is *the* prayer of the Christian church.) The point is this: when the disciples desired a prayer to set them apart, Jesus gave them a prayer that constitutes our bond with Israel, as Israel prays for forgiveness from "our Father . . . who art gracious and dost abundantly forgive" (from the *Amidah*); as Israel prays "Sanctified be his great Name in the world which he has created. May he establish his Kingdom . . . even speedily and at a near time" (from the *Kaddish*).

B. IN NO OTHER NAME . . . (ACTS 4:2)

1. The book of Acts pictures the apostles as wonder-workers. This is in continuity with the praxis and the beliefs, especially populist, both in Judaism, which had a strong tradition of wonder-working, and in the Greco-Roman culture. There is no other writing in the New Testament that is so colorful in its descriptions of Christian wonder-working as is the Acts of the Apostles, and if you want a treat, go to Acts 19:11ff. with the seven sons of Sceva and other colorful stories, which most of us don't like to think about too much. We may be embarrassed to find that magic worked wonders for the Lord. What is wrong with Simon Magus (8:10) is only one thing, namely that he tries to *buy* the power of Christian magic, not that there is such. Acts is a book rich in vividly religious behavior gloriously practiced by the early Christians, and it is all in the name of the Name. The phrase "to do something in the name of Jesus of Nazareth" is in all these passages related to the working of miracles. It is in the relation to the miraculous name-use, not in relation to the Shema (Deut. 6:4) that we must primarily read Acts 4:12—by this Name is salvation. Luke uses the Name more than any other New Testament writer. The Name is Luke's special term for expressing the Christian gospel at work. It is also worth noting that in these passages the faith of those healed is seldom stressed. Thereby the wonder-working effect of the Name is the more striking. For a study of how Jesus

(and the apostles) were perceived as wonder-workers in the Greco-Roman world, see Morton Smith, *Jesus the Magician* (New York: Harper & Row, 1977).

2. To what question is "In no other name" the answer? That question is found in Acts 4:7. It is the question of the temple authorities: "By what power or by what name did you do this?" "This"seems to refer back to the healing in chapter 3, although it could include the speaking in the court of the temple. The answer does, however, refer back to the healing. As we know from other such accounts, it was very important for these Christians to stress that they did not do such miracles in their own name, but in the name of Jesus. See for example Acts 3:12: "not as if we had done this in our own name."

3. Thus the primary and the simplest, the most obvious context of the words "In no other name is there salvation but in the name of Jesus" is: in the name of Jesus, and thus not in our own name. Pointing away from themselves, they made clear that they were not magicians within their own inherent powers. The power was in the name of Jesus. So that instead of answering all the questions of relations to other religions, the Jews, and all kinds of other things, the simplest level of this verse is: we didn't do it in our name but in the name of Jesus!

We may find such a minimalist exegesis almost unbelievably naive. We are all theologians and prone to milking the words of the Scriptures of their last drop of potential, but in listening to a story as Luke tells it, one should never miss that primary level, the light and quick meaning.

4. But there is a second context, and that one is obviously the Jewish people. Here, as in chapters 2, 3, and the rest of 4, the addressees are Jews, and in chapter 4 they are most specifically the temple authorities. Nowhere in these chapters enter any questions about Gentile gods, Gentile cults, or Gentile religion. Thus there is no way of knowing whether Luke, who wrote this, would consider this saying relevant to a discussion on Buddhism—if he knew anything about Buddhism, which is most doubtful. The setting is intra-Jewish and inter-Jewish. The "no other name" has no extra-Jewish referent, nor would I consider it proper to "smuggle in" such by supposing a flash back to the Shema, the confession that Yahweh (the Lord) is One.

Intra-Jewish and inter-Jewish setting highlights instead the distinction between the leaders and the people, a theme that Luke lets dominate the picture of the early days in Jerusalem and beyond (e.g., 4:21). That pattern is familiar to us all in contemporary terms: the Kremlin always thinks the American people are on their side as over against the capitalist and imperialist leaders and establishments. As a matter of fact, it is a timeless apologetic model for struggling revolutionary movements—of which the Jesus movement was one.

Thus we note that Peter here speaks within Judaism, fully identifying with Israel. Such an identification is of great importance for any interpretation. Jesus and the apostles are seen in the honorable and hard role of the Old Testament prophets. It is important to remember that with that role goes the identification with the people and its lot. But when such prophecies and words of warning and doom spoken within Israel, from and to Jews—when such prophetic words fall "into alien hands"—then they lose their original meaning, even if they are quoted verbatim. When Gentile Christians hurled Jesus' words at the Jews, something went seriously wrong. But here in Acts 4 the "debate" remains inter-Jewish. There is not a Jewish-Christian tension, but primarily one between the Establishment and the people, the latter being impressed by God's mighty deeds in Jesus' name.

5. To the Jewish Establishment, Luke here gives—through Peter's speech—the confession to Jesus Christ, apologetically sharpened by the reference to Psalm 118, used also elsewhere, including by Luke (20:17) in the parable about the vineyard. It is important to note what I have called an apologetically sharpened confession. Peter speaks when accused before the court. We should note that Peter has the Holy Spirit especially assisting him in making *this* speech (4:8), but not so in chapter 3. There is only one situation according to the Synoptic Gospels in which one can count on the assistance of the Holy Spirit and that is when one is brought into court, because the *martyrs,* the witness, is a witness before the powers, before the authorities. That is why we find that phrase "and Peter, filled with the Holy Spirit . . ." (Lk. 4:8). He is in court (cf. Mt. 10:19–20 par.). And in that situation the defense of the accused is a confession.

6. What is, then, the nature, the genre *(Gattung)* of such a

statement as "In no other Name"? It is a confession. What is the
nature of such a confession? And now comes the shocking
thought: it should be seriously asked if religious language, either
confessional, hymnic, or liturgical, that is to say, religious language that we call primary religious language, the language of
religious experience, should not be considered as love language,
as caressing language. That is why Protestants often have difficulties in understanding what liturgy is about. Liturgy is play, liturgy is repetitious; when you play, when you worship, you use
language in a caressing manner. It has the same sort of expression
as that kind of language by which one caresses the person dear to
one. That is proper, since the ultimate aim of our whole existence
is to praise God, glorify and enjoy God forever. Liturgy has a
caressing function; its language is a love language.

Or let me make my point differently: if a husband were to say
that his wife was the only one for him, and he were telling the
truth and nothing but the truth, then that is good and true. But if
he were witnessing in court and was under oath and the judge
asked him whether he could be sure that nowhere in the world
could there be another woman about whom he could have come
to say the same thing, then he could not take such an oath. For in
that setting the very same words would take on another meaning.
Just as would the words of Peter's confession if treated as an ax-
iom of dogmatic theology.

7. Now most of you would say that such an interpretation is too
subjective. I find, however, subjective/objective distinctions far
too blunt an instrument here. The issue is, rather, that of different
languages and intentions, and I think we should seriously ask one
another whether the nature of religious language is not, rather, to
be seen in the general direction here outlined.

8. Such love language is far from innocent or less threatening
to the Establishment, as we can judge from this story. (And those
of us who were part of the Establishment during the student revolution can witness to the power of the emotionally charged language that was spoken against us in those days. It was not harm-
less, not mere words, nor was it "objective" language, as
everyone might remember. It was a powerful witness, spoken with
the power of the powerless.)

9. The foregoing observations suggest to me that Acts 4:12 is

not a good basis for an absolute claim in an absolute sense, but that it is a natural confession growing out of the faith, growing out of the experience of gratitude. Also out of apostolic humility, that is, the awareness that they didn't do it themselves but that it was all in the power of the Lord. They thereby pointed away from themselves. Just as any reference to election is saying that one cannot understand how it could happen. Here is a confession, not a proposition. It is a witness, strangely enough not actually an argument, but just exactly a witness.

10. All thoughtful believers and believing communities that have taken monotheism seriously must sooner or later reflect upon how their *different* absolute claims somehow must fit together in God's mysterious plan. In stating this thesis it is clear that I move from the level of primary religious language (prayer, confession, hymn, liturgy) to the level of reflection, afterthought, namely, to theology.

11. They will do so "sooner or later." It would be a little much to expect that such reflection would loom large in the New Testament or in the first exuberant generations of the Jesus movement. And yet, as we shall see in the next study, that reflection happened already in the middle of the first century, in the mighty thoughts of the great missionary Paul.

C. THE PITFALLS OF UNIVERSALISM

Most of us take for granted that universalism is superior to particularism. Christianity is a universal religion, transcending shackles of particularism. As a matter of fact, we say, here lies one of the decisive differences between Judaism and Christianity. We might even argue that the very essence of monotheism requires a universalist stance.

I would like to take a second look at this comfortable and re-spectable model of Christian thought and teaching, as to both the Jewish and the Christian side of the ledger. I like to do so since I have been struck by the gruesome thought that universalist claims have often led to various kinds of imperialism and crusades. The connection is very simple. If my faith is universal in its claim, then woe unto those who do not see the world as I do.

As a student of Judaism in the time of the second temple, I

know that the Hellenistic rulers were universalists, convinced that their culture was true Culture. They could not stand people who did not accept it. Hence the Maccabean revolt. Cultural imperialism—the UNESCO approach in its early forms—builds on a universalism with little patience for the particularism of people and cultures. If that be so about cultures, how true it is about religions, where the one and true understanding of God is claimed in universalist form.

Now it is true that Israel's faith is particularist, resting in the grateful and humble conviction that it is called to a special faithfulness to God. But it is equally true that this particular and peculiar faithfulness is only part of God's universal work in the creation. At least from Second Isaiah's time it becomes crystal clear that Israel has a universal mission: to be a light for the nations, the Gentiles (Isa. 49:6, et al.). But not by making them Jews, but by being a faithful witness to the Oneness of God and the moral order—toward the day of a mended creation.

This witnessing particularism within a universal perspective led Jewish thinkers like Maimonides to the view that Christianity, and Islam, were "bearers of Torah"—bearers of the witness to the Oneness of God and the moral order—to the Gentiles. Such a model is remarkable in the history of religion, since it is rare indeed that one religion assigns a positive role to other religions, especially to religions that are hostile to one's own. But the greatness of this model consists perhaps in its concern for "the kingdom" rather than for oneself. It is the Eldad and Medad spirit from Numbers 11:26–29 (echoed in the teachings of Jesus in Mk. 10:38–41).

So let us move on to the New Testament. I would suggest that the image that emerges out of the New Testament is in more continuity with the Old Testament and postbiblical Judaism than we usually recognize.

It is obviously correct to speak of Christianity as a universalistic religion. The membership of the church is based on faith in and allegiance to Jesus Christ, and in Christ there is neither Jew nor Greek, neither slave nor free, neither male nor female. In that sense its base is universal. But as a new witnessing community the church understands itself as a minority community with a mission. And what—according to the New Testament—is the aim of its witness? Is it the Christianization of the world, the dream of the Christian Century? Or could it be something else? Something less self-glorifying and more centered in God's mysterious plan for a mended creation. A mission more in tune with being a light for the Gentiles?

We all know that phrase from the New Testament, both from the Song of Simeon (Lk. 2:32) and from the Sermon on the Mount (Mt. 5:13ff.). The images of Salt and Light are minority images. Who wants the world to become a salt mine? And note the saying: Let your light so shine before people that they see your good works *and give glory to your Father who is in heaven—* not: . . . and become Christians. And the Magi (Mt., chap. 2) did not start a church in Iran; they just got the lifting experience of their lives. And the one who gives a cup of cold water to you, since you are a disciple, that "outsider" shall not lose the reward (Mt. 10:42), a word that in Mark is part of Jesus' scathing critique of the cliquishness of the disciples (Mk. 9:41). And the whole world will be judged by how they have treated this little, witnessing community (Mt. 25:31–46).

This all indicates that the world is not divided between those who accept Jesus and the *massa perditionis*. The church is a new witnessing community, a minority whose witness somehow God "needs" in his total mission, the *missio Dei*.

It is urgent for us now—in a pluralistic world—to find our right place, our peculiar and particular place as faithful witnesses to Jesus Christ, leaving the result of the witness in the hands of God.

A significant event in the history of Christian reflection about how the Christian mission might fit into God's wider plan for the world is to be found in Paul's letter to the church in Rome. At a crucial juncture in his apostolic ministry Paul reflects on how his mission to the Gentiles fits into God's total plan (Rom., chaps. 9–11).

He begins by making clear that he certainly would like the Jews to accept Jesus as the Christ, yea, he swears that he is willing to be "accursed and cut off from Christ" if that would help to that end (Rom. 9:1, cf. 10:1). But before he is through, he will lecture the Gentile Christians (11:13) that they have no business in trying to convert the Jews. Paul seems to have discerned two things: *(a)* an attitude of superiority and conceit in the Gentile Christians

(11:25), which make them unsuited for such a mission; and *(b)* that the Jesus movement is to be a Gentile movement—apart from the significant remnant, the link by grace (11:5). That *is* quite perceptive in the mid-first century—but we know that that is roughly what happened.

For Paul these insights lead to a stress on the mysterious nature of God's mission: "Lest you be wise in your own conceits, I want you to understand this mystery . . ." (Rom. 11:25). And the mystery is that the salvation of Israel is in God's hands, and that the No of Israel was not toward her rejection (". . . have they stumbled in order to fall? By no means!") but in order to open up the salvation for the Gentiles (11:11).

Consciously or unconsciously Paul writes this whole section in Romans (10:18–11:36) without mentioning the name of Jesus Christ, and his final doxology is not—as is his usual style—in Christ-language but in God-language (11:33–36). It is as if Paul did not want them to have the Christ-flag to wave, since it might fan their conceit.

Here the most zealous of all missionaries, the very apostle Paul, has given us his reflection on the dangers of thoughtless universalism, his mature thought about how mission without mystery becomes oppressive. Perhaps he had been burned once by a religious zeal that took for granted that God's hottest dream was that all people believed like him—on the road to Damascus, set on bringing the Christians into line.

The issue at hand here is the church and Israel. But there is also the wider issue of a missionary style in which the mysterious *missio Dei* may call for new ways for us to sing our song to Jesus Christ without conceit. Not that Paul's Christians *felt* that conceit. They thought they were witnessing to the truth. And they were—but in a manner which suggested that God's only way was that everyone become like unto themselves. They did not understand their mission as a particular witness of their peculiar community in a world of communities. And in that, said Paul, they were wrong. They became proud, they did not "stand in awe" (Rom. 11:20).

II

The Lordship of Jesus Christ and Religious Pluralism

Stanley J. Samartha

How to confess the Lordship of Jesus Christ as we live and work together with neighbors of other faiths has become an urgent question for the churches today. For one thing, at a time when alternative claims are being made on behalf of other "lords," whether religious or secular, Christians need to make clear to themselves what it means to affirm that Jesus Christ is Lord. This should be regarded as both a theological responsibility and a pastoral concern. For another, the content and form of Christian witness in the coming years is bound up with this question, Does mission mean the conquest of other "lords"? Does universality mean simply the extension of Christian particularity? What happens if our neighbors of other faiths also have similar notions of universality, that is, of extending *their* particularities? These two questions, the meaning of the Lordship of Christ and the future of Christian mission, are inextricably bound together.

To these must be added a third reason why this subject should demand our utmost attention. While the Lordship of Christ is one of the central affirmations of the New Testament, the manner in which it was expressed was developed in the West where religious pluralism was not a particularly significant factor. True, they had other "lords" to contend with. Those of us whose history, tradition, culture, and social relationships are different from those in the West do not find it easy either to bear the burden of this heritage or even to lay it down. Our question today is not "How shall we sing the Lord's song in a foreign land?" (Ps. 137:4). Rather, it is "How can we sing a foreign song in the Lord's land?" But it must immediately be said that this task is far deeper than what usually goes by the name of "indigenization." In the sustaining fellowship of the *oikoumenē*, through mutual criticism leading to mutual enrichment, churches in different countries need to help each other to understand the universal meaning of the Lordship of Christ. This may well lead to the rejection of some of the terms used previously to express the Lordship of Christ. It demands a fresh look at the New Testament evidence and the traditions of the church. It must certainly mean that the involvement of Christians in pluralist communities should be taken far more seriously than before. The divine-human encounter in Jesus Christ is the basis for this confession.

i

The term "religious pluralism" is heavy. It is an academic concept, which should be broken open to reveal the vast number of people and the faiths they live by. It refers to millions of *people—neighbors* of other faiths—who share the common life of community with us. We are bound together in the bundle of life. Our destinies are intertwined. Christians share with their neighbors of other faiths the struggles and sufferings of human existence no less than its joy and satisfaction. Our neighbors too have their answers to the mystery of life and the tragedy of suffering. These answers, developed through centuries, satisfy them and they are not seeking alternatives, particularly in the Christian camp. In terms of spiritual depth, intellectual power, cultural richness, and social solidarity they do not regard themselves in any way inferior to Christians. Despising the religions of other people and claiming superiority for one's own can sometimes be a form of racism.

Several observations may be made about the religious situation today. The prediction so confidently made not too long ago by certain scholars and thinkers about the speedy demise of religions has proved to be incorrect. The rumors of their death have been exaggerated. They are very much alive and sometimes kicking. It was based on the assumption that the influence of Western education, the advance of science and technology, and the march of secularization would sweep away religions from the high roads of modern life. This has not happened. On the contrary, religious pluralism has proved itself to be a *persistent* fact of human life. Moreover, there are clear signs of religious *resurgence* everywhere. Whether it is in Judaism, or Islam, or Hinduism in India, or Buddhism in Sri Lanka, or the traditional religions in Africa, dogmas are being questioned and structures are disintegrating, but the core of different religions is becoming more alive. Even in socialist states where atheistic propaganda has gone on for many decades there are no signs of religions withering away. The recovery of religious values and their reinterpretation to meet contemporary needs sustain people in their struggle against meaninglessness and provide them with a vision for the future.

This point about religious resurgence should not, however, be overdone. Unwarranted market predictions should not be drawn from capsules of consumer religion that are sold in attractive packages to people in foreign lands who sometimes seem to be unable to differentiate between the lotus and the navel. There is indeed a *rejection* of institutionalized religions, especially by young people, who suspect all authority and all absolute claims on behalf of any one particular "lord." An absolutism based on religion can be as dangerous in its consequences as one based on a political ideology. Perhaps the turbulence of the times has contributed to the growth of a heightened religious sense, pushing people to search deeper for the spiritual roots of life. The rejection of institutions and the questioning of dogmas may be a product not so much of the influence of secularization as of a deepening spirituality seeking more satisfying expressions of religious life. Religion is both a way of life and a view of life. It is both *dharma* (law) and *dristi* (vision).* It helps people to connect the *pāramārthika* (ultimate) with the *vyāvahārika* (penultimate). A religious outlook enables its adherents both to look at the world in which they live and to look away from it. It is in developing the relationship between the way of life and the view of life, in suggesting how to look away from the world while looking at it, that particular communities of faith work out both their own sense of

---

* *Dharma* from the Sanskrit root *dhr*: to sustain or to uphold. Law or religion is a very inadequate English translation.

identity and their attitudes to people of other communities of faith. An element of exclusiveness is therefore built into the manner in which any community expresses its particularity.

While discussing the implications of religious pluralism there is a further observation which is pertinent to a theological discussion on the Lordship of Christ. This is the question of power relationships between different religious communities. By "power" we mean economic affluence, technological skill, political wisdom, and military strength—all those means that enable one community or nation to dominate and exploit others for its own benefit. When a particular country or nation is powerful in this sense, it is sometimes easy to assume that its own religion—the "lord" whom it professes to worship—is stronger and superior. It is often forgotten that the relation between different religious communities is very much influenced by the power factor. A clear example today is the manner in which Western Christianity is struggling to relate itself both theologically and politically to Jews, on the one hand, and to Muslims, on the other. In the case of the former, one of the factors is the abuse of power that led to the Holocaust. In the case of the latter, it is both the past history of Christian-Muslim relations in Europe and the growing economic strength of Muslim countries in the Middle East. People who suffered at the hands of the powerful can use the experience to intimidate those who inflicted such suffering. Powerlessness itself can be used as power. People tend to respect those whom they fear. Religions that emphasize "nonviolence" and "yoga" can always be commended and patronized for being "spiritual." "Soul power" is less of a threat than "oil power." Theological attitudes are not developed in a vacuum. They are always influenced by contemporary forces in history. Christ the Servant and Christ the King seldom coexist, although clever theologians can easily camouflage the latter by the trappings of the former. At a time when the histories of different nations are increasingly being drawn together, when different communities of faith are in dialogue with each other as never before, and when people of the world for good or bad share a common future, the exclusive claims of particular communities generate tensions and lead to clashes. Is there then a universal framework that can hold together particular claims without eliminating their distinctiveness? Can the church be an exclusive fellowship committed to Jesus Christ and, at the same time, be open to neighbors of other faiths? What does the Lordship of Christ mean in situations of religious pluralism?

ii

Kurios, or Lord, is the most familiar and characteristic word used to describe Jesus Christ in the New Testament. The obvious mark of a Christian is the confession that Jesus Christ is Lord (2 Cor. 4:5; Rom. 10:9; Col. 2:6, etc.). It signifies a new relationship of the believer to Jesus Christ, of commitment and loyalty, of surrendering oneself to God and to the one Lord, Jesus Christ. "For although there may be so-called gods in heaven or on earth—as indeed there are many 'gods' and many 'lords'—yet for us there is one God, the Father, from whom are all things and for whom we exist, and one Lord, Jesus Christ, through whom are all things and through whom we exist" (1 Cor. 8:5-6). In making this personal confession, the believer also joins the community of the faithful, the fellowship of those who believe in the resurrection of Jesus and have already acknowledged his Lordship. The personal confession "My Lord and my God" (John 20:28) is also the confession of the community about "God the Father and Christ Jesus *our* Lord" (2 Tim. 1:2). In addition, it is an affirmation that by virtue of his death and resurrection Jesus Christ has been exalted above all lords. "For to this end Christ died and lived again, that he might be the Lord both of the dead and of the living" (Rom. 14:9). This exaltation of Jesus Christ as the only Lord and as the Lord of all reaches its high-water mark in such well-known passages as Philippians 2:1-11, Colossians 1:15-20, and Ephesians 1:15-23. It is most extraordinary that when the church was weak and powerless Christians could sing such hymns of victory and praise to God through Jesus Christ without any sense of Christian triumphalism. It is equally extraordinary that the connection between suffering and victory, between emptying and exaltation, between the servanthood and the kingship of Christ should be missed in the triumphalistic advance of Christianity as a religion and the establishment of the church as an institution.

In discussing such a difficult and important subject as the topic before us, quoting scriptural passages can be an extremely hazardous business. Sooner or later the word "hermeneutics" may be thrown at us, both by theologians and by biblical scholars. Moreover, to jump from the context of the New Testament to the context of contemporary religious pluralism would be to ignore nearly two thousand years of church history during which period Christology has developed, the church has grown, and missionary attitudes toward other religions have been shaped. There has been continuing exegesis of cherished biblical passages, sometimes leading to differing interpretations. Our neighbors of other faiths also have the authority and the sustaining support of their Scriptures. They too have developed careful exegesis of their scriptures—the Jews of the Torah, the Hindus of the Vedas, the Upanishads and the Bhagavadgita, the Buddhists of the Tripitakas and the Muslims of the Qu'ran. The Bible does not give us "blueprints" to solve modern problems. The question of the relation between people of different religions today is in many ways a new problem, which cannot be compared to Israel's relation to the nations in Old Testament times or to early Christianity's relation to the religions in the Roman empire. It is, however, important and necessary for Christians, when faced with such a new problem, to go back to the Bible for insights, indications, and directions that can help them as they struggle with new problems. This has to be done in the light of the experience of the church and with the guidance of the Holy Spirit.

There are at least three points in the references made to the New Testament here that can be of help in understanding the Lordship of Jesus Christ in the context of religious pluralism. The first is the connection between the confession of Christ's Lordship and faith in his resurrection. The second is the relation between the exaltation of Jesus Christ as Lord and his humility, his suffering, his emptying himself, his servanthood. The third is the constant coupling of the Fatherhood of God with the Lordship of Jesus Christ. Taken cumulatively, these provide elements for a more helpful understanding of the relation between the universal dimension of the Christian faith and its particularity.

There is an intimate connection between faith in the resurrection of Jesus Christ and the confession that he is Lord. The two are inextricably bound together and mutually interpret each other. During one of the resurrection appearances "none of the disciples dared to ask him, 'Who are you?' They knew it was the Lord" (John 21:12). Without acknowledging the Lordship of Jesus Christ, one cannot believe in the resurrection; without accepting the resurrection, one cannot confess Jesus Christ as Lord.

Of all the ills human flesh is heir to, death is the most certain and most universal. No one can escape it. It is the ultimate in human suffering and the final stamp of meaninglessness on human existence. The longing to conquer death and gain immortality runs through all religions. The central problem of Buddhism is *dukkha* (suffering). "From death lead me to immortality" is part of one of the most ancient prayers in the Upanishads. During the funeral of Mahatma Gandhi, when flames engulfed his frail body and leapt to the sky, the cry that went up from the throats of thousands was, "Mahatma Gandhi has become immortal (*amarhogaya*)." To many people in Asia the suffering and the crucifixion of Jesus is not the difficulty. It is a deeply moving experience for many Christians to listen to the poems written by neighbors of other faiths on the suffering and death of Jesus Christ. Just because it was a "scandal" to the Jews and a "stumbling block" to the Greeks in Paul's time, it is foolish to insist that it ought to be a *skandalon* to all Hindus and Buddhists. In poetry, art, drama, and even the cinema, neighbors of other faiths have tried to bring out the profound implications of the suffering and death of Jesus Christ. It is the resurrection which seems to be the *skandalon*. Some years ago I delivered a lecture on the death and resurrection of Jesus Christ at the Institute of World Culture in Bangalore to an audience that was almost wholly Hindu. At the end, a well-known Hindu scholar and author told me, "I accept everything you have said about Jesus Christ except the last bit about the resurrection." When I asked him for the reason he said, "It looks like a happy ending to an otherwise powerful and tragic life. It makes it appear too much like some of the stories in our *purāṇas*" (popular religious stories).

To confess Jesus Christ as Lord is to recognize that by "death he has conquered death." The conquest of sin and death by Jesus Christ should not be subtly transformed as a call for Christians to conquer other religions. When there is the certainty and assurance that through this particular person death has lost its hold on life, there is the alternative of hope in the midst of death. That is the sure sign of Christ's Lordship. Those structures that oppress people through threats of death can now be challenged in the name of the Lord of life. The New Testament constantly emphasizes that it was God who raised Jesus from the dead, not that he raised himself. "You killed the Author of life, whom God raised from the dead. To this we are witnesses" (Acts 3:15). The witnessing finger points to Jesus Christ, but does not stop there; it points beyond to "the God of our fathers who glorified his servant Jesus" (Acts 3:13).

The church in history has tended to glorify, exalt, and deify Jesus Christ. The intensity of this glorification in doctrine, art, stained-glass windows, hymns, and attitudes to other religions has depended as much on Christian piety as on the degree of temporal power exercised by the church in history. The struggle between God and "many gods," between one Lord and "many lords," between truth and distortions of truth was often transformed into a struggle between Christianity and "non-Christian" religions. In doing so Christians have sometimes succumbed to the dangers of "a personality cult" where the underlying fact that "God is all in all" has been almost lost sight of. The hymn of praise gratefully sung to the exalted Lord by a humble group of Christians has often been transformed into a manifesto to conquer "God's enemies."

This Lord (*Kurios*) is also the slave (*doulos*) of all. One can reverse the statement "Jesus is Lord" to say "the Lord is Jesus"— "he who came not to be served, but to serve, and to give his life as a ransom for many" (Mk. 10:45). In the exercise of his Lordship there is a reversal of the usual practice. "You know that those who are supposed to rule over the Gentiles lord it over them, and their great men exercise authority over them. But it shall not be so among you; but whoever would be great among you must be your servant, and whoever would be first among you must be slave of all" (Mk. 10:43-44). The tendency to regard the Lordship of Jesus Christ as a reward by God for his willingness to empty himself and to humble himself even unto death (Phil. 2:8-9) is questionable. He did not surely suffer and serve in order that he might be exalted. On the contrary, he exercises his functions as Lord not through conquering people or ruling over them but through self-surrender and service and through accepting the burdens of others on himself. Only when the power of resurrection is related to the needs of people who are suffering and dying can the Lordship of the risen Christ be a sign of hope.

One of the points sometimes forgotten in confessing the Lordship of Christ is the fact that although the witness of the New Testament writers is Christocentric, Jesus Christ himself is theocentric. He habitually spoke of God as the Father. He was the man with God and for God before he could be described as "the man for others." True, there are sayings in which he identifies himself with God. For example, "I and my Father are one" (John 10:30). But he also says, "My Father is greater than I" (John 14:28). Further, belief in God and belief in Jesus Christ, the knowledge of God and the knowledge of Jesus Christ are often put side by side. "Believe in God, believe also in me" (John 14:1). Eternal life is "to know thee as the only true God, and Jesus Christ whom thou hast sent" (John 17:3). In the passages from the epistles referred to earlier the priority of God's authority in exalting Jesus Christ is repeatedly emphasized. God is there not only previous to Jesus Christ, but also at the final eschatological end. "When all things are subjected to him, then the Son himself will also be subjected to him who put all things under him that God may be everything to every one" (1 Cor. 15:28).

Attention is drawn to this point not in any way to ignore the divinity of Jesus Christ or to ignore his central importance to Christian faith and practice, but to avoid that kind of "Christo-monism" which is incompatible both with the evidence of the New Testament and with the tradition of the church, and which sometimes leads Christians to regard Jesus as a kind of cult figure over against other religious figures. It tends to regard Jesus Christ as "the Christians' God" and makes it impossible to have any meaningful dialogue with neighbors of other faiths. The divine-human encounter in Jesus Christ should not be distorted into an encounter between Christianity and "non-Christian" religions. The exclusiveness of *commitment* clings to the center of faith without closing the gates at the circumference. The exclusiveness of *possession* tends to petrify revelation and to monopolize truth. It fails to do justice to the mystery of human life and to the ambiguities of history. It does not recognize the need to leave

some doors unlatched in order that the gentle breeze of the Holy
Spirit may enter the Christian home, sometimes from unexpected
corners. Consequently, it can think of commitment only in terms
of firmness in closing the gates and of openness only in terms of
the dangers of relativism.

iii

How then is the particularity of God's revelation in Jesus Christ
to be understood in the larger framework of God's universal love
for all humankind? What about other particularities to which our
neighbors continue to cling with equal vehemence and devotion as
Christians cling to theirs? Does the Christian imperative demand
that they "proclaim" the Lordship of Jesus Christ, not just in the
midst of, but over against, the "gods" and "lords" of other religions?

Any firm and clear-cut answer to this question might be premature at a time when one era in organized missionary activities in
the world is coming to an end and another is just beginning. New
situations of Christian witness are developing in different parts of
the world. New wine is bursting the old wineskins. Boundaries
that marked different particularities are becoming blurred. Traffic across the borders is noticeable. Attempts to answer the question "What is the relation between the universal, creative, and
redemptive activity of God toward all humankind and the particular, creative, and redemptive activity of God in the history of
Israel and in the person and work of Jesus Christ?" should be
regarded as tentative at this time. Christians need to struggle together with this question more often; they need to enter not just
into the social life, but into the spiritual struggles of their
neighbors more deeply in order that the search for new relations
may become more genuine and the confession of Christ's Lordship more authentic. But one thing should be clear. Christians can
no longer talk of God's work in the lives of neighbors of other
faiths in purely negative terms. God's self-disclosure in the lives of
neighbors of other faiths and in the secular struggles of human
life should also be recognized as theologically significant. Therefore the relation of the particularity of the Lordship of Jesus

Christ to other particularities should be considered not in terms of rejection but in terms of relationships.

Two possibilities are obvious. One is to regard universality as the extension of just one particularity. To the Christians this would mean the conquest of other "lords" by Jesus Christ; it would mean the extension of the church and the extinction of other communities of faith. To the Muslims it would mean the extension of their particularity with similar consequences to neighbors of other faiths. This seems to be neither desirable nor possible. The other alternative is to recognize all particularities as equally valid and to demand that no particularity should claim universality. This popular attitude, which is often a reaction to the first, could lead either to a sterile coexistence or to an unseemly competition. Is there any other possibility that might enable us to move beyond these two, which have proved to be fruitless? This way cannot be described neatly as "the middle way" between the two. Neither can the word "dialectical" be thrown in to complicate matters. The web of religious relationships is complex and delicate. It does not easily lend itself to neat theological categories.

This other possibility, however, may be to recognize God alone as Absolute and to consider all religions to be relative. This means that religious particularities are not denied, but the fact is recognized that, as historical phenomena, religions are ambiguous. The relativization of religions would liberate their respective adherents from a self-imposed obligation to defend their particular community of faith over against others, in order to be free to point to the ultimacy of God who holds all things and all people in his embrace.

It is necessary to be cautious here to avoid misunderstandings. The standpoint has obviously to be within one's own community of faith. To acknowledge the fact of religious pluralism means that one cannot take shelter in neutral or objective ground. There is no theological helicopter that can help us to rise above all religions and to look down upon the terrain below in lofty condescension. *Our* standpoint, therefore, has to be Christian; but by the same token our neighbors are also free to have *their* particular standpoints.

However, while recognizing the distinctiveness of religions, one must look beyond them to that to which they point. I have often quoted a Buddhist proverb in this connection, which says: "When a finger points to the moon, it is foolish to look at the finger." In the depths of interreligious dialogue, where people meet in freedom and expectation, there are moments when the particular labels that partners wear lose their importance and that which is behind and beyond them breaks through in spiritual freedom, offering a vision of the ultimate that holds them together. Such moments may be few and far between; but they are profound and significant. Perhaps they will contribute to the transformation or transfiguration of particular religions in the future without denying their distinctiveness. We should, of course, be critically loyal to our own community of faith, the church, which is our spiritual home. But our final obligation as Christians today is not to Christianity as a religion, not to Western forms of Christianity, which some of us have inherited, or even to African or Asian expressions of Christianity, which some of us perhaps with a mixture of national zeal and religious enthusiasm are trying to promote, but to God who, at the very point where he reveals himself in Jesus Christ, liberates us from our particular bondages in order to have new relations with our neighbors in the larger community. Only then do we become truly free to share with our neighbors the inestimable riches of God in Jesus Christ.

The search for new relations may lead us to risk the breakup of cherished particularities of doctrine and structure, to break away from past captivities, and to develop new relationships in the *oikoumenē* of God. Christians are not called upon to be advocates of the Lordship of Christ; they are not called upon to make declarations about the inadequacy of other lords; their responsibility is to be obedient to him and to live in such a way that their life is a clear manifestation of the Lordship of Christ. In the incarnation God himself has taken the risk to become human. In Jesus Christ the Absolute has become relative in history. Why should Christians be afraid to live in the midst of persistent religious pluralism? Perhaps what we need at the moment is not a theology of dialogue, but courage for dialogue. Dialogue has been a controversial term in ecumenical debate in recent years, particularly after the Uppsala Assembly (1968) of the World

Council of Churches (WCC). Since then, a good deal of work has been done by way both of actual dialogues with neighbors of other faiths and of theological reflection on them. The theological significance of the data, namely the actual experience of numerous carefully prepared dialogues, is not sufficiently recognized. In earlier years the general feeling seemed to be for dialogue *or* mission. The two were regarded as alternatives that mutually excluded each other. Later on, it was reluctantly recognized that perhaps both have their own particular integrity and vocation in the life of the church in a pluralist world. Therefore dialogue *and* mission could exist side by side. At the WCC Nairobi Assembly (1975), however, the feeling seemed to be so strong against dialogue as to verge on panic and fear. Therefore it was felt that dialogue can only be *for* mission. The doubts and fears generated by the Nairobi debate have largely been overcome in subsequent years. It is significant that in 1979 the Central Committee of the World Council of Churches unanimously adopted a set of "Guidelines on Dialogue" together with a theological statement and commended them to the churches. This may well prove to be the beginning of a new stage in the relationship between Christian communities and their neighbors of other faiths. It is therefore in this changed ecumenical context of seeking new relationships that the question of the Lordship of Jesus Christ should be discussed. I hope the time will come, perhaps not in our generation, when we can speak of dialogue beyond mission, and mission beyond dialogue.

Dialogue is an attempt to understand and express our particularity not just in terms of our own heritage but also in relation to the spiritual heritage of our neighbors of other faiths. The tension in the relations between Israel and the nations in the Old Testament has implications for dialogue that are not always sufficiently recognized. Among the Priestly writers there is the tendency to consider other nations from the standpoint of Yahweh's relation to Israel. There is a feeling of exclusiveness, of being the only "chosen people of God." The prophets constantly challenge this assumption. Instead of looking at other nations from Mount Zion, they demand that Israel should look at itself from the standpoint of other nations. Mount Sinai should look at the river Ganga; and the river Ganga at Mount Sinai. There is no reason to claim that the religion developed in the desert around Mount Sinai is superior to the religion developed on the banks of the river Ganga. There is a persistent tension between the exclusiveness of Israel and the inclusiveness of Yahweh. Christians have tended to resolve it too quickly in favor of the former. "In that day Israel will be the third with Egypt and Assyria, a blessing in the midst of the earth, whom the Lord of hosts has blessed, saying, 'Blessed be Egypt my people, and Assyria the work of my hands, and Israel my heritage' " (Isa. 19:24–25). And Amos demands, "Are you not like the Ethiopians to me, O people of Israel, says the Lord. Did I not bring up Israel from the land of Egypt, the Philistines from Caphtor, and the Syrians from Kir?" (Amos 9:7). It looks as if other ancient people too have had their "exodus" no less than the captive people today waiting to be liberated.

In a situation of religious pluralism, therefore, dialogue is inevitable. It cannot be an optional activity. There are people, however, within every community of faith, who, for various reasons, deliberately reject new relationships and choose to remain isolated. That can only lead to a closed particularity that feeds on itself and in the process impoverishes the community. Dialogue is a mood, a spirit, an attitude of love and respect toward neighbors of other faiths. It regards partners as persons, not as statistics. Understood and practiced as an intentional lifestyle, it goes far beyond a sterile coexistence or uncritical friendliness. It does not avoid controversies; it does not emphasize only points of general agreement; it recognizes difficulties in relationships as well. It is not a gathering of porcupines; neither is it a get-together of jellyfish. Sensitively understood, it helps people not to disfigure the image of their neighbors of other faiths. In multireligious societies—and the world is indeed a multireligious society—dialogue cannot be just the activity of a few interested individuals. It can only be "dialogue in community." There must be dialogues *within* particular communities of faith and also *between* different communities in order that *new* communities might emerge—communities of concerned people ready to take risks, to move beyond safe boundaries, and to shape new profiles in place of old particularities.

Dialogue must therefore be accepted as a mode of relationship between people of different faiths, which has its own integrity. It has intrinsic values, not just instrumental use. Christian witness to the Lordship of Jesus Christ is not in danger in situations of dialogue. That suspicion itself is a symptom sometimes of pride and arrogance, sometimes of insecurity and fear. In a significant statement (January 1979) the Central Committee of the World Council of Churches said that dialogue is "not a secret weapon in the armoury of an aggressive Christian militancy." It has its own distinctiveness and integrity. "It is a joyful affirmation of life against chaos, and a participation with all who are allies of life in seeking the provisional goals of a better human community." Dialogue and witness do not stand in any contradiction to each other. Therefore they declared:

> Thus, to the member churches of the World Council of Churches we feel able with integrity to commend the way of dialogue as one in which Jesus Christ can be confessed in the world today; at the same time we feel able with integrity to assure our partners in dialogue that we come not as manipulators but as genuine fellow-pilgrims, to speak with them of what we believe God to have done in Jesus Christ who has gone before us, but whom we seek to meet anew in dialogue. (*Guidelines on Dialogue* [Geneva: WCC, 1979], p. 11).

The imperative of Christian witness in dialogue, however, places another obligation upon both Christians and their partners in dialogue. If Christians speak of "mission" they must be willing to recognize that their neighbors too have their "missions" in the same pluralistic world. The possibility of "mutual witness" to each other cannot be avoided. At an ecumenical consultation (July 1979) held at the Massachusetts Institute of Technology, Boston, on the subject "Science, Faith and the Future," Christian, Jewish, Buddhist, and Muslim members were present and read papers. In the section on "Humanity, Nature and God," the following statement was accepted:

> Among the achievements of our neighbors of other faiths to which we Christians should attend are the following: a deep piety and obedience to a merciful God who is close to the faithful; the awareness of the inter-connectedness of all things . . .;

the emphasis on the transient character of all existence, stressing continuities instead of discontinuities and eventuating in serenity, calmness, and acceptance of suffering as part of life; the spirit of non-attachment, the ability to find oneself by letting go of material possessions, to act according to the principle of causing least harm and disturbance to creation. Though all these may be found in our Christian tradition, we do not gain credibility by asserting in a triumphalistic manner that we ourselves already possess everything. We can only be credible witnesses to our faith if we are on "the way" (Acts 18:24f.) towards God's future [from Section II in *Faith and Science in an Unjust World*, vol. 2 (Geneva: WCC, 1980), p. 36].

iv

This immediately leads us to the question as to how Christians can witness to the Lordship of Jesus Christ as they live together with their neighbors of other faiths. The word "mission" perhaps should be avoided or even abandoned altogether. This is not to hide in any way the genuine Christian intention, but to remove a term that has become a threat to other particularities and a hindrance to open relationships. "Witness" is a biblical term. *Kerygma* in the sense of one-way "proclamation" and *diakonia* in the sense of patronizing service to others have obscured the *marturia*, the readiness to suffer and to die for the sake of others, through which the Lordship of Jesus Christ is confessed. Therefore, witnessing to the Lordship of Jesus Christ cannot be a mere verbal proclamation to the world at large. It has to be concrete and particular in the living context of relationships. It is not just a statement to be accepted, but a confession to be made at the end, not the beginning, of an experience. Demanding prior acceptance of the Lordship of Jesus Christ is against both the Old and New Testament experience where faith is the fruit of historical experience and is not imposed on people.

New situations offering new ways of Christian witness to the Lordship of Jesus Chrst are developing in different parts of the world. One can point to at least three. There are situations, for example, where people of different religious and ideological commitments are struggling for a community of justice seeking to break free from the chains of oppression. Jesus Christ as Lord does not stand apart from the struggle. His Lordship is over both the oppressors and the oppressed. This is not a matter of smuggling in a bit of liberation theology to the dialogue camp. It is a reminder to ourselves that Christian communities should confess the Lordship of Christ through their involvement in the struggle for justice. Only thus can Christians share in the *marturia* of Christ's Lordship today. Second, the pressures of contemporary history are such that practically every traditional religious community is now being challenged to seek new ways of relating religion and society, religion and politics, religion and science, religion and nature, religion and the inner life of human beings. The pressures are common to all, and some of the answers also may be similar in spite of, and sometimes because of, our particular commitments. Christians cannot witness to the Lordship of Jesus Christ by remaining isolated from this search. Accepting suffering as part of bearing the cross together with our neighbors is a form of Christian witness.

Third, there is what may be called the realm of "ultimate" values. In the last analysis, religious pluralism means that there are fundamentally different answers to the problems of existence. There seems to be no way out of this plurality. One may enlarge the boundaries of the church to accommodate "anonymous" Christians. One may extend the lineage of Christ before Abraham to relate him to larger humanity. One may emphasize the "cosmic" Christ to include principalities and powers, even nature, in his domain. But this kind of "co-option" may be regarded as patronizing by our neighbors of others faiths. It may satisfy an uneasy Christian conscience, but cannot cancel the persistent fact of religious pluralism. It is certainly not acceptable to our neighbors who are "listening in" to us. The mystery of life, the challenge of death, the agony of suffering, the purpose of history, the knowledge of truth, the nature of beauty, the structure of society, the meaning of freedom, and the courage to hope in spite of all odds—these are fundamental facts of human existence from which no one can escape and to which particular religions have provided particular answers at different times and in different cultures. There are different faiths, there are alternative ways of salvation, there are different hopes about human destiny, there are different affirmations as to what happens in the end. In the last analysis, religions should be recognized as having responded differently to the mystery of the Ultimate. While recognizing the plurality of these answers, Christians believe that in Jesus Christ the Ultimate has become intimate with humanity, that nowhere else is the victory over suffering and death manifested so decisively as in the death and resurrection of Jesus Christ, and that they are called upon to share this good news humbly with their neighbors.

And finally, one must note that all religions including Christianity have an "interim" character. This only reinforces their relativity in relation to God who alone is eternal. At depth, the essential feature of all religious life is its pilgrim nature. "Beloved, we are children of God now; it does not yet appear what we shall be, but we know that when he appears we shall be like him, for we shall see him as he is" (1 John 3:2). We are always on the way. Every arrival is a departure; every departure is a movement toward the next camp. Finality should not be claimed to the oases on the way. Lingering at a particular oasis as if it is the final destination may mean that we miss the larger caravan journeying further. "For here we have no lasting city, but we seek the city to come" (Heb. 13:14). God has exalted Jesus Christ to be the Lord. In this temporary *oikoumenē* we have to live with the full assurance of his Lordship, but its realization can only be partially understood in this world of particularities. We are called upon to witness to his Lordship as we share with our neighbors the hopes, the conflicts, and the ambiguities of human life.

To this end we would humbly share with all our fellow human beings in a compelling pilgrimage. We are specifically disciples of Christ, but we refuse to limit Him to the dimensions of our human understanding. In our relationships within the many human communities we believe that we come to know Christ more fully through faith as Son of God and Saviour of the world; we grow in His service within the world; and we rejoice in the hope He gives. (*Guidelines on Dialogue,* p. 9.)

1
Response

Arthur F. Glasser

INTRODUCTION

Since Dr. Samartha and I come from rather different traditions in the Christian church, it seems important for me to begin by stating the fundamental commitments that shape my response. These commitments have, of course, historic roots in my life. I have been a servant of the church in its witness to Jews in New York City and to Buddhists in Southwest China. Raised a liberal Protestant, I subsequently underwent a series of transforming experiences coupled with much study, and emerged a convinced evangelical. This means that I belong to that segment of the church which limits the ground of religious authority to the Bible: *the Scriptures are the Word of God written and have the force of law.* When Jesus of Nazareth was crucified by Pontius Pilate in Jerusalem, it was nothing less than "God in Christ reconciling the world to himself" (2 Cor. 5:19). By that act alone men and women lay claim to the presence and friendship of God.

I also affirm those *apostolic* emphases recovered for the church in the eighteenth century Evangelical Awakening: the essential importance of personal conversion to God and the "new birth," the call to holiness of life, and the mandate for making disciples of all the *ethne*—the peoples of every tribe and tongue and nation. The God who created all peoples and who is inescapably linked to all seeks to extend his righteousness and love to all. No individual and no people is excluded. It is God's purpose that all know the Creator who in Jesus Christ became their Redeemer.

I regard myself in the mainstream of the Christian church,

the tradition of Augustine, Luther, Calvin, and Wesley. But my posture is one of critical loyalty. The empirical church is no less than, and no more than humankind's response to God's self-disclosure in Jesus Christ. Being human, it is a historically shaped religious movement, a product of culture, and thus limited, as is any human institution. And yet, by God's grace, and with the faithfulness of many of his servants, the church has managed to preserve the proclamations and truth committed to its keeping (1 Cor. 11:23–25; 15:3–7; 1 Tim. 1:3, 14; etc.). It is those proclamations and truth that must be central in our deliberations concerning the subject before us.

THE ANTICIPATED RANGE OF THIS CONSULTATION

The brochure publicizing this consultation states that we are to explore the church's understanding of the universal Lordship of Jesus Christ vis-à-vis the reality of a religiously plural world. It adds that at the present time Christians seeking to be faithful to their understanding of Christ's Lordship can be roughly divided into three groups.

First, those whose response is to endeavor to enter into dialogue with other religious traditions, with a view to open interchange on matters of ultimate concern. Their concern is to deepen the sort of mutual understanding that furthers human reciprocity.

Second, those whose response beyond dialogue is to seek as Christians to be faithful to their tradition, working for human liberation as a Christian presence in a religiously plural society. Their concern is to be distinctly Christian in their efforts to further the humanization of society.

Third, those whose response is to press on in the task of calling people—regardless of religious tradition—to personal faith in Jesus Christ with a view to establishing churches where none exist. Their concern is to extend the knowledge of Christ's Lordship.

Thus far the brochure.

GENERAL REMARKS ON DR. SAMARTHA'S PAPER

We have all listened to Dr. Samartha's address with much care and great interest. In a warm and generous fashion he has called us to reason together, by listening and sharing, so that our consultation will not be in vain. We are all already in his debt. And yet, he chooses to address only two of the three options represented in the brochure.

Dr. Samartha wants Christians to deepen their "courage for dialogue" in order to develop harmonious "relationship between people of different faiths." This is the first option. And he calls us to cooperate in a distinctly Christian fashion with the adherents of other religious traditions in defining and seeking "provisional goals" that will lead to a better worldwide community. This is a second option.

What shall we say to this? Certainly, we can all commend Dr. Samartha for his urgent desire to further mutual understanding among peoples of different religious traditions and for his distinctly Christian sense of social concern. When he affirms these validities, he speaks for us all, and challenges my own tradition especially.

But what of Dr. Samartha's apparent disregard for those Christians whose commitment to the Lordship of Christ presses them to go forth and proclaim the gospel worldwide? They believe the church should issue the call to repentance and faith, and plant congregations for worship, fellowship, and service in every segment of the human family. Dr. Samartha, however, appears to have little respect for traditional missionary work. He identifies it with "conquest," with "triumphalism," with "exclusiveness," with "manipulation," with "the superiority complex," with "ideology," and with "aggressive militancy." Dr. Samartha regards the efforts of Christians to extend "Christian particularity" as worthless, even destructive. He judges them invalid because they bring about "the extinction of other communities of faith." In a most radical conclusion, he calls for the abandonment of anything approximating this kind of mission. The task of Christians, he contends, is to bear "witness"—the sort of witness that specifically excludes the "advocacy of the Lordship of Christ."

It is difficult to know what to say. I think I speak for all of you (and certainly I speak for my own tradition) when I affirm that none of us wants to defend all that missionaries have done down through the years. No more would we want to defend all that we personally have done in the service of the church. Indeed, all of us have suffered from the terrible blindnesses and arrogance of our day and generation. The best of us perceives the will of God only "through a glass darkly." It is hard not to agree with Bishop Neill that

> . . . much of church history is dreadfully depressing . . . with great betrayals . . . dark corruption . . . and, what is worst of all . . . the terrible and self-complacent mediocrity of the average Christian congregation.
> . . . Yet, while the Churches have on the whole been successfully sleeping, a worldwide church has come into being as a result of the modern missionary enterprise (1957: 13, 24).

A worldwide church—how can we regard its existence as a total misunderstanding of the issue of Christ's Lordship? I cannot do so. At this point, however, it seems important to identify and define more clearly those crucial questions that keep recurring whenever one reflects on Christ's Lordship and the reality of religious pluralism.

Let me be specific.

SOME CRUCIAL QUESTIONS

For instance, *what do we mean by the Lordship of Christ?* I want to endorse Dr. Samartha's desire that our discussions seek a biblical focus. Even though he grants that the Bible does not give us "blueprints" to solve modern problems—a thesis I heartily accept—he contends that it is "important and necessary" that Christians "go back to the Bible for insights, indications, and directions that can help them as they struggle with new problems." This and similar statements encouraged me to believe that our conference will be productive. And I liked his cautionary word that "quoting scriptural passages can be an extremely hazardous business." Exegesis must be careful and application must be contextual. On this issue Dr. Samartha and I agree. We must *think* as well as *"live* according to Scripture" (1 Cor. 4:6).

In our understanding of Christ's Lordship, however, there is less agreement, perhaps. According to the witness of the Gospels, Christ's Lordship is inseparably linked with the issue of truth.

Jesus himself said, "You call me Teacher and Lord, and you are right, for so I am" (John 13:13). Throughout the Gospels he unabashedly and with self-conscious authority claimed to be *the* Teacher and *the* Lord of all humankind. Hence, the test of one's submission to his Lordship is the acceptance of his teaching.

I was disappointed that Dr. Samartha's paper did not raise this issue. He affirmed Christ's Lordship but did not mention his teaching. And this, even though a careful reading of the Gospels uncovers the fact that Christ was not silent about many matters related to religious pluralism. Dr. Samartha's dichotomy runs the danger of reconceptualizing the Lordship of Christ into something bearing little resemblance to the reality described in Scripture. "My teaching is not mine, but his who sent me. . . . Why do you call me 'Lord, Lord,' and not do what I tell you?" (John 7:16; Lk. 6:46). John Stott summarizes for us this insistent obligation when he affirms:

> We must allow our opinions to be moulded by his opinions, our views to be conditioned by his views. And this includes his uncomfortable and unfashionable teaching —of God, of Scripture, of the radical sinfulness of man, of the fact of divine judgment and of the solemn and eternal realities of heaven and hell . . . with a great gulf fixed between them (1970:210).

This brings up a second question: *Can one be a true disciple of Jesus and not engage in the struggle for truth?* This struggle largely characterized his public ministry. It is a plain fact of the Gospels that Jesus was not only controversial, he was a controversialist. He was anything but reluctant to issue warnings against the false teaching of some of the religious leaders of his day (Mt. 16:6). He repeatedly engaged them in controversy over the issue of truth. They were critical of him and he was outspokenly critical of them. On one memorable occasion he told them they were "wrong" and then went on to state they were "quite wrong" (Mk. 12:18—27). And this because they were ignorant of the Scriptures and of the power of God.

Again and again he spoke his convictions without hesitation, apology, or diffidence. He taught the most profound truths with quiet, unabashed dogmatism: "His word was with authority"

(Lk. 4:32; Mt. 7:28, 29; etc.).And those who confessed him as Lord made no attempt to substitute their opinions for his, or to adopt any other stance than to contend earnestly for the faith he delivered to them. As Floyd Filson has admirably summarized:

> The ancient world was a ferment of competing philosophies and religions. Denunciations of false teachers in the New Testament show that not every Christian teacher avoided the danger of surrendering to the world something essential. The steadying content of Scripture, the Jewish heritage of monotheism and moral obedience to God, and above all the *teaching, example* and *work* of Jesus *himself* enabled the church to stay clear of the swirling waters of pagan syncretism (1973:707).

But Dr. Samartha does not call us to follow this pattern of making Jesus' teaching and praxis of truth the center of our witness. Rather, he states: "There is no reason to claim that the religion developed in the desert around Mount Sinai is superior to the religion developed on the banks of the river Ganga." And I can only reply: *"The question is not superiority but truth."*

If we accept the witness of the Gospels that Jesus Christ is God incarnate, there can surely be no fuller disclosure of God in terms of manhood than is given in his person and teaching. It is the task of the church to treasure this deposit of disclosure and proclaim its mysteries. At all times it is to be "the pillar and foundation of the truth" (1 Tim. 3:15). It holds this truth firm so that it is not moved and it holds this truth aloft so that all may see it (Stott 1970:26). No other religion makes such claims and endures such agonies to defend them. One is reminded of the sally C. S. Lewis wrote in a letter to Dom Bede Griffiths:

> Your Hindus certainly sound delightful. But what do they deny? That has always been my trouble with Indians—to find any proposition they would pronounce false. But truth must surely involve exclusions! (1966:267)

This brings up a third question. *What was the reaction of Jesus to the religious pluralism of his day?* Dr. Samartha affirms that "religious pluralism means that there are fundamentally different answers to the problems of existence." He is correct. Furthermore, there is no way to piece together the "revelation" claimed in each separate religion in order to form an intelligible, coherent whole. If anything, they are mutually contradictory. All of them, including Christianity, have an "interim" character. The future— well, we must leave it with God.

These statements are disturbing. I would set them aside and ask: *"What did Jesus command his disciples to do about the religious pluralism of his day?"* Has he given us any guidelines to follow? True, we find no evidence in the Gospels that Jesus ever expressed a judgment about non-Jewish religions as such, only about their futile patterns of repetitious prayer (Mt. 6:7). All we know is that he gave unquestioned allegiance to the Old Testament and did not challenge its witness against gods other than Yahweh. He saw no possibility of other gods beside the One he knew as his Father in heaven (Mk. 12:32—34). It seems impossible to contend that his attitude to other religious systems would have been at variance with the commandment: "You shall have no other gods before Me" (Exod. 20:3). His Father was supreme and unique; the service of other gods was totally forbidden (Deut. 4:39; Isa. 44:6—20; Jer. 10:11; etc.).

And yet, Jesus used the Old Testament in a selective and original fashion to attack certain practices of the Judaism of his day. He exposed and rebuked the Pharisees' self-righteousness, religious externalism, and exclusive nationalism. He made constant effort to make sharp distinctions between the infallible truth of Scripture and the flawed practice of that truth by his people. And he commended faith wherever he found it.

But what of Jesus' regard for Gentile religious pluralism? Had he approached the non-Jewish religions of his day we would have expected him to be serious, thoughtful, and free from prejudice. We would have expected him to commend every human expression of love and every human readiness to forgive. Dr. Samartha speaks for Christ when he rightly calls us to this same spirit of charity and impartiality.

Jesus would also have raised the issue of truth. Did he not say, "All things have been delivered to me by my Father; and no one knows the Son except the Father, and no one knows the Father except the Son and anyone to whom the Son chooses to reveal him" (Mt. 11:27)? Here we are face to face with the indisputable right of God to be God, and to be free to make distinctions and choices. In the light of his perception of truth, Jesus regarded even the Samaritan offshoot of Judaism to be inferior (John 4:22), and said so. Because of this it seems difficult to argue that in the midst of the religious pluralism of our day, we should confine our witness to endorsing all religious systems as relative and deepening mutual understanding between them. And is our focus of positive attention only to commend expressions of outgoing love and social concern?

Is this the sum total of the response Christ would have us make to the issue of religious pluralism? Of course, Jesus Christ was concerned that all peoples in their interrelation with one another attain the proximate goals of social harmony, civil justice and the alleviation of poverty. *But his constant stress on the ultimate goal of the kingdom of God led him to conclude and in a very real sense climax his ministry with a mandate that his people "make disciples" of the peoples of every tribe and tongue and nation.* This was his response to the issue of religious pluralism. Each of the four Gospels bears indisputable witness to this fact. And on this basis I must advocate his Lordship today.

My remarks are by no means conclusive of all the issues raised by Dr. Samartha's paper. Their purpose is to set forth a line of questioning, without which this consultation loses its context and meaning.

BIBLIOGRAPHY

Carnell, Edward John.
    1959. *The Case for Orthodox Theology.* Philadelphia: Westminster Press.
Filson, Floyd V.
    1973. "Bible: 14 New Testament History," article in *Encyclopedia Americana*, vol. 3, pp. 702—8.
Lewis, Warren Hamilton, ed.
    1966. *Letters of C. S. Lewis.* London: Geoffrey Bles.

Neill, Stephen.
     1957.   *The Unfinished Task.* London: Edinburgh House
             Press.
Stott, John R. W.
     1970.   *Christ the Controversialist.* Downers Grove, Ill.: In-
             terVarsity Press.

2

Response

Robert J. Schreiter, C.P.P.S.

Dr. Samartha deserves our thanks for a rich and stimulating paper. He draws together a number of important and interconnecting ideas, which not only embrace our concerns here but also will engage our interests for quite some time to come. What exactly religion is meant to be; what we mean (and what should happen) when we confess Jesus as Lord; what are the frameworks and attitudes for dialogue; what religious pluralism will mean for us in terms of all of these—this constitutes a powerful and provocative agenda.

These areas of concern are not new. But in posing his questions, Dr. Samartha brings some important dimensions to this discussion. First of all, he comes from a part of the world where other major religious traditions can equally claim a wisdom and depth of insight into the human condition as it touches the divine. Thus he avoids the kind of ethnocentrism which too often marks Christian discussion about the Lordship of Christ and religious pluralism.

Second, he reminds us that the question before us is not only a theological one, but a pastoral one as well. We are talking about millions of people, and not just a few ideas. And this deserves our attention.

The best compliment to be paid to Dr. Samartha's work here

might be to highlight a couple of points in his deeply textured presentation and follow them out to see where they might lead. This tracing out of a few implications may go beyond his intent, and may not represent where he would like to see his argument go; nonetheless, it could be a significant kind of undertaking. I would like to dwell on three interconnected points: (1) the Lordship of Christ as a pastoral as well as a theological problem; (2) religion as a way of life *(dharma)* and as a view of life *(dristi);* (3) what these affirmations mean for our confession of Jesus as Lord.

THE LORDSHIP OF CHRIST AS A THEOLOGICAL AND A PASTORAL PROBLEM

We Westerners have been struggling with how to understand the universal significance of the particularity of the Jesus-event for a long time. How can the activity of God in Jesus, confined to a particular time and place, have ultimate significance for all peoples in all places at all times? In the early periods of our history, the Apologists and later figures such as Lactantius provided us with alternate models of accommodation and combat. But the problem really became acute after the beginning of the so-called voyages of discovery, and especially after the introduction of the study of Sanskrit into the West in the eighteenth century. We were confronted with traditions of theology and logic at least as sophisticated as our own.

The West tried to resolve this problem for itself by turning to post-Enlightenment philosophy to relate the various traditions to Christianity. Hegel showed us that our chance for resolving this problem might be to follow a dialectical path, which would encompass all religions, including Christianity, in a process of movement toward a concrete universal.[1] Other nineteenth-century thinkers, drawing upon the burgeoning historical research into Indian and Buddhist traditions, developed a more historical dialectic, which showed both the historical and the philosophical plausibility of the superiority of Christianity. Perhaps Ernst Troeltsch would be the best example of this.[2]

I think it would be fair to say that, in relating the various great religious traditions, we have not made significant progress since the nineteenth century. A formal, philosophical approach, growing out of our disjunctive, either/or kinds of logic, simply cannot wrap itself around the problem. Our very modes of thought seem to fail us in solving this problem of the universal claim of Christianity in the face of other religious traditions.

But if our modes of thought do not lend themselves to solving the problem of how Jesus, living at a certain place and at a certain time, can have universal significance, even in a pluralistic world, then why do we keep trying? Perhaps we are looking in the wrong place, or not casting our net widely enough, to deal with our dilemma. Dr. Samartha has given us the glimmer of an insight when he suggests that the Lordship of Christ may be a pastoral as well as a theological problem. Let's carry this a step further.

If a problem remains intellectually intractable, perhaps there are other forces coming to bear upon it that cannot be encompassed by the cognitive categories we are using. Christian theology has become more aware of this fact in recent years. The sociology of knowledge has taught us that ideas do not fall from the sky; certain social conditions make certain ideas more plausible and acceptable at certain times than others. Likewise, social conditions may make certain problems more critical for a community at certain times than others. Second, the growing concern for contextual theology, that is, theology which is sensitive to and reflects its concrete context, has captured our imagination. Liberation theology, as one form of contextual theology, demands that we give place for social analysis as a necessary preliminary to any theological reflection.

While many theologians would be ready to admit all of this, are we really aware of how much our environment obtrudes upon our thought patterns? It goes far more deeply than we might imagine. Theology cannot be done in abstraction from its environment. While the revelation of God cannot be reduced to its historical and social circumstances, it cannot be understood or developed without them either. Why we as Christians attend to certain issues and not to others, why certain parts of the Scriptures are read more closely than others, why certain problems become burning at certain times—the motivations for all these are often more social and personal than cognitive. Some examples might be helpful here.

Why could the New Testament communities live with a gentle

pluralism of understandings about the divinity of Jesus, yet be torn apart by the Jewish-Gentile question? Why was Montanism considered a heresy in the second century and Egyptian monasticism included within orthodox Christianity in the fourth? When we read our history in this fashion, it becomes apparent that we are dealing in more than ideas. The pluralism in Christology of the New Testament became unacceptable in the fourth century; and the unacceptable Montanists of the second century became the saints of the Egyptian desert in the fourth. Why is this?

One cannot answer these questions purely on the basis of cognitive categories or some notion of a development of dogma. There are some clear pastoral problems underlying these questions about what constitutes the community of the church. To put it another way: we deal not only in ideas, but also in identity. Anthropologists such as Mary Douglas have pointed out that two key aspects in identity are group belonging, or relatedness, and world-view. She calls these "group" and "grid."[3]

Sociologists tell us that if group boundaries are relatively strong and people feel secure, they can withstand a lot of variance in ideas or cognitive dissonance.[4] But if the group is hard to define or threatens to break down, a more uniform world-view becomes important. And in many instances, the battle for one is actually fought on the field of the other: a threat to a group will be symbolized as a threat to some idea. Often to outsiders the difference in idea will seem small and not terribly significant. But the passion about group boundary gives uncanny vigor to the intellectual debate. Many of the so-called heresies in the Christian church were not terribly dissonant from the received view.[5] Yet the group supporting these ideas was tearing apart the body of Christ, and so the ideas needed to be attacked. The dispute with some Gnostic groups in the early centuries, or with the Albigensians in the Middle Ages, had not so much to do with their ideas (which diverged less from received views than some of the theological schools operant at those times) as with their threats to group definition.[6] In both instances, accepted concepts of authority within the group were being threatened. Perhaps the greatest example of this is the discussion on the justification by faith and works in the sixteenth century. Contemporary scholarship has shown that there really is no substantive difference between the Lutheran and Roman Catholic views; yet it provoked a major split in the Western church.[7] From a sociological point of view, what might have made Luther successful where Wycliffe and Hus failed was the readiness of German princes to give him shelter. There was a struggle over who would control both church and state politics. Luther put the spark to the tinder and provoked a regrouping in Western Christianity on the slender basis of a different emphasis in doctrine.

What does this have to do with the problem at hand? Perhaps our struggle with ideas is a transposed struggle with our communities. Our so-called problem of other religions is not a problem for those other religions, as Dr. Samartha has reminded us. Perhaps it is not how we understand others, but how we understand ourselves that is the problem. Is the often parallel doctrine of Indian and Buddhist traditions a threat to our group boundaries?

RELIGION AS A WAY OF LIFE AND AS A VIEW OF LIFE

Dr. Samartha reminds us that religion is both *dharma* and *dristi*. To put it another way, it is people, not theological systems, which are religious. For most of the world, religion is a way of life, interwoven into a larger fabric. Views within religion are seen as feeble attempts to formulate the experience of the way. Veteran dialoguers are aware of the gentle bemusement with which Buddhists or Hindus sometimes greet our seriousness about doctrinal matters, and ask why we think doctrine, rather than experience, should constitute the stuff of dialogue. That the idea of double-belonging in the Buddhist/Christian dialogue (i.e., that one can be a Buddhist and a Christian at the same time) is a growing one reflects this same reality.[8] Why is it that the interreligious dialogues among monks of East and West seem to have been more productive than those of theologians?

But we Christians insist that membership in our group is first and foremost a matter of belief. Why did the *view* of life come to predominate over the *way* of life in Christianity (perhaps a similar case could be made for Islam)? Judaism is the source and sharer of much of our religion, yet does not share what we give to religion as a view of life. To be a Jew today encompasses a wide range of possibilities.[9] Nor can we claim the shift on the basis of the historicity of our founder; the Buddha, Gautama Śakyamuni, is deeply etched in history, yet his followers do not share our intense concern for dogma and belief. (Dr. Samartha's comments about Jesus' theocentrism and our Christocentrism are apropos here.)

Does our way of life as Christians demand this explicitness in our view of life? Or is this a product of moments in our history? Does it grow out of Catholic Christianity's unique relation with the Roman empire, where to be a citizen was to be a Catholic Christian? Take, for example, the fact that the emperor called the first great councils. Ideas were causing division and unrest; Arian Christianity was a rallying point for the Goths. Constantine seemed to be willing to accept either Christological view, as long as there was consensus. And according to some accounts, unity rather than orthodoxy was a major concern in the deliberations.[10] If this is the case, our concern for right believing may reflect historic policing functions within a social polity more than any mandate of Jesus. We were commanded by Jesus to believe in the coming of the kingdom; but nowhere do we discover what exactly the kingdom is.

Another source of our giving primacy to view of life over way of life may stem from the Reformation. The role of the principle of *sola scriptura* (impossible to implement before the advent of the printing press) placed the core of group definition on a text, rather than on a more ambiguous tradition or magisterium. One could thus argue church order on ideas to which all had access, rather than on fuzzy precedent. The so-called Protestant Principle would require this primacy of view over way. Does this historical situation explain why Roman Catholics have been able to move toward the accommodationist approaches we find in such official documents as *Nostra Aetate* and *Redemptor Hominis,* which leave Protestant Christians uncomfortable?

What I am trying to say here is that Christianity's giving predominance to religion as a view of life rather than a way of life cannot be traced to Jesus or the New Testament as such. We have too many examples within the New Testament and later Christianity that speak differently. To cite one final example: liturgy, the gathering of people, and tradition have always been the prime determiner of ideas for Orthodox Christians.

Thus we need to shift the base for our reflection on a theology of dialogue. Why are ideas so important to us? What does this emphasis on ideas say about our pastoral experience of community in the Lord Jesus Christ? Dr. Samartha alluded to Psalm 137 and wondered whether the problem is singing the Lord's song in a foreign land or singing a foreign song in the Lord's land. He is on the mark here.

CONFESSING JESUS AS LORD

What does all this have to do with how we confess Jesus as Lord? It is interesting that Dr. Samartha chose three aspects of confessing Jesus as *Kurios* out of all the possibilities: *kurios* as relating to resurrection, as servant, as related to the Father. In other words, *kurios* as life-giver, as servant, as familial relation. How different this Lordship is, this Lordship centering upon nurture and group belonging, from the territorial and military metaphors we Westerners often use! Dr. Samartha has selected out references to Lordship rooted in Jesus' identification with God *(Kurios* as the Septuagint translation for the Hebrew *YHWH* and *Adonai)*. We often select meanings of *kurios* to talk of "establishing Jesus' Lordship," "overcoming the powers of this age," "winning souls for Christ."

To go back a last time to the group and grid distinction: Why do we talk of Lordship in terms of expanding our territory or group? Words of control, of possessiveness, of extension, of inclusion and exclusion run rife. What does this have to do with the understanding of Jesus' becoming *Kurios* by emptying himself (Phil. 2:6–11)? What is wrong with our group boundary and sense to urge us into all of this?

In conclusion, we need to look more closely at the social context which gives shape and urgency to our quest to understand better the meaning of the Lordship of Christ. We need to become more keenly aware of why we are impatient with dialogue and insist on conversion, why we are worried about our motivation for mission, why we select certain meanings of Lordship that are peripheral to its central meaning in our Scriptures. This is not a plea for a massive psychoanalytic project. But I feel we shall not make significant progress on the question at hand until we understand the context better. The question has as much to do with the state of our communities and our sense of belonging as it does with our formulation of ideas. The perspective that Dr. Samartha has brought should make us all see that a bit more clearly. Our problem may indeed not be singing the Lord's song in a foreign land; perhaps it is our songs which have become foreign in God's world.

NOTES

1. G. W. F. Hegel, *Lectures on the Philosophy of Religion*, trans. E. B. Speirs and J. B. Sanderson (London: Routledge, 1895).

2. Ernst Troeltsch, *The Absoluteness of Christianity*, trans. David Reid (Richmond: John Knox Press, 1971).

3. Mary Douglas, *Natural Symbols* (London: Barrie and Jenkins, 1970).

4. See particularly the work of Lewis Coser, *The Functions of Social Conflict* (New York: Free Press, 1956).

5. Walter Bauer, *Orthodoxy and Heresy in Earliest Christianity* (1934), (Philadelphia: Fortress Press, 1971), is an important figure in this area. See also the discussion in John Gager, *Kingdom and Christianity* (Englewood Cliffs, N.J.: Prentice-Hall, 1975), pp. 76–92.

6. On the Gnostics, see Elaine Pagels, *The Gnostic Gospels* (New York: Random House, 1979); on the Albigensians, see Emmanuel LeRoy Ladurie, *Montaillou: The Promised Land of Error* (New York: Basic Books, 1978).

7. See especially Harry McSorley, *Luther: Right or Wrong?* (Minneapolis: Augsburg, 1969).

8. See the discussion in Joseph Spae, "The Buddhist-Christian Encounter," *Pro Mundi Vita Bulletin*, no. 67 (July–August 1977).

9. See the helpful discussion on Jewish attitudes to this question in Eugene Borowitz, "The Lure and Limits of Universalizing Our Faith," in Donald Dawe and John Carman, eds., *Christian Faith in a Religiously Plural World* (Maryknoll, N.Y.: Orbis Books, 1978), pp. 59–68.

10. Robert M. Grant, "Religion and Politics at the Council of Nicaea," *Journal of Religion* 55 (1975): 1–12.

3

Reply

Stanley J. Samartha

I am grateful to Dr. Glasser and Dr. Schreiter not only for their thoughtful comments, but also for the sensitive manner in which they have made their points. The difference in the approach of these two responses is striking—one coming from a Roman Catholic background and the other described as an "evangelical" response. Because of this difference I find it difficult to discover common points in them to which I can respond together. I am a member of the Church of South India, which means that, among other factors, my experience of living together with neighbors of other faiths has inevitably influenced my Christian life and thinking. Does not this mean that within the larger fellowship of the worldwide church a plurality of approaches to such a fundamental matter as the Lordship of Christ should be given greater recognition than any demand to conform to a particular interpretation? This plurality, of course, is not in the central affirmation of the Lordship of Christ to which the New Testament bears witness, but in the manner of understanding its content and in ways of confessing Christ in a pluralist world.

Since Dr. Glasser has described his comments as an "evangelical" response, some of his critical points did not come as a surprise to me. I have many evangelical friends both in India and abroad. I share with them their love of the Bible, their commitment to Jesus Christ, and their desire to bear witness to Jesus Christ. These points, together with a deep religious experience, come out in Dr. Glasser's paper with great intensity. However, I have considerable hesitation about some of his assumptions. For example, he claims "to be in the mainstream of the Christian church," which he understands to be "the tradition of Augustine, Luther, Calvin, and Wesley." The spiritual insights gained through the Reformation are certainly important to me, particularly when the roots of my own church tradition go back to it. But how can one talk of "the mainstream of the Christian church" without referring to the Roman Catholic and Eastern Orthodox churches? How can we exclude church fathers like Clement of Alexandria, Origen, the two Gregorys, Aquinas—to mention only a few—from the list? Further, there are little tributaries that sometimes contribute in some measure to the ongoing flow of the mainstream. Therefore, the insights gained and lessons learned by communities of Christians outside Europe and North America who are actually living together with neighbors of other faiths cannot be ignored, especially in discussing a topic like the Lordship of Christ.

The authority of the Bible is obviously important to any discussion on the Lordship of Jesus Christ. But there are differences among Christians in understanding the nature of this authority and its application to particular situations. I find it difficult to accept the view which "limits the ground of religious authority to the Bible" alone and to regard the Scriptures as having "the force of law." Without taking into account the long experience of the church in interpreting the Bible down the centuries and without being open to the guidance of the Holy Spirit there is the danger of scriptural texts being misused. I am sure Dr. Glasser too recognizes this, but I must confess that his statement that the Scripture, as the written Word of God, has "the force of law" bothers me. In asking for a greater recognition of the church and the Holy Spirit in interpreting the Bible, at least one question may be raised. Is any exegesis by itself—for example, of Israel's relation to the nations in the Old Testament or of those few passages such as Paul's speech at Athens in the New Testament —sufficient basis to conclude that the entire religious life of Hindus and Buddhists extending to more than three thousand years of spiritual struggle and devotion has no share "in the struggle for truth" at all or is "wrong" or "quite wrong"? The limitation is surely not in the Word of God, but in historical and cultural circumstances, which inevitably change from time to time.

The question of truth is indeed important, but God's love is even more important. The Sanskrit word *sat*, applied to God, means both "being" and "truth." The Hebrew word *emeth* emphasizes God's "truthfulness," his abiding "trustworthiness." The Greek word *alētheia* contrasts that which is true from that which is false. That Jesus Christ is "the way, the truth, and the life" is the affirmation by which we live as Christians. When the question of truth is introduced into a discussion on neighbors of other faiths, there is often a hidden assumption that other religions are "false." The struggle between truth and falsehood, which goes on within every religion, should not be subtly transformed into a struggle between Christianity and other religions. The combination of grace and truth in Jesus Christ should not be forgotten. We are possessed by God's love; we do not possess it. We are illumined by God's truth in Jesus Christ; we are not the source of that illumination. C. S. Lewis is not the only one who had "trouble with Indians." Others too have had that experience. If he had taken a little more trouble and probed deeper into Hindu spirituality, perhaps he would have understood why Mahatma Gandhi described his autobiography as "The Story of My Experiments with Truth." Love takes precedence over truth. The demand for a prior acceptance of Jesus Christ as Truth before sharing with our neighbors the love of God in Christ is unhelpful.

Dr. Glasser misunderstands me when he says that I advocate "the sort of witness that specifically excludes the advocacy of the Lordship of Christ." This is quite wrong. He also says that I appear "to have little respect for traditional missionary work." This too is quite wrong. But for the traditional missionary work I and many of my fellow countrymen and-women would not have experienced the joy of God's grace in Christ transforming personal and community life in history. We are grateful to God for his gift in Christ brought to us by our missionary friends. All missionary institutions, insofar as they are human institutions, stand under the judgment of God, which sometimes means human criticism as well. I am occasionally surprised at the sensitiveness of some missionaries and their feeling of being hurt when attention is drawn to attitudes of paternalism, "conquest," "triumphalism," and so forth, which sometimes get mixed up with some of the missionary methods. Drawing attention to them is not "disrespect," but a means of recognizing them together in order that our common witness may be purified and come closer to the spirit of Christ. Further, should not Christians also take into account the sensitiveness of our neighbors of other faiths about whose cherished religious life and convictions Christians have been making enormously negative statements in the name of mission? Even today when one listens to certain types of radio broadcasts and reads certain types of literature advocating strident evangelism I ask myself whether such militancy is in accord with the spirit of Christ. What I am pleading for, therefore, is a different type of spiritual attitude on the part of those who witness to the Lordship of Christ—an attitude that is less aggressive, but far more humble, far less dependent on sophisticated organization, technological devices, and finance, but far more dependent on the instrumentality of quiet, simple, and committed Christian communities and on the self-sufficiency of the grace of God in Christ to transform human lives working as leaven, as salt, as light, as the mustard seed. "If you are sugar, the ants will come to you. If you are light, the moths will fly to you," said another troublesome Indian. Therefore, far from excluding the advocacy of the Lordship of Christ from Christian witness, I call for that kind of Christian witness which is more in harmony with the spirit of Jesus Christ who emptied himself and became obedient even unto death.

I am in general agreement both with the interpretations Dr. Schreiter has given to some of my suggestions and with the framework in which he puts them. He has drawn attention to the inadequacy of cognitive categories to do justice to the complexity of interreligious relationships where communities are concerned. In this respect *tarka* (logic) seems to be less helpful than *anubhava* (experience, intuition). Further, his call to take into more serious account the sociology of knowledge to understand why certain aspects in Christ's Lordship are stressed by the Christian community at certain times in history is helpful to reject notions that are obsolete and sometimes become hindrances to Christian neighborly life. When a community is expanding or is threatened, "words of control, of possessiveness, of extension, of inclusion and exclusion" seem to help people to guard their identity. But if we recognize that Jesus became *Kurios* by emptying himself, then the "talk of Lordship in terms of expanding our territory or group" becomes questionable. Thus he points out that in my presentation I have selected those aspects of Christ's Lordship that touch the resurrection, that is, life through death; his role as servant, that is, not of domination; and his filial relation to the Father.

I have two observations to make. There are indeed pastoral elements in the church's treatment of the Lordship of Christ. That is, the Christian community needs to clarify to itself the meaning of the Lordship of Christ in order to strengthen its commitment, its growth in maturity, and its life of witness. The credibility and joy of Christian worship is bound up with the Lordship of Christ. However, one has to be careful not to subordinate the need for rigorous theological thinking to the pastoral requirements of the community. Even when the pastoral needs of the community are met more or less, the theological problem of how to confess the Lordship of Christ in a pluralist world remains. Therefore what is essentially a theological problem should not be reduced to just a pastoral concern.

Second, it is true that I have emphasized those aspects of Christ's Lordship which seem to be most helpful to confess him in a religiously plural world. However, my choice is not because of any expediency, but because to me these points are central; it is the notion of "control," "extension," "possessiveness," and so forth that are peripheral. It may be that at this time we need more a sociological understanding of the theological enterprise than a theological interpretation of sociology. My choice of these points, however, is not because of contemporary social needs of the church but because they are basic to the New Testament witness to Christ. In fairness, I must point out that Dr. Schreiter himself recognizes this when he says that "the revelation of God cannot be reduced to its historical and social circumstances." But I felt it necessary to emphasize this point in order to avoid any ambiguity or misunderstanding.

III

"No Other Name"—
An Evangelical Conviction

Waldron Scott

By way of introduction let me acknowledge the obvious: I am using the term "evangelical" as a matter of convenience. I am aware that it is properly appropriated, for example, by German Lutherans as well as by Latin American Protestants of all kinds. But I employ the term in a narrower sense to refer to those Christians who, in some circles at least, are commonly called "conservative evangelicals." While that phrase is not altogether inappropriate, I find it a bit cumbersome.

When I speak of evangelicals I have in mind those who are associated in various ways with the World Evangelical Fellowship, as well as those who would find themselves in general sympathy with the first three sections of the Lausanne Covenant of 1974, particularly paragraph 2, "The Authority and Power of the Bible." Elsewhere I have described evangelicals as those who, historically, have placed a high premium on the authority of Scripture, the necessity for new birth, the cultivation of private devotional habits, and the imperative of world evangelization.[1] Many evangelicals are found in separatist churches but others, including myself, are members of mainline denominations.

THE HISTORICAL JESUS

Evangelicals are a biblically oriented people. Precisely because the theme of Christ's Lordship is biblically grounded, it becomes

58

inescapable to evangelicals. It is not a human insight but a divine revelation, which must be maintained and obeyed at all costs. "Flesh and blood has not revealed this to you," the Lord Jesus said to Peter after his confession at Caesarea Philippi, "but my Father who is in heaven" (Mt. 16:17). I take it that as Christians we do not question but, rather, assume Christ's Lordship and therefore simply seek to understand the meaning, implications, and expressions of it in the context of religious pluralism.

To begin with, evangelicals cannot separate the Lordship of Christ from the historical figure of Jesus, nor from the historic name of Jesus. The historical Jesus whom doubting Thomas was invited to touch is the very one who invokes the response, "My Lord and my God" (John 20:28). After Jesus' ascension, angels declared, "Men of Galilee . . . *this Jesus,* who was taken up from you into heaven, will come in the same way as you saw him go into heaven" (Acts 1:11, italics added). It is the Jesus of Nazareth who came to Israel preaching good news of peace who is proclaimed Lord of all by Peter to a Gentile seeker (Acts 10:36). And it is at the name of this same Jesus that "every knee should bow and every tongue confess that he is Lord, to the glory of God the Father" (Phil. 2:10–11). Thus the Lausanne Covenant declares:

We also reject as derogatory to Christ and the Gospel every kind of syncretism and dialogue which implies that Christ speaks equally through all religions and theologies. Jesus Christ, being himself the only God-man, who gave himself as the only ransom for sinners, is the only mediator between God and man. There is no other name by which we must be saved. All men are perishing because of sin, but God loves all men, not wishing that any should perish but that all should repent. Yet those who reject Christ repudiate the joy of salvation and condemn themselves to eternal separation from God. To proclaim Jesus as "the Savior of the world" is not to affirm that all religions offer salvation in Christ. Rather it is to proclaim God's love for a world of sinners and to invite all men to respond to him as Savior and Lord in the wholehearted personal commitment of repentance and faith. Jesus Christ has been exalted above every other name; we long for the day when every knee shall bow to him and every tongue shall confess him Lord.[2]

The issue of the translatability of the name of Jesus, which Donald Dawe has raised,[3] is therefore of special concern to evangelicals. We would agree that the name of Jesus is no magical formula. Nor should it be the basis for a new legalism. But we are uneasy with the idea that the name of Jesus is merely the "disclosure of the pattern of God's action in human history," which Dawe takes as the basis for understanding the particularity and universality of Christianity.

What disturbs me as an evangelical is the phrase "pattern of . . . action." There seems to be something cyclical, something repetitive, implied in the phrase that stands in opposition to the definitiveness of the one, universally efficacious act at Calvary.

> But as it is, he has appeared *once for all* at the end of the age to put away sin by the sacrifice of himself. And just as it is appointed for men to die once, and after that comes judgment, so Christ, having been offered *once* to bear the sin of many, will appear a second time, not to deal with sin but to save those who are eagerly waiting for him (Heb. 9:26–28, italics added).

This passage does not suggest that Jesus' atoning death was the pattern for God's saving acts in Jewish history but, rather, that God's saving acts in history pointed to (were a pattern for) his definitive act at the cross. Thus to evangelicals there is much more to the death and resurrection of Jesus than "the encoding of a pattern of existence" marked by finding life through dying to self and operating throughout the world under the names of many religious traditions. At Calvary the sins of "the many" were borne once and for all. This information, this good news, is relevant to men and women of all religions, including nominal adherents to Christianity.

Rather than translating the name of Jesus into some universal philosophical or religious concept, evangelicals are more concerned to proclaim the universal and definitive consequences of the concrete once-for-all event that occurred at the cross. We would be less likely to utilize Calvary to illumine patterns of self-giving in other religions than to utilize such patterns in other religions to illumine the significance of Calvary.

THE GREAT COMMISSION

Another facet of Christ's Lordship relates to the Great Commission. *"All authority* in heaven and on earth has been given to me. *Go therefore* and make disciples of all nations . . ." (Mt. 28:18–19, italics added). The missionary movement—traditionally focused on cross-cultural evangelism, conversion, church-planting, discipling, and service—has been and continues to be for evangelicals an authentic expression of the Lordship of Christ in a religiously pluralistic world. It is not the only expression and, in a given situation, not necessarily the initial expression, but it is nevertheless a major expression. Within the missionary movement evangelicals see concepts of Christian presence, dialogue, and the struggle against unjust social systems as contributing to, in one way or another, the actual proclamation of Jesus' death, resurrection, and kingly rule.

When I speak of the missionary enterprise I do not mean the Western missionary movement only. Today there are over four hundred so-called Third World missions. Most of them are evangelical in orientation, engaged in cross-cultural discipling activities in obedience to the Lord's command. To date they have fielded more than three thousand missionaries in at least fifty countries. The missionary department of ECWA (the Evangelical Churches of West Africa), for instance, has sent out over two hundred missionary couples. Eight indigenous missionary societies have banded together to form the Indian Evangelical Missions Association, headquartered in Bangalore. The World Evangelical Fellowship (WEF) has established an international Missions Commission, one objective of which is to promote cooperation among these Third World missions, and between them and the older Western missions.

Another objective of WEF's Missions Commission is to stimulate the development of a new missiology more relevant to a world of religious pluralism. While not convinced that the continuity/ discontinuity debate is fruitless, we do recognize that it has been carried on primarily by and from the West. New conceptual categories may therefore by required if the Great Commission is to be fulfilled in our day and age, as Gerald H. Anderson has suggested.[4] We suspect that these will emerge from the experience of Third World mission leaders submitted to the Lordship of Christ, and from Christian communities of Asia and Africa that undergird them. It is doubtful, however, that the line Choan-Seng Song has taken in his book *Christian Mission in Reconstruction— An Asian Analysis* is likely to be accepted by Third World evangelical leaders.[5]

TRIUMPHALISM

An earlier generation of evangelicals (indeed, churchpeople of all shades of theological opinion) expected Christianity to prevail over all the earth. They saw the then embryonic missionary movement as a means to this end. As early as the mid-eighteenth-century the great evangelical Jonathan Edwards anticipated this expansion of Christianity and prophesied, "Then all countries and nations, even those which are now most ignorant, shall be full of light and knowledge. . . . There shall then be universal peace and a good understanding among the nations of the world. . . . Then shall all the world be united in one amiable society. . . . All the world shall then be as one church, one orderly, regular beautiful society."[6]

This truly triumphalistic vision characterized a great deal of both evangelical *and* liberal thinking in the nineteenth century as well. Nearly one hundred years ago (1884) Josiah Strong served as general secretary of the Evangelical Alliance in the United States. According to Strong, "God, with infinite wisdom and skill, is training the Anglo-Saxon race for an hour sure to come in the world's future. . . . This race of unequaled energy, with all the majesty of numbers and might of wealth behind it—the representative, let us hope, of the largest liberty, the purest Christianity, the highest civilization—having developed peculiarly aggressive traits calculated to impress its institutions upon mankind, will spread itself over the earth."[7] Similarly, around the turn of the century Henry Churchill King, then president of Oberlin College and a spokesman for the liberal cause, could denounce American imperialism while virtually underscoring the religious triumphalism of Edwards and Strong.[8]

In the twentieth century, however, evangelical thinking has changed considerably. Under the influence of dispensational theology, with an associated premillennialism, evangelicals have accepted the fact of continuous religious pluralism. We do not expect the walls of Islam, Hinduism, Buddhism, or communism for that matter, to come tumbling down. To change the metaphor, and to quote Jesus in a context some may find offensive, we expect the wheat and the tares to "grow together" until the harvest, the end of the world (Mt. 13:30). In place of the disintegration of entire religious systems and their replacement by the Christian faith, evangelicals today speak more often of the Lord "taking out a people for his name" (Acts 15:14). In this perspective evangelicals see the missionary movement as a means of planting churches within as many cultural units of the world's population as possible. A great deal of current evangelical interest focuses on the estimated 16,750 cultural units ("hidden peoples") still unreached by any Christian witness.[9]

This too is a kind of triumphalism, of course, but of a more modest nature. It is anticipated that by sowing the gospel like seed throughout the great religious regions of humankind evangelical communities will spring up, which will (in the gloomier scenarios) act as lifeboats rescuing men and women from ungodly cultures, or (in the more optimistic scenarios) ferment like yeast to make the surrounding cultures "more Christian." In other words, contemporary evangelical concern focuses on evangelization as the proclamation of the gospel in every nation rather than the conquest of religions *per se*, or the total conversion of religiously based cultures. If as a result of proclaiming the gospel a particular people—tribe, caste, or other—turns to Christ *in toto*, well and good. If it does not, the mandate to preach the gospel to every culture and make disciples in all nations remains. The Great Commission has never been rescinded.

THE SERVANT LORD

After the Lord Jesus had defended the right of his disciples, against the religiously based socioeconomic system of his day, to pluck grain on the Sabbath to assuage their hunger—and after he had healed a man on the Sabbath, again in confrontation with the

leaders of his nation—Matthew the evangelist interprets Jesus'
action in these words (12:17–21):

> This was to fulfill what was spoken by the prophet Isaiah:
>
>> "Behold, my servant whom I have chosen,
>> my beloved with whom my soul is well pleased.
>> I will put my Spirit upon him,
>> and he shall proclaim justice to the Gentiles.
>> He will not wrangle or cry aloud,
>> nor will anyone hear his voice in the streets;
>> he will not break a bruised reed
>> or quench a smoldering wick,
>> till he brings justice to victory;
>> and in his name will the Gentiles hope."

Jesus the Lord is the lord of justice. He is the Spirit-filled Servant whose mission it is to proclaim justice to the nations. He is
the persevering one who will bring justice to victory. He is the
ultimate hope of the nations. Followers of Jesus Christ will acknowledge and respond to his Lordship by working for justice
everywhere. It is common knowledge that much of the injustice
present in our global society is the result of religious bias and
intolerance. Within the context of Christianity *apartheid* comes
immediately to mind. But the phenomenon is not limited to Christianity.

In the midst of religious pluralism Christians must be prepared
to cooperate with people of other faiths in rectifying situations
inimical to human welfare and promoting activities that aim at
establishing justice. Whether all evangelicals are prepared to cooperate so intimately is still a moot question. At the very least all
of us should strive to correct injustices that exist within our own
communities or that stem from the impact of our activities, not
least our missionary activities, in other countries.

SIN AND THE BIBLICAL WITNESS

Underlying the evangelical perspective and approach is a biblically informed theology of human sin and its religious expressions

that is in stark contrast to that held by many Christians engaged in interreligious dialogue today. For example, in the earlier consultation on religious pluralism Donald Dawe, citing Ezekiel's admonition of Jerusalem ("she has wickedly rebelled against my ordinances more than the nations") suggested that this meant other nations had a knowledge of the law to which they were more faithful than the Chosen People.[10] Evangelicals reading the same passage would understand Ezekiel to be evaluating levels of rebellion, not levels of faithfulness! That the nations have a knowledge of God is admitted. But Ezekiel's emphasis is on the fact that all peoples react to that knowledge by rebellion, not obedience, some more so than others, perhaps. "Although they knew God they did not honor him as God, or give thanks to him" (Rom. 1:21).

I draw attention to Dawe's comment, not to take issue with the main point he was making in context—that the Covenant People are not exempt from divine judgment while all other peoples can expect only judgment—for this point is surely valid. Rather, I am suggesting that Dawe's reading of Scripture and his objection to triumphalism appears to stem in part, at least, from presuppositions regarding man and religion that evangelicals would seriously question. Clarifying these presuppositions may be a useful exercise in this consultation, though I realize they are already familiar to many.

The Lausanne Covenant states: "We recognize that all men have some knowledge of God through his general revelation in nature. But we deny that this can save, for men suppress the truth by their unrighteousness."[11] Evangelicals see in the biblical testimony a low view, not a high view, of people's religions. Surely this is true of the Old Testament witness where idols are known to be human-made and consequently powerless to save (Isa. 44:9ff.). Evangelicals do not perceive a significantly different evaluation in New Testament writings. The Roman Cornelius, for example, was a prayerful, benevolent, sincere man who, nevertheless, had neither salvation nor life (Acts 11:14, 18) until the gospel was proclaimed to him.

Furthermore, the biblical witness cannot be said to stem from an isolated experience vis-à-vis the religions of the world. Israel's contact with Egypt, Canaan, Syria, Babylonia, and Persia, and the early church's experience with the intense and highly diversified religious ferment of the Greco-Roman world, was both extensive and intensive.

Evangelicals are aware that God is constantly active in the Christian and the non-Christian world alike. He has not left himself without witness. He is not far from anyone. He gives light to everyone. He reveals himself in nature and his light, which "is plain" and can be "clearly perceived" (Rom. 1:19–20), may very well be reflected, in greater or lesser degree, in the religions of humanity. Yet people reject the awareness they have. They do not acknowledge God in truth. They utilize their religiosity to escape from God. This is as patently true of the Christian religion in its cultural expressions (for at best Christianity is a flawed, human response to the revealed gospel of Jesus Christ) as it is of non-Christian religions.

I am aware that this relation of the gospel to the world's religions is hardly distinguishable from Hendrik Kraemer's thesis of "radical discontinuity" and that many Christian thinkers, including my good friend Gerald Anderson, see this as a dead-end concept. Yet evangelicals would insist that a low view of religions as means of ultimate revelation does not preclude appreciation for, and even a high view of, world religions as cultural expressions of humankind's drives and, consequently, a high view of the possibilities of interreligious dialogue. That is, evangelicals do not see interreligious dialogue as a means for discovering God but as a way of understanding *humankind*, and an opportunity to experience and express solidarity with our fellow human beings.

A biblical view of the faiths of humankind is not a dead end. Far from it. Rather, it is a narrow way provided by a gracious Providence to guide us into fruitful dialogue with others. "Salvation is of the Jews," Jesus explained to the Samaritan woman (John 4:22). Was this merely a chauvinistic assertion? Hardly! Was it not, rather, his candid evaluation of the Samaritan religion? And was it not a pointer to what God has done (or was about to do) for humankind in a particular historical person and event?

EVANGELICALS IN DIALOGUE

At a recent consultation on theology and mission, David Hesselgrave of Trinity Evangelical Divinity School called on evangelicals to review their attitude of disinterest and nonparticipation in dialogue. In a world of religious pluralism, he said, evangelical witness, preaching, and teaching should become increasingly dialogical. Hesselgrave had several types of dialogue in mind. These included dialogue on the nature of dialogue, interreligious dialogue to promote freedom of worship and witness, dialogue concerned with meeting human need, dialogue designed to break down barriers of distrust within the religious world, and dialogue that has as its objective mutual comprehension of conflicting truth claims.

Obviously this brief list does not exhaust the possible dialogical responses to religious pluralism. Indeed, it is as revealing for what it leaves out as for what it includes. What is of more immediate interest, however, is the response that participants in the consultation—all evangelicals—made to Hesselgrave's call. Their response was virtually nil. Consequently Hesselgrave concluded that "for whatever reasons, evangelicals are not really ready for any of the five types of interreligious dialogue proposed in my paper."[12] Hesselgrave went on to note that perhaps that is the way it should be. "Certainly," he said, "until such a time as the position of evangelicals is clearly understood by both non-evangelical participants and a wider evangelical constituency, the cause of biblical Christianity, at least, is better off without their participation."[13]

It would be neither fair nor accurate to extend Hesselgrave's conclusions too far. He was speaking in a North American context. Evangelicals outside North America frequently have a more open approach to non-Christian religions and to interreligious dialogue. Even within the North American evangelical community there are a number of individuals and groups prepared to dialogue with others, anticipating mutual benefit in doing so. I hope that this paper will contribute to clarifying the evangelical position to both the "non-evangelical" participants and the wider evangelical constituency that Hesselgrave referred to.

At this point it may be useful to indicate briefly the extent to which evangelicals are currently engaged in interreligious dialogue. The Overseas Ministries Study Center at Ventnor, New Jersey, regularly sponsors gatherings in which evangelicals have opportunity to interface with ecumenically oriented Protestants and Roman Catholics. In 1978 in Venice, under the patronage of Cardinal Luciani (later Pope John Paul I), eight evangelical leaders met with an equal number of Catholic theologians to discuss "signs of convergence" in their respective understandings of mission.[14] A follow-up consultation is being planned. I myself maintain regular contact with the Catholic charismatic office in Brussels. Evangelical and Jewish leaders also have met together to discuss issues of theology and history.[15]

The Evangelical Alliance of Great Britain has authorized a special commission "to clarify the issues of inter-faith dialogue." Last year the Fellowship of European Evangelical Theologians emphasized the necessity of dialogue between evangelicals and non-Christians, including Marxists. Not long after, Ernest Oliver, past chairman of the Missions Commission of the World Evangelical Fellowship, called on "faith missions" (a peculiarly evangelical phenomenon) to get better acquainted with the psychological and religious sources of non-Christian religions. Oliver spoke positively of the "strength and comfort" other faiths provide their adherents. Meanwhile in Singapore, at the 1978 Asian Leaders Conference on Evangelism, S. V. Bhajjan of the Henry Martyn Institute reported on an evangelical dialogue with Muslims in India which started in 1963 and continues to this day.

All of this together does not add up to very much, perhaps, in the eyes of those who have been involved in interreligious dialogue for many years in a wide variety of circumstances. Yet I submit that it is an indication of the fact that some evangelicals are coming to understand dialogue as an expression of the Lordship of Christ and are more actively engaging in it. To this extent Hesselgrave's conclusion, noted above, can be modified somewhat. In the final sections of this essay I would like to suggest areas in which evangelicals might learn, indeed should learn, from others engaged in the current discussions, as well as areas in which, it seems to me, evangelicals have useful contributions to make to the ongoing enterprise.

THE SEARCH FOR NEW MODELS OF MISSION

If I am not mistaken, the living memory of Christians provides three basic contextual models for relating to other faiths. These are (1) the Greco-Roman model, which presumes mission in the context of a highly civilized (i.e., urbanized) culture in process of decay; (2) the tribal model, of which Europe after the fall of the Roman empire is the prototype; and (3) the Islamic model, which represents mission to a cohesive, self-confident, even aggressive culture. (The relationship between Christians and Jews is, of course, another and in some respects the most important model. But it seems to me to present a very special case for which the limitations of this paper do not allow discussion.)

Drawing upon its collective memory the church in mission in modern times has responded by (1) trying to create alternate societies within supposedly corrupt cultures—in our time by planting "Christian" villages, (2) providing the religious base for a civilizing or Christianizing mission—again in our time, for example, by establishing liberal arts colleges and vocational training institutions, and (3) treating other faiths as "the enemy" by adopting a polemical, confrontational approach. The inadequacies of all three approaches have become obvious to our generation, including thoughtful evangelicals. Ever since the Jerusalem missionary conference in 1928 the church at large has been searching for a new model. A new model has not yet emerged, though various trial balloons, such as Anton P. Stadler's "dialogical apologetics," have been floated.[16]

Evangelicals have participated in this quest to only a limited degree. As a consequence of our failure to interact seriously with other religions (the "lifeboat" and "yeast" responses referred to earlier can hardly be classified as serious attempts to interact in depth), evangelicals are confronted by a range of troublesome questions. Some of these have been listed by Dr. Jack Shepherd of the Christian and Missionary Alliance. They include the sheer incredibility to the modern person of an exclusivist approach, the partialness of the Bible's teaching on the subject (for in spite of what I noted earlier about the extensive and intensive experience of Israel and the early church with surrounding religions, the Bible is silent on the specific religious cultures of India and China), the true meaning of "faith" in biblical terms, the real significance of "no other name" (especially when it is acknowledged that people of faith lived and died within the Old Covenant before the coming of Jesus), and the consequence for the redemption of in-

dividuals of the realization that God is always at work in the
world outside the range of gospel proclamation.[17]

Another troublesome issue relates to the fact that the world's
religions appear to meet the psychological and religious needs of
many people, as Ernest Oliver noted. My own experience as a
missionary to Muslims confirms this. Along the same line, I personally have long been disturbed when trying to come to grips
with the apparent evidence of true faith and awareness of grace in
Sufi writings and in the lives of some Muslim individuals. Is the
God they worship the God and Father of our Lord Jesus Christ?
Is theirs true faith, true grace? Only God knows the hearts of men
and women. How can I be certain, short of total immersion in the
other religious experience (with the risk of my own conversion)
that Raimundo Panikkar seems to suggest?[18]

EVANGELICAL CONTRIBUTIONS

Shepherd asserts that evangelicals have been impoverished because they have allowed themselves to be isolated from the enrichment and discipline that could have resulted from a direct and
creative relationship with those who do not share their concept of
evangelism and mission, even though this relationship obviously
contains elements of tension. With this judgment I agree.

At the same time I wonder if evangelicals do not have some
positive contributions to make to others engaged in interreligious
dialogue, even though the "traditional" evangelical approach
carries the onus of familiarity? After all, evangelicals make up the
greater part of the Protestant missionary force in our time. This
being so, it would seem to be advantageous for ecumenically
oriented leaders to interact with evangelicals. Yet such interaction
can hardly be expected if there is not a mutual readiness to listen
and learn.

It is not at all uncommon to hear evangelicals express the wish
that ecumenists would exhibit the same irenic spirit toward evangelicals that they do toward non-Christians. Not long ago, in reviewing the symposium *Faith in the Midst of Faiths,* a report of
the Chiang Mai Consultation sponsored by the World Council of
Churches, the reviewer dismissed out of hand one Bible study
contributed by a respected evangelical theologian. Two other Bi-

ble studies, by other scholars, he suggested, could be read profitably by all Christians concerned with dialogue.[19] Presumably they were more compatible with his own thinking. This kind of brush-off, all too common, causes evangelicals to approach dialogue with other Christians skeptically.

The specific contribution evangelicals might make to the larger enterprise will be evaluated ultimately by the actual participants. But if I were to suggest possible contributions, they would include our concern for faithfulness to what the Bible positively teaches on relevant subjects (e.g., dialogue), insights on the phenomenon of "conversion" with which we have extensive experience and which should throw light both on the gospel and on other religions, and the corrective influence brought to bear by our insistence that all religious systems, including our own, carry demonic elements and therefore stand under God's judgment.

First, the positive biblical witness in relation to dialogue. It is well known that Luke, for example, frequently employs the verb *dialegomai* to describe Paul's approach to people of other faiths. Yet this is dialogue of a particular kind, significantly different from that advocated today. It is dialogue subordinate to proclamation. This shows up clearly in Paul's ministry at Thessalonica (Acts 17:1–4). Here five verbal forms are brought together: proclaim, explaining, argued (*dielexato*), proving, and persuaded. John Stott, one of the architects of the Lausanne Covenant, points out that the subject of Paul's dialogue was always one he chose himself, namely, Jesus Christ as Lord, and his object always was conversion to Jesus.[20]

I cite this example not to suggest that contemporary concepts of dialogue are altogether wrong, but that they do not do justice to the full biblical record and therefore are inadequate. Even if they should prove to be very useful at a certain stage of relationships between people of different faiths, it would be a pity if other biblical dimensions of dialogue were lost sight of.[21] True dialogue inevitably leads to encounter, which may engender confrontation as well as harmony and understanding.

Second, the possibility of losing sight of the very real phenomenon of conversion. At the 1976 consultation held at Washington and Lee University, Alfred Krass, co-editor of *The Other Side*, a magazine of evangelical social action, described his conversion to

Christ from an agnostic Jewish background. According to Krass, when as a college student he first heard the message "Jesus Christ is Lord," he understood it in an exclusivist sense:

> If the Christians I had met there, when I was an agnostic Jew, had been less exclusive, I would have had no trouble with them. But as it was I could not help but see that, no matter how warm and loving and accepting of persons they were, their whole being addressed me with the question: "Will you recognize as Lord the one to whom we have committed ourselves? Will you confess that he is *the* Lord?" They exercised no moral suasion. They were ready to continue their friendship whether I accepted their creed or not. They refused to manipulate me. I had sought them out, not they me. But my question to them— "Why are you so wonderfully different from everyone else around?"—could only be answered by reference to their faith.
>
> The agnostic in me yielded long before the Jew in me did. I came to believe in the reality of God because I saw God alive and powerful in the lives of these disciples of God. But I still kept asking, "Is there not, under God, any other way? Only the way of Jesus? Must it be so exclusive? Could we not accept Jesus, perhaps, as Teacher and Prophet alongside, even as the greatest of, others? Rather than as Lord, Shepherd, High Priest, and King?"
>
> I searched the Scriptures and I saw no other way conformed to the records; it was not just a matter of pruning the "utopian" statements and leaving the essentials. It was a matter of recognizing that either Jesus was who he claimed he was and who his disciples confessed him to be, *or* he was a megalomaniac or a dangerous *poseur,* and his disciples were therefore deceived. . . .
>
> It was *after* I had accepted this unbending Christ that I first was able to make the historically prior affirmation (which had always earlier struck me as an affront to the modern mind): that *my* people, Israel, were God's chosen people. In both matters it was "the scandal of particularity" that had offended me. But in both cases I found, after that, in his strange economy, God does work through the historically particular. . . .[22]

In my own ministry as general secretary of the World Evangelical Fellowship I continually meet women and men of Muslim, Hindu, Buddhist, and other religious backgrounds who have been converted to Jesus as Lord precisely as that has been traditionally understood by Christians for centuries and is still understood by evangelicals today. At the human level I have even been the instrument of a number of such conversions. This is a phenomenon that our contemporary generation should investigate in depth for insights that would surely emerge, and the findings applied seriously to interreligious dialogue. Are all these conversions to be regarded as blunders? Is God to be faulted for overtaking the impeccable and zealous Pharisee, Saul, and bringing him to acknowledge Jesus Christ as Lord? I do not see evidence of this kind of serious investigation in ecumenical discussion.

Third, the necessity of keeping alert to the demonic in religion. It seems to evangelicals that contemporary dialogical theology underestimates the reality of the demonic dimension.[23] "Even Satan disguises himself as an angel of light" (2 Cor. 11:14). Consequently God sends his messengers "to open their eyes, that they may turn from darkness to light and from the power of Satan to God, that they may receive forgiveness of sins and a place among those who are sanctified in me" (Acts 26:17-18). Thus the evangelical emphasis on proclamation (admittedly often to the neglect of legitimate dialogue, Christian presence, and social action) is nevertheless a prophetic ministry that is fully warranted, even necessitated, by the biblical perspective. Will this be lost sight of in Christian approaches today apart from evangelical participation?

NOTES

1. Waldron Scott, *Karl Barth's Theology of Mission* (Downers Grove, Ill.: InterVarsity Press, 1978), p. 46, n. 71.

2. J. D. Douglas, ed., *Let the Earth Hear His Voice* (Minneapolis: World Wide Publications, 1975), p. 4.

3. Donald G. Dawe and John B. Carman, eds., *Christian Faith in a Religiously Plural World* (Maryknoll, N.Y.: Orbis Books, 1978), p. 30.

4. Gerald H. Anderson, "Religion as a Problem for the Christian Mission," in *Christian Faith in a Religiously Plural World*, p. 107.

5. See Choan-Seng Song, *Christian Mission in Reconstruction—An Asian Analysis* (Maryknoll, N.Y.: Orbis Books, 1975).

6. Jonathan Edwards, in *Works,* vol. v, pp. 226–27, cited in Richard F. Lovelace, *Dynamics of Spiritual Life: An Evangelical Theology of Renewal* (Downers Grove, Ill.: InterVarsity Press, 1979), p. 403.

7. Josiah Strong, *Our Country* (New York: Baker and Taylor, 1884), p. 161.

8. William R. Hutchison, "Modernism and Missions: The Liberal Search for an Exportable Christianity, 1875–1935," in John K. Fairbank, ed., *The Missionary Enterprise in China and America* (Cambridge, Mass.: Harvard University Press, 1974), pp. 116–24. I am indebted to Arthur Glasser for this reference.

9. See Ralph D. Winter, *Six Essential Components of World Evangelization* (Pasadena, Calif.: William Carey Library, 1979), p. 10.

10. Dawe and Carman, p. 21.

11. Douglas, p. 4.

12. David J. Hesselgrave, ed., *Theology and Mission* (Grand Rapids, Mich.: Baker Book House, 1978), p. 269.

13. Hesselgrave, p. 270.

14. See "Report on Evangelical/Roman Catholic Dialogue on Mission," *Occasional Bulletin of Missionary Research,* April 1977, pp. 21–22.

15. See Marc H. Tanenbaum, Marvin R. Wilson, A. James Rudin, eds., *Evangelicals and Jews in Conversation on Scripture, Theology and History* (Grand Rapids, Mich.: Baker Book House, 1978).

16. Anton P. Stadler, "Dialogue: Does It Complement, Modify or Replace Mission?" in *Occasional Bulletin of Missionary Research,* July 1977, pp. 2ff.

17. Jack F. Shepherd, "Understanding Other Religions from an Evangelical Point of View," unpublished notes of a lecture given at the Fuller Theological Seminary School of World Mission.

18. Compare Raimundo Panikkar, *The Intra-Religious Dialogue* (New York: Paulist Press, 1978), p. 27.

19. *International Review of Mission,* October 1978, p. 490.

20. John R. W. Stott, *Christian Mission in the Modern World* (Downers Grove, Ill.: InterVarsity Press, 1975), p. 63.

21. See, for example, Richard R. de Ridder, "God and the Gods: Reviewing the Biblical Roots," *Missiology,* January 1978, pp. 11ff.

22. Alfred C. Krass, "Accounting for the Hope That Is in Me," in *Christian Faith in a Religiouly Plural World,* pp. 158–59.

23. Cf. Arthur Glasser, "Mission and Cultural Environment," in Clark H. Pinnock and David F. Wells, eds., *Towards a Theology for the Future* (Carol Stream, Ill.: Creation House, 1971), pp. 310–11.

1
Response

Margrethe B. J. Brown

This response comes from one who presently holds responsibility to interpret denominational mission locally and regionally. I see that task primarily focusing on the need to provide education and information to the members of the congregations in northwestern New York for which I have administrative responsibility, so that they may know and understand mission as an integral part of Christian living in today's world of religious pluralism. Thus my daily environment is not one of the "foreign mission field" but of a part of America where one nevertheless cannot avoid acute awareness of the worldwide connections of such large corporations as Kodak and Xerox, which dominate life in Rochester, New York, and its immediate surroundings. The daily challenge to witness to the Lordship of Jesus Christ there also takes place in a world context, albeit at a somewhat different angle from that of the traditional missionary movement.

My response to Dr. Scott's presentation is not one that challenges the notion of the actual Lordship of Jesus Christ, but one that seeks to understand its particular basis within the history of the missionary movement and to search for its proper expressions and implications in a contemporary worldwide context of religious pluralism.

It is good and well that evangelicals seek not to separate the Lordship of Christ from the historical figure of Jesus or from the name of Jesus. However, that is not what causes problems for us today. The need for criticism of the uses of the notion of the Lordship of Christ arises not out of the biblical material but out of the practices of nineteenth- and twentieth-century Western cultures and their projections throughout the missionary movement. Al-

though Dr. Scott rejects Josiah Strong's triumphalistic understanding of the responsibilities of the Anglo-Saxon race to develop strong Christian institutions across the world, triumphalism still pervades his presentation.

First of all, the statement quoted from Strong must be rejected
not merely for its overt triumphalistic tone, but even more so for
its explicit racism. The majority of the Christian community today has acknowledged its need to be racially pluriform. A statement and a significant movement within our past which can har-
bor in its core such racist declarations will have to be thoroughly
examined in its claims.

Second, we must examine the tendency to see "the Great Commission" as the sole and primary biblical expression that gives
direction to Christian mission. It obviously caught the imagination of the churches at a time when the cultures within which they
were rooted in the North Atlantic area spread victoriously out
across the nations of the earth, making their peoples political and
economic dependents of the West. There are other "sending" accounts in the Gospels, such as Luke 10. Here the seventy were
commissioned to proclaim a rather different message of life on a
subsistence level rather than economic expansions, peace rather
than conquest, and healing rather than impoverishment. The understanding of the sending authority of Jesus vested in that passage offers a very different content to Lordship from that of
Western-style dominance easily discerned behind the preoccupa-
tions with Matthew 28:18–19.

Third, we must be cautious where interreligious dialogue is suggested for the purpose of understanding the object beyond the
perimeters of the Christian faith. If faith is *used* by one in the
relationship to the partner, then the initiator has failed to communicate that faith before entering into a dialogue by declaring
his or her own superiority. Genuine dialogue presupposes equality
of the partners, and a continuity of relationship within which no
one "uses" the other.

Fourth, we shall have to consider many more different models
for interfaith relationships today than the three described by Dr.
Scott. Contrary to the Greco-Roman model, it may be that we
have to acknowledge that our Christian Western cultures are suffering decay, as we are still pretending to rest upon the conquests

of our aggressive colonizing. A historical criticism is required of us as we begin to examine the conditions under which we have claimed the right—or duty—to expand the Lordship of Christ over those whose religious convictions challenged the Lordship. Conquest of economic and political life does not necessarily lead to conversion of cultural and religious life.

In summary of these points, I find it difficult to enter into a discussion about others, as if they had rejected the Lordship of Jesus Christ. All I really can affirm is that they have rejected the particular Western, imperialistic style of understanding that Lordship, which was embedded in the modern missionary movement as it went hand in hand with the colonial expansion of the (Christian) West. It is nearly impossible for us today to differentiate between the refusal to "convert" to a Western lifestyle and submit to Western political power, and the genuine call to turn to Christ. We need first to join the struggle to free the Lordship of Christ from its bondage to exclusive imagery and notions. That means freeing it from its inherited racism and from its claim to political and economic superiority, and allowing it to be filled with the biblical perceptions of Jesus Christ as the servant Lord. It seems that we have come to a point where we, when we say "Jesus is Lord," have filled the name Jesus with the notions of Lordship as found in a recent historical period. Instead we need to change the emphasis and understand the sentence as one that counterpoints precisely such traditional understandings of Lordship in their imperialism with the claim that indeed the *Christian's Lord* is Jesus, the Servant, the Crucified One.

It is significant for us to remember that the call to dialogue has come predominantly out of the so-called younger churches. Not only are they younger, they also are churches that live amid people of other faiths, with whom they share in all kinds of human relationships. We must, therefore, take seriously their urging of reconsideration of our culturally filled concepts of Lordship. Much discussion has been given to define the Christian message in a non-Christian world, arguing whether or not "others" had a natural understanding of God, and whether such natural revelation might measure up to Christian standards. That discussion misses the contemporary key issue for an understanding of the Lordship of Christ vis-à-vis religious pluralism, which calls us first to reexamine our culturally biased understanding of Lordship, which so sorely is missing recognition of Christ as Servant Lord.

Lest you think I merely project distant images of military glory unto the missionary movement, let me assure you that the arena of so-called home mission was no less free of the interweaving of military and commercial conquests with the convictions that proclaimed the gospel. A few blocks from my home, at the head of the Irondequoit Bay, stands a marker placed there by the State of New York and the local Park Commission. It bears the following inscription:

> This is the site of Indian Landing. Here were scenes of adventure and romance for a period of three hundred years involving *Indian wars,* struggle for *Empire* between French and English and *Revolutionary* and Pioneer period. RELIGION, COMMERCE AND WAR made this territory a famous battleground bringing here many noted PRIESTS, TRADERS and SOLDIERS. [Italics added.]

The local monument clearly suggests the parallelism between conquest of whatever kind and Christian faith. Repeatedly we now claim that our commitment to the Christian gospel as a gospel of good news to all enables us to accept cultural, ethnic, political, and economic pluralism. If that is accurate and faithful, then the cultural, ethnic, political, and economic notions of glory that fill our understanding of Lordship will have to be stripped from our presentations of Jesus Christ as Lord.

Integrity of faith requires of us that we now listen to those from the younger churches, who live among people of other faiths, as they offer to lead the way to new understandings of Christ's Lordship, which may indeed offer guidance to those of us who are called daily here to witness among people of no faith. The theological issue at stake is not whether or not there is a natural revelation of God, but how we understand our faith and its claims to Lordship in the midst of our own culture.

2
Response

Thomas F. Stransky, C.S.P.

i

As a Roman Catholic who has fullsteam entered the ecumenical arena ever since Pope John XXIII officially encouraged Catholics to do so, I have seen during the 1960s and 1970s a shift in the paradigm of Christian mission cleavage. No longer side-by-side existence of Protestant denominations/mission groups; no longer a simple, competitive Roman Catholic versus Protestant/Orthodox. The main gap now appears between the mainstream Protestant/Roman Catholic/Orthodox, and the commonly called "conservative evengelicals."[1] Waldron Scott implies the same rift. But this is not the occasion to explain and defend the thesis.[2]

What is clear is that the harsh terms that had once marked too much of mainline Protestant and Roman Catholic discourse now have too often been transferred to descriptions of another segment of the Christian family. Disdain, or what Waldron Scott calls the brush-off, spawns its furies in a joint effort to diminish that word about God from our evangelical brothers and sisters. For example, if I mention with conviction to many mission-minded companions that for various reasons, the evangelicals are emerging out of their low, defensive profile of the 1960s and early '70s and are looking energetically and afresh at the total mission agenda, and that in many areas of common concern they could very well give leadership to Roman Catholics and other Protestants, I hear from some friends a refreshing willingness to learn how to bridge the acknowledged gap; but I also hear from others the snobbish, "The evangelicals are only catching up to us," or worse, "Witness the last, shrill gasp of a dying movement."[3]

With eloquent tongue we all describe the dialogue with those of other world faiths as the discipline of at least trying first to understand others as they understand themselves, and then to judge that understanding with Christian criteria. How well do we Christians exercise that discipline in trying to understand each other? The quality of Christian witness we give to those who claim other religious beliefs and have other names for the divine often depends not only on the witness we Christians offer to the God whom we share together because of his initiatives and gifts, but also on the way we handle our differences concerning the implications of being committed to the Lord, "the Faithful and True Witness" (Rev. 3:14).

Furthermore, the classic phrase "exporting our divisions" still holds. In the context of Western mission power overseas, one need look only at the North American scene to discover that by far the largest and fastest-growing force, in numbers and income, embraces those evangelical confessional groups or missionary agencies that are not related to either the National or the World Council of Churches.[4] In fact, less than 15 percent of United States Protestant missionaries is related to the Division of Overseas Ministries of the National Council of Churches. By including United States Roman Catholic overseas personnel, over 90 percent of the total is Catholic/evangelical! In the places of their assignment, most of these are ministering in areas where the majority of people is not of committed Christians. For these missionaries, consensus and differences in understanding "Christ's Lordship and Religious Pluralism" have direct implications in mission practice, in the whys and hows of relationships with others, and in the content of catechetical instruction and preaching about others, Christian or not. The same implications hold for home mission; for example, in Christian teaching and conduct carried out on American campuses by the various churches and by agencies, such as Inter-Varsity, Campus Crusade, and the Navigators.

As does Waldron Scott, I question David Hesselgrave's conclusions that "evangelicals are not really ready" for interreligious dialogue—all five types, and that "until such a time as the position of evangelicals is clearly understood by both nonevangelical participants and a wider evangelical constituency, the cause of biblical Christianity, at least, is better off without their participation." Isn't it through the dialogue itself that the understandings are shared and sharpened, at least nuanced, in discovering first-hand who these "nonevangelicals" are and what "biblical Christianity" is?[5] Otherwise, I see the same unrealistic position as that taken by a bishop at Vatican Council II: no dialogue by any Catholic with any non-Catholic, Christian or otherwise, until the whole church becomes filled with perfectly equipped apologists who then, and only then, would be launched onto the non-Catholic stage, with all cues well learned, including the humble bows to be taken after the final curtain falls and opens for the applause.

Formal dialogues usually collect a peculiar type of trained participant. I doubt the other types—99.9 percent of our constituencies—are all marshaled to keep quiet and remain aloof until .1 percent work out the theses and conclusions with myriad qualifications. In practice, far more dialogue is going on than some present theories will permit or than information offices can catalogue. The non-self-conscious, person-to-person varieties defy our computers of "success" or "failure." True, there may be little dialogue-about-dialogue; this type is already two steps removed from a state university dormitory buzz-session between a committed Church of the Nazarene student who chats with a "Moonie" roommate, another friend who "dumped that religious junk" in a Catholic high school, and a foreign student who is a firm Muslim believer from northern Nigeria. Even the majority of evangelical students in seminaries is no longer coming out of a closed society at home to another closed society circumscribed by seminary walls.

Again, in my contacts with North American evangelical missionaries in East and West Africa, I met many who had personal contacts of a dialogical quality with Muslims and those of traditional African religions. A few admitted, with smiling grace, that such contacts were more pronounced than their home-sending churches or boards judge as fitting the acceptable categories of direct person-to-person evangelism.

And where I met in missionaries resistance to dialogues with those of other world faiths, I found these resisters are closed also to contacts with other Christians, foreign or indigenous. Often this resistance, I suspect, is forged not out of a theological construct but out of a cultural isolation in their American backgrounds, including their missionary formation. Some missionaries, it seems to me, are just psychologically threatened or at least made uncomfortable when they meet, eyeball to eyeball and heart to heart, another who does not share the same religious labels, unless they (the missionaries) in some way have the upperhand with unchallenged Christian answers. Lest this last evaluation seem harshly one-sided, I add that the same kind of resistance for the same reasons is found also among, alas too many, other Protestant and Roman Catholic missionaries.

ii

At stake today is not only the right view of salvation but the right of Christian commitment to function as a world-view;[6] that is, such a commitment has the overriding, indeed the final authority over all other commitments and provides the framework, models, and basic patterns through which all experience is grasped and organized, and all ideas are judged. The distinctively *Christian* world-view is shaped by reference to the God who has broken into our space-time and is actively present in it through Jesus Christ, the Lord of all. Jesus of Nazareth is, in Hans Küng's words, "ultimately decisive, definitive, *archetypal,* for man's relations with God, with his fellow man, with society. . . . All those can be called Christian for whom in life and death Jesus Christ is ultimately decisive."[7]

The very *right* to such a claim and the *content* of that claim are being questioned, but the two are so interrelated that, although logic distinguishes, the contexts of "Christ's Lordship and Religious Pluralism" remain the same for all Christians. May I in shorthand style give a few tentative comments on the *contexts*? I do this as one whose Christian ministry has not been strictly academic but pastoral/missionary.

1. "Suicide of thought" is a phrase G. K. Chesterton used to describe the intellectual helplessness of those who are too humble to be convinced of anything, including the multiplication table.[8] I have no right, one says, to think at all, especially if my thoughts emerge into any "exclusive" or "inclusive" claims, religious or

otherwise, whether these convictions come from myself or from any person or group dubbed an "outsider." One can analyze and analyze again the causes of this peculiar skepticism, but along with other influences it does affect the religious quest.

True, the Protestant Reformation in the sixteenth century formulated questions that today are still asked, especially in classroom and formal dialogues among Protestants, and between them and Roman Catholic/Orthodox. This same Christian movement, later intensified by the Great Awakenings, became in the Christian West "the great instigator of choice."[9] But notice, the freedom of religious choice of "answers" remained, until recently, in the context of Christian faith and Christian community or church.

Today, however, questions among Christians are no longer confined to "Who is Jesus Christ, the Lord of all?" or to its ecclesiastical version, "What and where is the church of the Lord?" but expand to "Is any religious existence at all viable, intelligible, or creative?" Not only "How is the 'Ungospeled Non-Christian' justified by grace through faith?" but "How do I justify faith at all?"

These broader questions should not imply that a godless, cool, human-in-control is emerging as the inevitable future prototype. Nor do I see that Chesterton's overmodest skeptic's image of the Noble Doubter dominates the fantasy life of every "modern" person. One continues to take a stand, to plot out for oneself a segment of ground from which one can view the ultimate and make sense of reality. What has really changed is that one must more and more intentionally choose from a bewildering variety of available meaning systems, including those that are not explicitly religious or may even be explicitly nonreligious. And on the Western religious scene, the expanding religious pluralism has broken the monopoly once held by the Judeo-Christian tradition and the variety of choices within it: Zen Buddhism, Meher Baba, Subud, Krisnamurti, Sufism, Tibetan Buddhism, Black Muslim, Vedanta, Healthy-Happy-Holy Organization, types of Transcendental Meditation and of the Human Potential Movement, the Church of Satan, and so forth. To these one can add the secular enchantments of psychedelic drugs, psychokinesis, astrology, and sorcery.[10]

For some people these are too many options to choose from

and cope with, so they withdraw from an authentic religious quest. Sometimes they rationalize the escape by a professed skepticism or a tolerating "I'm okay, you're okay." But others have the opposite reaction. If one does cling to a claim with conviction, one wants to guard the rare gift, and sees "dialogue" as a threat to self-security. A few years ago, in a discussion among Catholic college graduates, a lawyer revealed to us his anxiety over the text from 1 Peter, "Give an account of the hope that is in you." "I'm afraid," he admitted; "such public articulation may lead others unwittingly to destroy the only hope I have." He was threatened even by the old adage: not to share the faith is eventually to lose it. He preferred the risk to keep quiet, unless perhaps, in his sharing the other would only listen.

Yet others welcome any clear world-view message, especially if it provides an ultimate shield against meaninglessness and an institutionalized way of life that can cope with painful and unmanageable experiences, along with joyful, more controllable ones. In 1972 Dean Kelly stirred up the ecumenical brew with his analysis of *Why Conservative Churches Are Growing.*[11] A church functions effectively when it provides ultimate meaning, demands *serious* commitment, does not apologize for its beliefs, loyalties, or practices, and does not allow itself to be treated as though it makes no difference or should make no difference in its adherents' personal and communal behavior. Kelly in no way wants his analysis to reinforce a popular notion that a religious organization can be "serious" only if it is authoritarian and that the only content it can be serious about is "fundamentalism."[12] Nor should one write off the whole church-growth phenomenon as an enterprise of conservative evangelical churches to provide secure comfort islands for the religiously immature and culturally captive.[13]

My only point here is that the right to a Christian world-view is very human; that its best defense is not nervous defense or anxious isolation, but "serious" witness; and that Christians should honestly recognize that their ultimate faith-commitment today is one among several possible commitments. One must choose. And the choice is made or reconfirmed in the context of dialogue with the others.

Although it is understandable for one to observe the barrage of so many proposed world-views and so to search for some higher point of view that brings together clashing ultimate commitments in a single framework, that search is impossible. As Lesslie Newbigin has written:

> The framework which I devise or discern is my ultimate commitment or else it cannot function in the way intended. As such a commitment, it must defend its claim to truth over against other claims to truth. I have no standpoint except the point where I stand. . . . There is no platform from which one can claim to have an "objective view" which supersedes all the "subjective" faith commitments of the world's faiths; every man must take his stand on the floor of the arena, on the same level with every other, and there engage in the real encounter of ultimate commitment with those who, like him, have staked their lives on their vision of the truth.[14]

Much of the foregoing contextual descriptions may be limited to Europe/North America. Walter Kasper, for example, searches for the place of his whole Christology, including Lordship, in the context of a "crisis of meaning in modern society," a meaningless nihilism intensified by the dichotomy between faith and life. Read Sartre and Camus, Novalis, Fichte and Schelling, Nietzsche and Hegel, and German Romanticism.[15] Well and good, as Kasper writes for Europeans who hunger for meaning but find a banal world without and emptiness within. But are we to suppose that the crisis of meaning, enlightened skepticism, overt or disguised neo-fundamentalism in contemporary Europe, or in North America, are paradigmatic for the rest of the world? "Life" in the central marketplace of Kumasi at high noon or in a moon-bathed Tanzanian village cannot be described by *angst, ennui,* or boredom. An Ingmar Bergman film festival would not fill the cinemas of Karachi.

2. The *content* of the Christian claim immediately shows that it is more than a competitive world-view, but also and fundamentally *persons*—Father, Son, and Holy Spirit. Thus the claim cannot be presented solely in biblical, doctrinal, or theological terms, but must proclaim what is primary, namely, the specifically Christian experience of God in Jesus through the Spirit. Evangelicals

rightly stress experiential faith, the personal relationship with Jesus Christ as Savior and Lord of one's life. Christology may begin with our questions about Jesus, but it ends with his question to us, the same as his to Peter: "Do you love me?" (John 21:15.) The content of "the uniqueness of Jesus Christ, the Lord of all" should thus be seen in the primary context of recalled love-experiences or shared memories, not world-view headtrips.

Some of these experiences that claim to be Christian are, however, the very support for those who question or deny the supposed content. The cringing before Christian claims vis-à-vis other religions also comes from a consciousness of the horror of historical evil done in God's name, and via his Word, the transferral of human pathologies to God for his sanction and approval. Too often and too consistently the worst aspects of ourselves masquerade under the name of God, under "Scripture tells us so." Our statements about Lordship and about those of other world faiths must be analyzed also to find out what they are saying about us. What we call "our religion" may not in fact be ultimately authoritative in much of our thinking and acting. We may be afraid of dialogue precisely because dialogue will show us this, demand penance, and call for the purification of our so-called Christian claims so that they remain indeed Christian.

Even many Christians may be rejecting unique Lordship to Jesus of Nazareth because they are afraid of committing acts of spiritual violence (use Jesus as a club with which to herd people into salvation); or of being intolerant of others ("You are nothing in God's eyes or God's heart unless you explicitly believe in Jesus as Lord and Savior"); or of repeating past imperialisms (the rights of God-squads prevail over "mere" human freedoms, including the right to be free from the manipulative hard-sell).

In other words, it's not the Lordship doctrine itself that is first questioned. Authentic human instincts are rebelling against what claim to be consistent conclusions for perceived quasi-inhuman evangelistic attitudes, motivations, and practices. And even here, the argument of then disposing of the Lordship doctrine presupposes that right practice is exclusive one-way traffic, which starts far up the logical line with that one, pure biblical truth that refuses any entrance into the arena of dialogue.

iii

My task here is not to explain or defend Roman Catholic official understanding(s) of "Christ's Lordship and Religious Pluralism"; that is Pietro Rossano's assignment.[16] But I shall comment, again in shorthand, on the present state of both biblical research and theological studies in which our subject is being discussed.

Waldron Scott describes evangelicals as those who subscribe to the statement of the 1974 Lausanne Covenant, which deals with the authority of the Bible. If, as the Covenant states, "the only written Word of God" is "without error in all that it affirms," then for us Christians who accept that formula—as a Roman Catholic I indeed do[17]—the question is: What *do* the Scriptures *affirm* about the efficacious sovereignty of Yahweh in the Hebrew Bible, and in the New Testament about the Lordship of Christ in a biblical world of religious pluralism? As I try to follow discussions on the biblical data, I see the main difficulty among scholars, whether professedly evangelical or not, whether Roman Catholic or not, not in the authority of the Bible as such, but in the different ways they are both understanding and doing biblical theology precisely in order to answer: What does the Bible affirm as supremely normative in and above its cultural conditioning?[18] Two examples from Roman Catholic writers. Paul Knitter is proposing that the claim of Christ's uniqueness, as described above by Kung, is "not necessary for fidelity to Christian tradition." One of his summary arguments:

> Given the prevailing Jewish eschatological-apocalyptic mentality, it was natural that the early Christians should interpret their experience of God in Jesus as final and unsurpassable. Their peculiar philosophy of history was such that they expected a new and definitive stage; also, it was a stage that was to break forth on the world *only* from Jerusalem. So when they encountered the overpowering presence of Jahweh in Jesus, the spontaneous conclusion was that this stage had arrived. Furthermore, since at least in the early New Testament writings, the end of history was thought to be immanent, possibili-

ties of other revelations or prophets were simply beyond one's consideration. [So Knitter asks,] Is not such an apocalyptic mentality, understood in the literal sense, culturally limited? Must it be taken as part of the essence of the Christ-event? If Jesus had been experienced and interpreted in another philosophy of history, e.g., that of India, would he have been said to be final and unique?[19]

Another supportive argument comes from Gregory Baum. He proposes that the exclusivist claims of the New Testament, namely that, apart from its message there is no salvation, were "survival language." "The trusting surrender to Jesus Christ as source of salvation, experienced in a small threatened community within the hostile Roman Empire, surrounded by competing religious groups, demanded a language of survival and self-identity." Baum adds, "However, when the Christian church became the religion of the Roman empire and later identified itself with Western society, the same doctrinal statements acquired a different meaning. The Church's exclusivist claims became a language of power and domination."[20] Does this mean that the historically conditioned affirmation is not transcendent to the times and does not remain part of the central, permanently valid assertions of Christian texts?

Knitter's and Baum's questions are not mine, and their assertions are not generally accepted by Roman Catholic biblical scholars. I mention them only to illustrate the lack of consensus, not in what biblical authority is but in what biblical data are really affirming and thus "should be held as affirmed by the Holy Spirit."

Furthermore, if all theology is biblical, that is, its point of departure and primary datum are the revealed Word of God, not every theology is biblical theology. The sustained, systematically elaborated interpretation of faith is the need of the believing intelligence, which brings to bear on the Christian message historical experience, psychological insight, philosophical perspectives, ontological reflection, and whatever rational, experiential, and scientific achievements are germane. This form of theological effort is nothing else but a law of the living mind that by its very nature must strive to search out the intelligible structure of what, through the grace of faith, it believes.[21] Thus Anselm could term the enterprise *fides quaerens intellectum*, faith seeking understanding.

To apply this to our theme of Christ's Lordship and the rule of God in those human lives of other world faiths, one sees that the origins and historical developments of descriptive categories like the "low" or "high" views of creation and of the human; nature and grace; general and special revelation; salvation "inside" or "outside" ecclesial frontiers and explicit proclamation—these are not obvious, unchangeable, directly derivative biblical formulae, which have been and are *un*influenced by prevailing historical pressures, philosophical currents, and also, lest we forget, by prevailing intra-Christian debate and confrontation and, only recently, by the ecumenical dialogue.

As with biblical theology, as I follow these theological discussions on "exclusive" or "inclusive" Christologies and on the relationship of the Christian fact (i.e., the written texts seen from the horizon of the past and present experience of men and women in society) with other individual and collective religious experiences (*their* facts!), I see the main difficulty in the variety of ways we are both understanding and doing theology. If the 1970s are far enough behind us to submit to our historical diagnosis, that decade can be characterized as emphasizing method more than content; this emphasis is in "Third World theologies" as much as in the North American/European enterprise. What M. Colin Grant has called "The Theological Smorgasbord" or David Tracy, more politely, "The Blessed Rage for Order"[22] is already laden with several models on a table going from the very rationalistic (e.g., the evangelical Carl Henry's rational theology) to the extreme experiential (e.g., story theology). I suspect that much of our differing viewpoints that appear in our discussions here can be traced back not just to differing denominational traditions, certainly not just to an evangelical-and-the-others variation, but to different theological methods, even vocabularies.

For example, I wholeheartedly agree with Waldron Scott that we all lose credibility in stating our case if we downplay or ignore what he calls "the phenomenon of conversion." Such experience stories are a *locus theologicus*. But what about the Islamic, Hare Krishna, Zen "conversion experiences," and significant for us here, the subtle conversions that take place within Christians by the very experience of authentic dialogue with others, as Stanley Samartha describes dialogue? Yet the methods that theologians use to evaluate such experiences, or the way these experiences challenge the theologies of theologians, is the very point of frequent disagreements, even within Christian communities. For example, glossolalia may be regarded as a way of letting off steam, as a symptom of hysteria, as a religiously significant experience of demonic possession, or as a genuine religious experience of God.

To enlarge Waldron Scott's remarks, I do see that a primary agenda topic for these further conversations, which need the evangelicals as equal partners, is the Christians' *experience* of being a community of believers in Jesus Christ in today's world,[23] and today's experience more and more includes the everyday and more formal dialogue with those who are of other world faiths, of secular ideologies, or of utter skepticisms. Furthermore, today's and tomorrow's world shows that the Christian community is growing more and more outside of the northern Atlantic arena, and there becoming more articulate. These new voices in the Christian choir of biblical and theological reflection may be able to release many of us from our present sounds stifled because of impasses erected by a narrow and overargumentative history.[24]

NOTES

1. At least on the American language scene, "liberal" and "conservative" labels are seldom voiced without either an enhancing or a pejorative tone, and these tones shift according to general cultural moods. In trying to transcend such language partisanship, the Anglican evangelical John Stott reminds us that the church of every age is called to hold fast to that "completed revelation," which God has providentially preserved in Scripture. "It is in this sense that every Christian is (or should be) 'conservative,' because it is his duty to conserve the truth which has been handed down to him from Christ and the apostles. In everything else, however—in social and ecclesiastical structures, in patterns of ministry and liturgical forms, in Christian living and missionary outreach, and in much else besides—the Christian is obliged to be as radical as Scripture commands and is free to be as radical as Scripture allows" (John Stott, *Christ the Controversalist* [Wheaton, Ill.: Tyndale House, 1970], p. 37).

2. Thanks to a one-year fellowship from the Maryknoll Center for Mission Studies, the author was able in 1979 to evaluate North American evangelical mission thinking, training programs, and overseas practices, especially in East and West Africa.

3. See my "Mission Power in the 1980s," *International Review of Mission* 69, no. 273 (January 1980), esp. pp. 46–48. Because of their long reaction against liberalism, American evangelicals admit that their "combative instinct is deeply

ingrained, and when thoroughly aroused in a battle for fundamental truth, is slow to subside" (see interview with Kenneth Kantzer, editor of *Christianity Today*, in the April 7, 1978, issue). This stance, from the heat of battle, influences not only the intramural debates among evangelicals, but also their handling of conciliar or Christian consensus statements. "Evangelicals have learned to be suspicious—and with some good reason—of the orthodox tones of ecumenical documents. They have learned not to take the language of mainstream Christianity at face value; indeed, they come close to assuming that the better a document sounds, the more reason they have to be suspicious" (Richard J. Mouw, "New Alignments: Hartford and the Future of Evangelicalism," in *Against the World for the World*, ed. Peter L. Berger and Richard John Neuhaus [New York: Seabury Press, 1976], p. 114).

4. As Waldron Scott reminds us, even here sharp structural distinctions, like membership in the National or the World Council of Churches and in the World Evangelical Fellowship, can be artificial impositions on convictions. The recognized evangelical leader John Stott is a priest of the Church of England, which is a member of the British Council of Churches and the World Council of Churches. Scott's denomination, the United Presbyterian Church, is a founding member of the NCC and the WCC. The same comparison would hold for many who subscribe to the Lausanne Covenant of 1974.

5. What complicates the intra-Christian dialogue could be the very naming of the gaps *without* dialogue! If evangelicals admit, in good humor, that they find it hard to agree on self-descriptions, it is even harder, I reply with equal good humor, to know what evangelicals mean by those Christians they call "non-evangelicals" (sometimes more politely, "ecumenical, conciliar Christians").

6. Cf. David Wells, *The Search for Salvation* (London: InterVarsity Press, 1978), p. 45.

7. Hans Kung, *On Being a Christian* (New York: Doubleday, 1976), pp. 123 and 125.

8. G. K. Chesterton, *Orthodoxy* (New York: Doubleday, 1959), chap. 3, "The Suicide of Thought."

9. Martin Marty's expression in "Religious Thought and Assumptions," in *Evangelicals Face the Future*, ed. Donald C. Hoke (Pasadena: Wm. Carey Library, 1978), p. 116.

10. Charles Y. Glock and Robert N. Bellah, eds., *The New Religious Consciousness* (Berkeley: University of California Press, 1976); Jacob Needleman and George Baker, eds., *Understanding the New Religions* (New York: Seabury Press, 1978). In discussing religious pluralism, we need to reconsider what we mean by religion in America, and not too quickly declare cloture by narrower definitions and classical typologies.

11. New York: Harper and Row, 1972; rev. ed. 1977.

12. So insists Dean Kelly, in Dean R. Hoge and David A. Roozen, eds., *Understanding Church Growth and Decline* (New York: Pilgrim Press, 1979), pp. 340–42. Losing out to his editors over the 1972 title, Kelly had preferred, "Why Strict Churches Are Strong," whether "theologically conservative or not, whether growing at a particular time or not" (Ibid. p. 340).

13. "Nonevangelicals," with a slightly patronizing tone, often caricaturize the reasons for "growing" churches; e.g., Thomas R. McFaul's review of Kelly, " 'Strictness' and Church Membership," *Mission Trends, No. 2*, ed. Gerald H. Anderson and Thomas F. Stransky, C.S.P. (New York: Paulist Press, 1975), pp. 56–63. Most evangelical leaders, I find, are very aware of this danger in their churches, as in any other Christian community that is "serious."

14. Lesslie Newbigin, *The Open Secret* (Grand Rapids, Mich.: Wm. B. Eerd-

mans, 1978), pp. 185, 190. Newbigin is responding to John Hick's "Christian Theology and Inter-Religious Dialogue," *World Faiths,* no. 103 (Autumn 1977), pp. 2–19.

15. Walter Kasper, *Jesus the Christ* (New York: Paulist Press, 1976), p. 16. "The road travelled by the modern spirit leads to nihilism" (ibid.).

16. See my commentary, "The Declaration on Non-Christian Religions," in *Vatican II: An Interfaith Appraisal,* ed. John H. Miller, C.S.C. (Notre Dame: Notre Dame Press, 1966), pp. 335–48, 371.

17. Vatican Council II's *On Divine Revelation*(n. 11) is even more explicit than Lausanne: "Since everything that the inspired authors, or sacred writers, affirm *[asserunt]* should be held as affirmed by the Holy Spirit, so the books of Scripture must be acknowledged as teaching firmly, faithfully and without error that truth which God wanted to entrust to the sacred writings for the sake of our salvation" *(Constitutio dogmatica de divine Revelatione [Dei Verbum],* in *Enchiridion Vaticanum,* 9th ed. (Bologna: Edizione Dehoniane Bologna, 1971), p. 501 (quotation trans. Stransky).

18. So also John Stott, one of the drafters of the Lausanne Covenant, in his commentary on clause 2, "The Authority and Power of the Bible": ". . . In declaring that Scripture is 'without error in all that it affirms' we commit ourselves to its study, to the responsible work of biblical interpretation, so that we may discern the intention of each author and grasp what is being affirmed" (*The New Face of Evangelicalism: An International Symposium on the Lausanne Covenant,* ed. C. René Padilla [Downers Grove, Ill.: InterVarsity Press, 1976], p. 37). Arthur Johnston, however, criticizes the Lausanne phrase as a loophole; it "appears to leave an opening for another *subjective* authority on what the Bible teaches: a theologian, a Church, a Tradition or a tradition, etc." (*The Battle for World Evangelism* [Wheaton, Ill.: Tyndale House, 1978], p. 326).

19. Paul Knitter, "World Religions and the Finality of Christ: A Critique of Hans Küng's *On Being a Christian,*" *Horizons* 5, no. 2 (Fall 1978): 154. Knitter proposes that a claim for Christ's uniqueness is not necessary for one's commitment to him, not necessary for Christian identity and living, and is even not possible according to the norms of theological and historical-critical method. His theses have provided an outline for continuing and most lively discussions by the Catholic Theological Society of America. Cf. *Proceedings* 33 (1978): 192–98.

20. Gregory Baum, "Is There a Missionary Message?" in *Mission Trends, No. 1,* ed. Gerald H. Anderson and Thomas F. Stransky, C.S.P. (New York: Paulist Press, 1974), pp. 83–84.

21. Cf. Eugene M. Burke, C.S.P., "Dogmatic Theology," *New Catholic Encyclopaedia,* vol. 4, pp. 949–56.

22. M. Colin Grant, "Who's Catering the Theological Smorgasbord?" *The Christian Century* 94 (May 4, 1977): 428–31; David Tracy, *Blessed Rage for Order* (New York: Seabury Press, 1975).

23. "While it is artificial to separate Christology from soteriology, and theology will continue to grapple with the questions surrounding the identity and ontological reality of Jesus, Christian theology is certainly embarked on a more functional approach to understanding Jesus. What we are searching for is a more accurate understanding of what Jesus actually did—in his life, death, and resurrection—and of what he continues to do as the Lord of history. Here, again, Christology and ecclesiology will become indistinguishable; theology about the present salvific action of Christ will inevitably lead us to a Christian pneumatology; but the only starting-point for a realistic pneumatology is the experience of the Christian community, for it is this experience which manifests the activity of the prophetic and

creative Spirit" (Bernard J. Cooke, "The Church: Catholic and Ecumenical," *Theology Today* 36, no. 3 (October 1979): 366.

24. See the bibliography in *Mission Trends, No. 3* ("Third World Theologies"), ed. Gerald H. Anderson and Thomas F. Stransky, C.S.P. (New York: Paulist Press, 1976), pp. 250–54. And on Jesus Christ in African and Asian perspectives, see *African and Asian Contributions to Contemporary Theology,* ed. John S. Mbiti (Celigny, Switzerland: Ecumenical Institute/Bossey, 1977), passim.

3
Reply

Waldron Scott

Both of my respondents have favored me—Margrethe Brown by drawing attention to certain weaknesses in my presentation (and doubtless in my understanding of mission today) and Thomas Stransky by reflecting on several strands of the larger context in which evangelical mission occurs.

I'm not sure all readers will agree with Ms. Brown that triumphalism "pervades" my presentation. Yet she is surely justified in pointing out my failure to acknowledge the extent to which an unwarranted (I do not say totally unbiblical) triumphalism, and even racism (I *must* say unbiblical), still characterizes some sectors of missionary activity today. This is inexcusable and evangelicals must take the criticism seriously.

As for the Great Commission of Matthew 28, few evangelicals today see it as the sole or even primary biblical expression of Christian mission. In my presentation I stated explicitly that "it is not the only expression and, in a given situation, not necessarily the initial expression." Ever since the Lausanne Congress of 1974, and even before, we have been seeking guidance from other accounts in the Gospels. For many of us Jesus' charge, "Even so I send you" (John 20:21), with its clear contextual overtones of servanthood, provides the basic mandate.

Nevertheless the Great Commission cannot be dismissed out of hand, nor tied exclusively (as Ms. Brown seems to suggest) to nineteenth-century imperialism. It was directed initially to a first-century band of believers witnessing from the underside of history and has captured the imagination of numerous emerging Third World missionary societies today, most of whom are as powerless and oppressed as their apostolic predecessors.

I agree wholeheartedly with Ms. Brown's aversion to using *persons*, for whatever end. But is this the same as using *dialogue* as a method for understanding persons of other faiths with a view to bearing witness to our own faith more effectively?

From my point of view all three historical models of mission described by me are inadequate for our time. For that reason I welcome, with other evangelicals, the search for new models. In that search we do need to reexamine, as Ms. Brown suggests, the historical conditions under which we Western Christians claim the right or duty to expand the Lordship of Christ. The intensity with which the Ayatollah Khomeini inveighs against the "Christian" West and our moral decadence is clear warning of this.

Nevertheless, although Ms. Brown and I share the same denominational background, I feel her generalizations about missions past and present are too sweeping. Christian witness has not been as monochromatic as she pictures it. Servantship, not imperialism, cultural or other, has motivated and still motivates the precepts and practices of thousands of missionaries. Having said this I find I do respond positively to the overall thrust of Ms. Brown's remarks. Evangelicals, with others, do need to rethink the overt and covert content of the claim "Jesus is Lord." I am grateful for her insistence upon this.

As regards dialogue, I agree with Thomas Stransky's observation that far more occurs at the grass-roots level in every continent than is commonly acknowledged, and that evangelical missionaries and laypersons are involved in dialogue to an extent not always recognized. Evangelical mission executives need to encourage this formally and make more systematic, or at least more regular, provision for it.

The curricula of evangelical seminaries also needs significant revision to allow not only for the academic study of comparative religion but also for "neighborhood" dialogue with local adherents of other faiths. For would-be missionaries Father Stransky's contention that ultimate faith commitment in our time is only one of several possible commitments, and that "the choice is made or reconfirmed in the context of dialogue with others" should be underscored.

Father Stransky agrees with Margrethe Brown that it is not the doctrine of Christ's Lordship that is challenged in the first instance by those of other faiths, but, rather, those imperialistic attitudes that frequently belie the biblical content of the doctrine. The fact that both Brown and Stransky stress this point marks it in a special way for evangelical concern.

But I also see, in Father Stransky's gentle challenge to my comments about conversion, the need for evangelicals to review more carefully and critically our methods of doing Bible study and theology. These are more historically, culturally conditioned than we ordinarily recognize. I think it is fair to say that some of our younger missiologists are ready to come to grips with this.

IV

Christ's Lordship
and Religious Pluralism
in Roman Catholic Perspective

Pietro Rossano

As a representative of the Vatican Secretariat for Non-Christians, I shall relate my comments to what was stated in Vatican Council II and in the subsequent documents of the Roman Catholic Church, from Paul VI's 1975 Exhortation on Evangelization (*Evangelii Nuntiandi*), which resulted from the 1974 Synod of Bishops, to John Paul II's 1979 Encyclical on the Redemption of Man (*Redemptor Hominis*).

FROM THE RELIGIOUS QUEST TO RELIGIONS

In its declaration *Nostra Aetate* Vatican Council II started from the existential religious quest that today, as in the past, springs up in the human heart: "What is man? What is the meaning, the purpose of life? What is the moral good and what is sin? Whence suffering, and what purpose does it serve? Where lies the path to true happiness? What is the truth about death, judgment and retribution beyond the grave? What, finally, is that ultimate inexpressible mystery which encompasses our existence: whence do we come, and where are we going?" (n.1).[1]

Clement of Alexandria (ca. 150–215) saw these same questions raised in his own time.[2] They had been formulated in the same terms some centuries before Christ in the Svetasvatara

Upanishad (1, 1). Such questions have not ceased; today they have become more acute by developments in science and technology.[3]

These universal questions are rooted in the very structure of humankind, and therefore reveal a specific dimension of the human person. Psychologists speak of "psychogenous" or spiritual needs, before which "science" is impotent. Such questions contain a spectrum of elements and different nuances according to different ethnic and cultural families. But they also indisputably reveal convergent and analogical features: a search for origins, for the ultimate cause and final destiny; a reaching out beyond what is visible and transient; a flight from the river of suffering to reach the banks of quiet and peace; an aspiration toward a highest good that does not deceive or disappoint; a search for what is permanent amid the contrasts of change; a thirst for a life that is fulfilling and happy; a desire for perfect relationship and for social and cosmic harmony; a fleeing from fear, frustration in the face of death and unavoidable evil; a longing for protection and security; an unspoken expectation of liberation and salvation; a rebellion against limits and injustice; the torment of being torn between the experience of transcendence and the experience of finitude, between the good that one wishes to do and the evil to which one is inclined; the thirst for communication with a perfect Thou. The human person searches for more, for a *novum* that liberates and heals, develops and fulfills.

The Christian pursues this religious quest in common with Muslims and Buddhists, with Taoists and with the followers of the African religions; in fact, with every human being, even with those who declare themselves alien to any religious faith.

From the religious quest it is but a small step to the religions as sociocultural structures with doctrinal, moral, and ritual elements. These religions represent the social and ritual codification of the replies to the existential quest of entire generations. They are the "accumulated traditions" on which the "personal faith" of individuals rests.[4] To the variety of religious quests there corresponds a plurality of replies. It is here that the plurality of religions is born. The history and phenomenology of religions are concerned with their distinction and classification. One evident distinction is between the religions of historical-prophetic monotheism (Judaism, Christianity, Islam), and those of a monistic nature, with their theo-cosmo-anthropic character. One could also speak of religions of self-realization (Hinduism, Buddhism), of cosmic and social integration (Taoism, Confucianism, Shintoism, African religions), and of submission to and dialogue with God (Judaism, Christianity, Islam).

Historically, whence does this plurality of religions arise? Besides the very complexity of the religious quest, itself the bearer of a multitude of particular queries, we should consider the ethnic particularity (the so-called genius or character of each people), the variety of ecological, historical, and cultural experiences, the elusiveness of the goal and of the object pursued, and the limitations of the human subject. But, in answer to that question, we must not undervalue the crucial importance of religious founders and leaders, whose experience has become the paradigm for innumerable numbers of followers. Here the aphorism *Paucis vivit genus humanum* is apt: the entire human family lives under the influence of a few persons.

RELIGIOUS PLURALISM AND THE SEARCH FOR TRUTH

The experience of the variety of religious traditions creates a great problem for every human conscience. This pluralism is, in fact, irreducible. It is marked by exclusions, contrasts, jealousies, absolutisms, all of them well known to the science of religions. They have drawn upon religions the accusation of being elements of division in the human family. Sometimes they have aroused contempt and skepticism toward the religions themselves.

The problem must not be minimized. Despite every attempt at establishing the union and harmonization of religions, it is scientifically certain that the Christian "way" is different from the Buddhist "path"; that Hindu "liberation" is not the "submission" of Islam; that the "life" sought in African religious practices is not comparable to that offered by Gnostic or Tantric traditions; that the aim of *bhakti* is not that of Zen; and so on. To this historical-phenomenological diversity one must add that every religous tradition has its own way of evaluating other religions. Each has its own "theology of religions"; they stretch from writing off and rejecting all others as aberrant, to the legitimization of all, as with Hinduism (although by doing this, Hinduism imposes its own specific dogma of the equivalence of every religion).[5]

A reasonable person concludes that systems of such diversity and contrast cannot possibly be considered equally valid and true. In fact, from the very origins of the church, the inquiry concerning the true religion and the true worship of God (*de vera religione; de vero Dei cultu*) has been a feature of the Christian conscience. The religious journeys of Justin, Augustine, Hilary of Poitiers, to name only a few, are widely known. Nor can the quest for truth along the human religious pilgrimage be disregarded today even in the name of a legitimate pluralism in the social field. The person is bound to search for truth as it affects both one's manner of life and one's destiny.

That is why at the beginning of its Declaration on Religious Freedom, Vatican Council II states: "All are bound to seek the truth, especially in what concerns God and his Church and to embrace the truth they come to know, and hold fast to it. . . . It is in accordance with their dignity as persons . . . that all should be at once impelled by nature and also bound by moral obligation to seek the truth, especially religious truth. They are also bound to adhere to the truth, once it is known, and to order their whole lives in accord with the demands of the truth. . . . Truth, however, is to be sought after in a manner proper to the dignity of the human person and his social nature. The inquiry is to be free."[6]

FOR THE CHRISTIAN,
CHRIST IS *THE* RELIGIOUS TRUTH

For the Christian, the truth is Christ, who is "the way, the truth and the life" (John 14:6), "the center of the universe and of history."[7] Christians are obliged to justify rationally and historically their act of faith in Christ, in whom "one finds the fullness of religious life,"[8] the *novum* that God the Creator has given and offers to human beings within their history, and the key to decipher all the religious traditions of humankind.

In fact, the New Testament bears witness to a significant process of development in the Christian's knowledge of Christ. This begins with the amazement of the crowds and the disciples (the "pre-Easter" period, cf. Mk. 1:27–28), then moves on to the Easter faith that acknowledges him to be Lord and God (cf. John, chaps. 20, 28, 29), and further on to the proclamation of him as the sole mediator of salvation (cf. Acts 4:12). Then later, in the

apostolic age, Christian reflection begins to unravel the implications of what faith in him involves in the context of Jewish
monotheism and the religious traditions of the time. The prologue of John, the Christology of the letters to the Ephesians and
to the Colossians, and of the book of Revelation, speak of the
universal sovereignty of Christ over time and history. He is "the
Alpha and the Omega, the first and the last, the beginning and the
end" (Rev. 22:13; 1:17–18). He is "the Lamb, slain before the
foundation of the world" (Rev. 13:8; cf. 1 Pet. 1:19–20; Rom. 16:
25–26), the Lamb slain and victor, who holds the scroll of the
historical events (Rev. 5:6–8; "in Him we have been chosen before the foundation of the world" (Eph. 1:4). Saint Paul identifies Christ with the Wisdom of God (1 Cor. 1: 24–30). In Paul's
catechesis, as reflected in the letter to the Romans (2: 9–11,
28–29), in the Pastoral Letters (1 Tim. 2:5; Tit. 2:11), and in the
discourses recounted in Acts (14:15–17; 17: 22–28), he recognizes
the universal dimensions of the salvific action of God centered in
Christ.

The New Testament thus furnishes authoritative premises for a
reflection on the universal sovereignty of Christ over history and
over the world religions. Such premises gave rise to a difficult but
fruitful development in the first five centuries of the church. This
reflection was later halted by a historically understandable religious isolationism, and emerged only in some outstanding figures
who, as it were, passed on the torch through the centuries: from
the philosopher Justin Martyr, who recognized in Christ a spiritual sovereignty over humankind even before his appearance in
history, to Irenaeus, Clement, Origen, Augustine, the Pseudo-
Dionysius, and Basil. Later we find the solitary figures of Raymond Lull, Bonaventure, Nicholas of Cusa, Thomas More, Mat-
teo Ricci, John Henry Newman, J. N. Farquhar, and Otto
Karrer, until such time as the change in the historical situation
urgently called Christians courageously to resume their reflection
on Christ, "the center of the universe and of history." Such mediation sees Christ as the One in whom all things were created; to
whom all is directed; in whom all subsists (Col. 1:16–17); in whom
God will reconcile all things with himself (Col. 1:16, 17–20);
Christ who comes into the world where his light is already present
(John 1: 1–10); Christ the same today as he was yesterday

and will be forever (Heb. 13:8); in whom every person finds salvation, whether one lived before or after him.[9] As John V. Taylor, the Anglican bishop of Winchester, incisively observes, this means that "from the beginning the world was held in existence by the Redeemer who was to die. . . . Being forgiven is therefore a more primary condition of man than being a sinner. Being in Christ is a more essential human state than being in ignorance of Christ."[10]

THE RELIGIONS IN THE LIGHT
OF CHRIST PANTOKRATOR

For the Christian, every theological evaluation of the human religious phenomenon is based on this image of Christ. It was already delineated in the New Testament and then developed in the early centuries when the churches were confronted with the religious traditions prevalent in the Mediterranean area. Today, as we face the immense problem of the religious pluralism of humankind, let us see what can be drawn from this same image of Christ.

Above all, this Christology allows us theologically to interpret and appreciate the religious quest. This religious search, a constant feature of the human heart, is perceived as the expression and existential epiphany of the creaturehood of human beings and of their being called to Christ. God moves men and women to seek him and, it may be, to touch and find him, though he is not far from any of them (Acts 17:27). This "instinct of the inviting God"[11] is Christocentric because Christ is the future of humanity, the image of the perfect human on whom we are modeled (1 Cor. 15:48-49; cf. 2 Cor. 3:18). The unity and the variety of the religious quest are thus seen as the fruit of the inexhaustible riches of the human family, which the creative Wisdom of God has apportioned among individuals, families, and nations. The Christological hymn of the letter to the Colossians (1:15-20) turns on the axis "He-and-all," namely, the multiplicity of creatures, and their origin and destiny in Christ.

In the light of Christ Pantokrator a theological understanding of the religions in their diversity, continuing presence, and vitality becomes possible. If it is historically true that the variety of religions depends on the particular genius and character of each people, and on their history and existential situation, one may also theologically assert that each religion represents the traditional manner of response of a given people to the gift and enlightenment of God. It is a response given within a particular frame of culture and language, which often makes extremely difficult the relation and communication of religions among themselves.

By stating this we do justice both to the divine and to the human element present in each religion. In his encyclical *Redemptor Hominis* (no. 12), Pope John Paul II writes of religions in this sense as the "marvellous heritage of the human spirit," and of their values as "the work of the Spirit of God who breathes where he will" (John 3:8). The assertion does not imply that the religions contain different revelations of God, as if God had revealed himself in one way to one people and in another way to another. The historical revelation in Jesus Christ is one thing, the "light that enlightens every man" (John 1:9) is another.

If the illumination given by the Word is the same, the responses are different. An analogy may be found in the colors that shimmer on a surface touched by the same ray of light, or in the different sounds that come from various musical instruments in the hands of the same musician. From the striking polyvalence or difference of the human subject there is born the variety of human response. But this is also the consequence of that transcendence and immeasurability of the light of the Word: no human language or culture can express or reflect it in an adequate way.

Yet the human person can also resist, even refuse the inner action of the Spirit. One is capable of disobeying God and turning in on oneself, even to the point of subordinating religion to one's ego. "Both the obedience and the disobedience gets built into the tradition and passed on to later generations. And they, in their turn, may respond more readily to the unceasing calls and disclosures of the Spirit, and so be moved to reform some part of the tradition."[12] The religions in history are in a continual process of transformation, of progress and reform, of conservation and development, both under the influence of circumstances and, at best, under the action of the Spirit of Christ active in their adherents. As for the salvific function of these religions, namely, whether they are or are not paths to salvation, there is no doubt that "grace and truth" are given through Jesus Christ and by his Spirit (cf. John 1:17). Everything would lead one to conclude, however, that gifts of "grace and truth" do reach or may reach the hearts of men and women through the visible, experiential signs of the various religions. Vatican Council II is explicit on this point.[13]

A more problematic area is the theological judgment on the significance and role of spiritual leaders and the founders of religions. In the light of Christ, Lord of the universe and of history, spiritual gifts may be given to individual people at particular moments of history and society, in order that they may give witness to, and promote values fundamental to humankind's ultimate good. Such values may be the primacy of God, detachment from self and from worldly values, ascesis and mastery over body and spirit, submission to the will of God, the law of conscience, the urgency of seeking salvation, the practice of justice, the upholding of harmony and order in family and society, methods of truth and nonviolence, and so on.

In the biblical tradition, personalities who have the characteristics of religious leaders, such as Melchizedech, Job, and Cyrus, are related to Christ as signs and images of his coming. The seer of the book of Revelation sees underneath the altar of heaven, along with the souls of those martyred "for the word of God," also those witnesses who gave their life "for the witness they had borne" (Rev. 6:9). Could it not be that he is speaking of those who have struggled and suffered in order to affirm spiritual and moral values among men and women?[14]

A UNIVERSALIST READING OF THE BIBLE

There is a further step. Contemporary experience of religious pluralism not only stimulates Christians to meditate on the vast horizons of Christology, but also invites them to reread the Bible itself from Genesis to the book of Revelation, and so to discern the divine plan in universal history. It is often said that the Bible is ethnocentric because its dominant theme is the action of God toward the Jews and toward Christians. This is true, but the very experience of our age calls us to rediscover also the universal perspectives of the Bible.

The Vatican Council's *Dei Verbum* and *Nostra Aetate* distinguish two dimensions, or if one prefers, two moments in God's action toward men and women. Both moments are documented in the sacred books: a universal aspect and a Jewish-Christian aspect. There is the economy of the covenant granted to Israel and to the Christians, and there is the sapiential economy in which all people are embraced. The Priestly Code already recognized a plurality of covenants, and the rabbis distinguished between the covenant of Moses, established with the Israelites, and that of Noah, a covenant embracing all the peoples of the earth.

By "sapiential economy" I refer to the action of God through Wisdom. This is described in the great collection of the so-called Wisdom literature, but also in the first chapters of Genesis, in parts of Deuteronomy, in the prophets, and in the New Testament writings. Both economies, that of the Mosaic covenant and that of Wisdom, are, in a New Testament perspective, joined and fused in Jesus. He is the "elect," the "beloved of God," and the "son" in whom Israel is resumed. But he is also the "Wisdom of God," present throughout the universe. We could say that in one hand Jesus holds the children of Israel, and in the other hand, all the peoples of the earth.

This is not the place to develop and illustrate the Wisdom economy in any detail. I only present it as the backdrop upon which the Jewish-Christian economy with its own function and specific purpose is woven, and I emphasize that the significance and value of the religious traditions of humankind are illuminated by it. Wisdom is with God and proceeds from God (Prov. 2:6; 8:22–23; Sir. 24:1–3, 9; Wis. 7:25–26; 8:4; 9:4). Wisdom is present throughout all creation, among every people and nation, and rejoices to dwell among human beings (Prov. 8:23–31; Sir. 24:6; Wis. 8:1). Indeed Wisdom is given to every one as the "eye of God in the heart" (Sir. 17:6–8), and in every generation "she passes into holy souls and makes them friends of God and prophets" (Wis. 7:27).[15] She is the source of right and perfect conduct because she teaches fear of God and justice toward men and women (Prov. 3:7; 8:13; Sir. 17:14). Wisdom is the source of salvation for those who welcome her and brings assurance of immortality near to, and in friendship with God (Wis. 6:19–20, 24; 7:14; 8:27–28). She is life for the person who finds her (Prov.

8:35), and her fruits are virtues (i.e., the virtues of the Greeks: self-control and prudence, justice and courage, cf. Wis. 8:7). However, Wisdom is incarnated in a special way in the Torah of Israel (Sir. 24:8–11; Bar. 4:37–38). The Bible sees, then, a link between Wisdom and the ethical religious life of humankind.

I mentioned that besides the Wisdom economy, a rereading of the Scriptures with the plurality of religions in mind throws light on other aspects which are useful for a theological evaluation of these same religions. For example, from Genesis to the book of Revelation, the covenant and revelation—namely the relationship of God with his people—are regularly presented according to the categories and religious forms of the milieu (Mesopotamian, Egyptian, Canaanite, Hellenistic), and Israel responds to the covenant, positively or negatively, in the framework of the religious psychology of the time.

Thus the religions as such do not appear in antithesis to God's self-communication but as the providential means, the concrete and historical instruments of the God-human relationship in the Bible, even if many of their elements clearly require purification and transformation before being assumed or taken up. Friedrich Heiler observed that in the biblical tradition the religious nature feasts *(Naturfeste)* were transformed into celebrations of the history of salvation *(Heilsgeschichtliche Feste)* without, however, entirely losing their original meaning: thus the Sabbath, the Pasch, Pentecost, the feast of the Tabernacles, the feast of Purim, the Hanukkah, and, we could add, the Christian Christmas. At this point we are confronted by one of "the greatest revolutions in the history of religions."[16] According to the biblical tradition, therefore, a bond and a theological relationship exist between religious expressions and the historical event of salvation. Examples could be multiplied both for the Old and the New Testaments. We may conclude that the creating and enlightening Word, present in history even before his incarnation, secretly prepares, sustains, purifies, and finally takes up what humanity achieves in its laborious search for the absolute and for salvation.

The Bible appears to be hostile toward the religions only when they represent a threat to the covenant, or assume forms of a cosmic and vitalistic monism, or draw people to worship idols and thus substitute the creature for the Creator. But when the Bible encounters forms of pure religion or forms that are reconcilable with faith in the God of the Covenant, it welcomes them and takes them up. One need only refer to the cases of Melchizedech, or Jethro, or Job; these are non-Jewish religious personalities who are nevertheless recognized and praised for their faith.

A NEW ATTITUDE OF THE CHURCH TOWARD THE RELIGIONS

At this point a query arises on the relationship of the church to the religions. *Nostra Aetate* represents the first time in its history that the Roman Catholic Church has faced this question in such an official way. This declaration in many ways implies a new mentality, and in it we can distinguish two approaches. There is, first of all, a global approach to the world religions. In comparison with the attitude prevalent in many past centuries, this approach is certainly new and uses such terms as *esteem, respect, dialogue, proclamation, witness.* Second, there is a differentiated approach to the individual religions according to the nature of each; this had already been delineated in *Lumen Gentium* (n. 16).

What is the global approach? It can be summed up in two words: *proclamation* and *dialogue.* Proclamation is something the church cannot deny itself. The very reason for the church's existence is to proclaim the marvelous deeds of God *(mirabilia Dei)* in history, which culminate, in the "fullness of time," in the death and resurrection of Christ. In Pauline terminology, the purpose of the church is to proclaim, announce, make known, manifest, tell, enlighten, teach[17] the *mysterion* hidden through previous centuries but now revealed and made known so that it may be proclaimed to all peoples and nations. In the context of religious pluralism, this proclamation must be carried out with fidelity and frankness.

But every time that the Vatican Council documents mention mission or proclamation, they also speak of esteem and respect for the religions, and of dialogue. Dialogue means that the herald of the gospel should know the persons to whom one speaks and respect them in their cultural and religious identity. This requires a high degree of spiritual maturity and an ample measure of patience. Dialogue means listening to the other in depth, to let oneself be judged by the other and to understand the other's objections toward ourselves. It also means we give an account for the hope that is in us (1 Pet. 3:15), putting forward the gospel in its own identity, free from the cultural accretions with which it is clothed in ourselves, and offering it not as a destructive force but as liberating and perfecting the values the other already possesses.

Dialogue thus requires a long and thorough hermeneutical effort both to enter into the other's horizon of meaning and to point out the meaning the message has for that other. As a consequence, dialogue brings the happy experience that every opening to the values and objections of the other implies a deepening and a fuller knowledge of the very message that the church proclaims.[18] That is why, in the context of dialogue, among all the images used to designate the gospel I find the most inspiring are those which refer to it as "little seed," "leaven," "salt," "graft," "unction," "seal"; namely the gospel as a principle that does not destroy but "conserves, purifies and perfects," "heals, ennobles and perfects," as key expressions of Vatican II's vocabulary put it.[19] "Mission and dialogue," as the Protestant scholar Horst Bürkle observes regarding this couplet that constantly recurs in the documents of the Vatican Council, "are so related to one another as to constitute a reciprocal guarantee against possible abuses: that the missionary effort does not become a plagiarism of Western-type Christianity, and that dialogue does not degenerate into the exercise of making sterile historical comparison."[20]

While I have referred to the global approach of the council toward the religions, I must immediately add that the church's approach varies in tone and emphasis in relation to particular religions. The church stands in a different existential relationship with each: *Nostra Aetate* moves from the simpler and less structured religions to Hinduism, Buddhism, Islam, and to the Jewish people with whom there is a unique "spiritual bond." *Lumen Gentium* (n. 16) begins with "the people from whom Christ was born according to the flesh," and goes on to the Muslims who, adhering to the faith of Abraham, "along with us adore the one and merciful God, who on the last day will judge humankind." The document then speaks of those who seek an unknown God "in shadows and images," then concludes with those "who have not yet arrived at an explicit knowledge of God, but who strive to live a good life, thanks to His grace."

Each religion is seen in terms of its specific relationship to the church: the relationship with Judaism, which was the church's forerunner, expressed the church, and then rejected it, but which still accompanies it in history in accordance with "a mystery" of God; the relationship with Islam, with which the church is linked by faith in Abraham and the prophets, by faith in Jesus, son of the Virgin Mary, Word and Spirit of God, and Judge of history; the relationship with Hinduism in its numerous historical expressions, some of them clearly influenced by Christianity; the relationship with Buddhism in its journey toward the Permanent; the relationship with Confucianism, Taoism, and the African religions.

In each of these religious groupings the Christian finds various values, and responds to them accordingly in a process of give-and-take. A consequence of the mutual presence of mission and dialogue in the church is that Christians find themselves in the uncomfortable but stimulating situation of being at one and the same time heralds and disciples, pilgrims and eschatological witnesses, people-with-others and people-for-others. Christians journey with others, seek with others, are enriched together with others, enrich others and are enriched by them, by their anthropological, metaphysical, ascetical, mystical, and ritual values, "to share with them" in the gospel of Christ (cf. 1 Cor. 9:23).

This twofold fidelity of the Christian to the "riches of creation" and to the gospel message, to the religious traditions of humankind and to the Christ-event, depends ultimately on the acceptance of the universal sovereignty of Christ: Christ is the Word of God already "present in the world" and yet who "comes into the world," as we see in the double image of John's prologue, to give to all "the power to become children of God" and to walk in His light (John 1:12; Rev. 21:23–24; cf. AG 1).

In this perspective we can conclude by saying that Christ is seen as the origin, center, and destiny of the various religions, as the One who brought them to birth, takes them up, purifies them, and fulfills them in order to take them to their eschatological goal, so that "God may be all in all" (1 Cor. 15:28; cf. LG 17; AG 11). This does not mean that our journey will be easy or that we can see the route it will take. There remain many difficult and complex questions to which Christians must devote attention and energies. For example, how in practice may the universal nature of the Christian message be reconciled with a respect for the spiritual traditions of others? If and how can fidelity to Christ and a particular religious tradition be reconciled? What is the relationship between the universal gift of God to those of goodwill and that communicated in the faith and sacraments of the church community? How are we to relate what is received through faith in Christ with what was given previously? What is the relationship between the universal enlightenment through the Word and the historical revelation of the gospel? How can a religious tradition be called a vehicle of the grace of God if it appears to be alien to him and even opposed to him? What is the real contribution of various religions to the Christian message if it only means our making explicit what is already in them?

This is why the Christian's attitude to the religions of the world is one of humility and respect, and of frankness in giving witness to Christ, the Word that enlightens every person, *paratus semper nuntiare, paratus semper doceri,* always ready to announce, always ready to be taught.

NOTES

1. Vatican Council II documents are here cited by abbreviating the first two Latin words which are each document's official title; thus: NA: *Nostra Aetate* (On the Relation of the Church to Non-Christian Religions); LG: *Lumen Gentium* (On the Church); GS: *Gaudium et Spes* (On the Church in the Modern World); DH: *Dignitatis Humanae* (On Religious Freedom); AG: *Ad Gentes* (On the Missionary Activity of the Church); DV: *Dei Verbum* (On Divine Revelation). The numbers refer to the document's paragraphs. Citations trans. by T.F. Stransky.

2. *Excerpts from Theodotus,* 78, 2.

3. Cf. GS, n. 10.

4. Distinction and terminology from Wilfred Cantwell Smith, *The Meaning and End of Religion* (New York: New American Library, 1964).

5. Cf. R. J. Werblowsky, *Beyond Tradition and Modernity: Changing Religions in a Changing World* (London: Athowe, 1976), chap. 6.

6. DH, nn. 1–3. The duty of seeking religious truth, the right to seek it freely and of not accepting inner constrictions in religious commitment and public profession was the subject of thorough reflection at Vatican Council II.

7. John Paul II, encyclical *Redemptor Hominis,* n. 1.

8. NA, n. 2.

9. LG, n. 2.

10. John V. Taylor, "The Theological Basis of Interfaith Dialogue," *International Review of Mission,* October 1979, p. 379. Cf. the vigorous expressions on humanity's relation to Christ in *Redemptor Hominis,* n. 14.

11. *"Instinctus Dei invitantis,"* Thomas Aquinas, *Summa Theologiae,* II–II, q. 2, art. 9, ad 3.

12. J. V. Taylor, "Interfaith Dialogue," p. 376.

13. Cf. AG, n. 3; GS, n. 32.

14. Cf. A. Feuillet, "Les martyrs de l'humanité et l'Agneau égorgé. Une interprétation nouvelle de la prière des égorgés en Ap. 6:9-11," *Nouvelle Revue Théologique* (March-April 1977), pp. 183-207.

15. Origen had already interpreted this text as referring to the saints and wise men of the ancient world, *Contra Celsum*, IV 3.7.8.

16. F. Heiler, *Erscheinungsformen und Wesen der Religion* (Stuttgart: Kohlhammer, 1961), p. 155.

17. Cf. "proclaim," 1 Cor. 2:1; "announce," Eph. 3:8; "make known," Rom. 16:26; "manifest," Col. 4:3; "tell," Col. 4:4; "enlighten," Eph. 3:9; "teach," Col. 1:28.

18. *Redemptor Hominis*, n. 11.

19. Cf. LG, n. 17; AG, nn. 3, 9, 11.

20. H. Bürkle, *Einführung in die Theologie der Religionen*, Darmstadt: Wissenschaftliche Buchgesellschaft, 1977), pp. 27-28.

1

Response

Gerald H. Anderson

Monsignor Rossano has given us a remarkably helpful summary and synthesis of official Roman Catholic thought on our subject since Vatican Council II. It is difficult to realize that the office he represents and the documents he discusses have developed in less than fifteen years—from the creation of the Vatican Secretariat for Non-Christian Religions in May 1964 during the council, to the issuance of the papal encyclical *Redemptor Hominis* by John Paul II in March 1979. His study leads me to suggest that Roman Catholic mission theology has undergone more radical change in those fifteen years than in the previous century. And there is obviously a great deal more ferment to come in the last fifth of the twentieth century. What we see so far, in my judgment, is but a foretaste or the first fruits of a radical realignment of Catholic mission theology that by A.D. 2000 will be as far from our thinking today as our thinking today is from where Catholic mission theology was twenty years ago.

Let me suggest some flashing signals already pointing in that direction. First, Monsignor Rossano referred briefly to *Redemptor Hominis,* Pope John Paul's first encyclical. But there is considerably more in that pastoral letter for our purposes than has been mentioned. In fact, the most creative and important point in the whole letter is precisely that it relates the redemption in Christ to each and every person, without exception. The pope says:

> The human person—every person without exception—has been redeemed by Christ; because Christ is in a way united to the human person—every person without exception—even if the individual may not realize this fact. "Christ, who died and was raised up for all"—for every human being and for all human beings—"can through His Spirit offer man the light and the strength to measure up to his supreme destiny" (n. 14).

Notice the explicit emphasis that *"every person without exception—has been redeemed by Christ,"* and that *Christ is already united to "every person without exception—even if the individual may not realize this fact."* This is the single most significant doctrinal statement of the Catholic church for mission theology since Vatican Council II. For while this view is grounded in biblical and patristic testimony, and has never been entirely absent from Catholic doctrine, it has seldom—if ever—been singled out in the official teaching of the church with such clarity and visibility for the kind of unqualified emphasis that is given to it here by Pope John Paul II.

The far-reaching import of this has not been lost on those who have studied the encyclical carefully. For instance, Catholic theologian Gregory Baum in Toronto says that

> what is new and startling in the encyclical is the emphasis, many times repeated, on the redemptive presence of Jesus Christ to the entire human family—to people everywhere, to every single human being in his or her concrete historical situation. . . . The Pope takes sides here with modern theologians like Karl Rahner who, assimilating an ancient patristic theme, look upon the incarnation as the revelation of God's union with the entire human family. In Jesus is revealed that

God is present to every single person. What follows from this is that each human life is supernatural, each human life is constituted through a dialogue in which God is redemptively present.[1]

Protestant theologian Roger Hazelton, in his comments on the encyclical, says that redemption here

is conceived as nothing less than the total re-creating of humanness itself. . . . Moreover, there is no suggestion of a condescending, self-confident "evangelism" asking those outside the Christian fold to come in and be saved. On the contrary, it is repeatedly declared that our redemption is a *fait accompli,* for each and every person "without any exception whatever" is already redeemed—united with Christ—by virtue of the incarnation.[2]

If I could ask the pope just one question, it would be this: "Your Holiness, since you have said that everyone without any exception whatever is already redeemed by Christ and united with Christ, even where they are unaware of it, why is there any urgency or need at all for persons of other faiths to hear the gospel, to proclaim their faith in Jesus Christ, to be baptized into membership in the visible church and to partake of the sacraments?" This is not clear in *Redemptor Hominis.* It is also not entirely clear to what extent the pope is speaking only about the redemption of individuals who are not members of the visible church, and to what extent his teaching implies salvific values in other faiths to which those individuals may belong. And while we are raising questions for clarification perhaps we should also ask whether or not "redeemed by Christ" implies or is synonymous with "everlasting salvation."

What the pope has said does not, of course, constitute a radical departure from recent trends in Catholic mission theology. What it does is to confirm officially some of these trends and encourage further developments along the same lines. For instance, the trend in American Catholic mission theology since Vatican II has shifted from an "anonymous Christian phase" in the attitude toward other religions to a more radical reexamination not only of

Christianity's universal claims, but of its self-identity.[3] This is seen in the following statement by Roger D. Haight, an American Jesuit, who says:

> Not only is the doctrine "No salvation outside the Church" wrong, but also, statistically speaking, the common, normal, and "ordinary" way and place of salvation is outside the Church. Up to now, and in the foreseeable future, salvation has been and will be achieved for the vast majority of people without any empirical historical connection with Jesus of Nazareth.[4]

Father Haight recognizes that when one takes this position, the crucial question is no longer "What is the church?" but rather "Why the church?" and even "Why be a Christian?"[5] Thus the Catholic church, as it enters the 1980s, is asking itself the most radical questions in its history, questions that deal precisely with the issues of mission in relation to the Lordship of Jesus Christ and religious pluralism.

One of the problems that I find in Monsignor Rossano's paper and in what I have been discussing is that Catholic teaching on our theme since Vatican II has developed largely along only one tradition or line of thought that is found in Scripture and in the history of Christian doctrine. This is the broad, inclusive tradition that emphasizes the revealing and redeeming activity of God, which is both longer and larger than the Christian response to that activity. This tradition emphasizes the *continuity* of God's activity in Christ with his activity among all persons everywhere. It views God's actions in Jesus Christ as the climax of a divine revelation and relationship that has been available to everyone from the beginning. Jesus Christ in this view is crucial, normative, and definitive, but not exclusive. What is true of Jesus Christ in a focal way is pervasively true of the whole cosmos. He is the key or clue to the rest of God's working. But the Word of God is not limited to and did not end with the revelation in the historic person of Jesus. Prior to Vatican II this tradition was minimized in Catholic teaching; since the council it has been maximized. As Karl Rahner suggests, this is a belated corrective and recognition that "theology has been led astray for too long by the tacit assumption that grace would no longer be grace if God became too free with it. . . . We have no right," says Rahner, "to assign arbitrary limits to the grace of God outside the Church."[6]

But there is another tradition—equally if not more strongly represented—in Scripture and in the history of Christian doctrine. It is the narrow, particular, and exclusivistic tradition that emphasizes a radical *discontinuity* between the realm of Christian revelation, which is absolutely unique *(sui generis),* and the whole range of non-Christian religious experience. In this view the non-Christian religions are the various efforts of human beings to comprehend their existence, whereas Christianity is the result of the self-disclosure of God in Jesus Christ. God, according to this tradition, has spoken to humanity only in the person of Jesus Christ and "there is salvation in no one else" (Acts 4:12). The tradition of discontinuity would emphasize Christ's saying in John 14:6 that "no one comes to the Father but by me."

Prior to Vatican II this tradition was maximized in Catholic teaching; since the council it has been minimized. The point I want to make is that both these traditions are part of the Christian heritage. Both have solid support in Scripture and patristic teaching. Both are included in the holistic gospel and mission of the church. The problem is that the church tends to swing its emphasis in different periods from one extreme to the other, and thereby distorts its message and mission. It is imperative that both of these traditions in Christian thought be maintained in balanced tension. This is difficult to do when those from one tradition offer continuity with doubtful uniqueness, and those from the other side urge uniqueness without continuity. What is needed in our theological understanding about Christ's Lordship and religious pluralism is uniqueness *with* continuity.[7]

In conclusion, I want to raise an issue of fundamental importance, a cornerstone issue in mission theology, which Monsignor Rossano did not discuss, but which I feel must be addressed. It is an issue about which the Catholic church has been sensitive and has tried to refine its position. I refer to the issue of the church and the Jewish people. In my remarks at the Washington and Lee conference in 1976, I made reference to this issue, but did not include it in my published remarks. Since that time, however, a major Roman Catholic statement on the subject has been issued.

While not an official document of the church, it is being viewed as authoritative, because—as reported in the *New York Times* (April 3, 1977)—"the prestige of the [Vatican] delegation [presenting the statement] lends its views far-reaching significance and commends them as compatible with Vatican thinking."

The document to which I refer is a "Study Outline on the Mission and Witness of the Church," prepared by Dr. Tommaso Federici of the Urban University in Rome for the Vatican's Commission for Religious Relations with the Jews. It was presented by the representatives of that Vatican Commission at the sixth meeting of the Liaison Committee between the Roman Catholic Church and the International Jewish Committee for Interreligious Consultations at Venice in March 1977. Jewish leaders have described Federici's work (sometimes referred to as the Venice statement) as a "watershed paper," because—in their words—"it calls into question the concept of mission to others and focuses instead on mission to self."[8] They anticipate that the new understanding represented by the document "will eventually change the course of the Jewish-Catholic relationship."[9]

There are two or three issues regarding this document, and the way it is being interpreted by some Christians and Jews, that I want to comment on briefly, and then to say something in general about the issue of the church and the Jewish people. In one sense this might be seen as a case study in our larger concern for the Lordship of Christ and religious pluralism.

First of all, Professor Federici rightly distinguishes between Christian mission and witness on the one hand, and proselytism on the other hand. Mission and witness, he says, are essential to the nature of the church. Proselytism, however, which is "anything that forces and violates the right of every person or human community to be free from external and internal constrictions in matters of religion," is a corruption of witness (II, A, 12).[10] "Therefore," he says, "the Church clearly rejects every form of unwarranted proselytism . . . every kind of testimony and preaching that in any way becomes physical, moral, psychological or cultural constraint on the Jews, as individuals or as a community, that could in any way destroy or even diminish personal judgment, free will, full autonomy to decide, either personal or communitarian" (II, A, 13). The document then rejects "any ac-

tion that aims at changing the religious faith of the Jews . . . by
making more or less open offers of protection, legal, material,
cultural, political and other advantages, using educational or social assistance pretexts" (II, A, 15). And in this context of proselytism, the statement affirms that "the temptation to create or-
ganizations of any kind, especially for education or social
assistance, to 'convert' Jews, is to be rejected" (II, A, 18).

This is quite proper and necessary, and has been widely acknowledged, not only among Roman Catholics but also by the
World Council of Churches. However, some Jewish authorities
are now citing the Federici/Venice statement as an indication, not
only that the Catholic church condemns proselytism, but also that
it rejects "any effort 'to change the religious faith of the Jews.' "[11]
This is *not,* however, what the document says in context. In effect,
the careful distinction in the Federici/Venice statement between
affirmation of mission and witness, and rejection of proselytism,
has been confused, and is now being interpreted by some as a
categorical rejection of Christian mission and witness to the Jewish people by the Catholic church. This is unfortunate and requires clarification.

Why am I concerned about this? I am concerned because our
understanding of the relationship of the church and the Jewish
people is of fundamental importance for our understanding of
the relationship of the gospel to *all* other faiths. I am concerned
also because in our North American context Jews are the largest
non-Christian religious community among our neighbors; therefore it is particularly important that we seek for clarification in
our self-understanding and relationships. And, finally, I am concerned about this issue because of the direction of much contemporary theological discussion on the subject.

The whole tenor and thrust of thought among Roman Catholic
theologians in North America who are writing on this issue is that
Christians have no mission to the Jewish people. They maintain
that Jews do not need the gospel or faith in Jesus Christ as the
Messiah because they have their own covenant with God, which is
adequate. Let me give three examples.

Father John T. Pawlikowski, O.S.M., from the Catholic Theological Union in Chicago, says that "as Christians we must come
to view the Jewish 'no' to Jesus as a positive contribution to the

ultimate salvation of humankind." He proposes "radical surgery" on "parts of our traditional Christology," and he is willing to "profoundly alter Christianity's self-definition" so as to "make possible a more realistic relationship to Judaism and to all other non-Christian religions." By "realistic" Pawlikowski means "that Christianity must look anew at its contention that the Messianic age, the time of fulfillment . . . took place with the coming of Christ."[12]

Writing in a similar vein is Gregory Baum, professor of theology at St. Michael's College of the University of Toronto. Baum, who comes from a Jewish family and is a former Catholic priest, says:

> After Auschwitz the Christian churches no longer wish to convert the Jews. . . . The major churches have come to repudiate mission to the Jews, even if they have not justified this by adequate doctrinal explanations. We have here a case, frequently found in church history, where a practical decision on the part of the churches, in response to a significant event, precedes dogmatic reflection and in fact becomes the guide to future doctrinal development. Moved by a sense of shame over the doctrinal formulations that negate Jewish existence, the churches have come to recognize Judaism as an authentic religion before God, with independent value and meaning, not as a stage on the way to Christianity.[13]

For Baum, the Christian "message of hope does not imply that people are called to become Christians out of the great world religions. The church's claims to be the unique source of saving truth is a judgment on the systems of the world, not on the great world religions." The witness of the church, he says, "can be followed and obeyed by people wherever they are, in any spiritual tradition."[14]

Dr. Rosemary R. Ruether, coming from the Catholic tradition and teaching at Garrett-Evangelical Theological Seminary, says that Christians must reckon with the "inescapable fact that the messianic age has not come."[15] Therefore, in her view, if we ask, "In what sense is Jesus the Christ, we must say that he is *not yet* the Christ."[16] For Dr. Ruether, the Jew is "a brother in faith, who does not necessarily need to know about this faith through the story of Jesus, because he already has other stories that tell him the same thing, such as the story of Exodus."[17]

What do we say in response to this trend in Catholic theological thinking? First, Christians must indeed bear a profound sense of regret and repentance for the discrimination and suffering inflicted on the Jewish people through the centuries, to a large extent as a result of anti-Semitic ideology fostered by teachings and attitudes perpetuated in the churches, which culminated with the extermination of six million Jews in the Holocaust. And Christians must commit themselves to correcting the negative stereotypes and sub-Christian concepts that have stained the church's attitude toward the Jewish people through the centuries.

Second, Christians should affirm their appreciation for the positive influence and contributions of Judaism to the Christian faith.

Because Christians and Jews share a covenant with God, their relationship is one of *continuity.* More important for us as Christians, however, is the fact that Christ *fulfills* and *completes* the covenant with Israel (as anticipated in Jer. 31:31-33). Jesus said he came not "to abolish the law and the prophets . . . but to fulfill them" (Mt. 5:17).

Inherent in the Christian affirmation that Jesus is the fulfillment of the promise given to Israel is the understanding that what God has done in and through Jesus Christ is of unique, ultimate, and universal significance. He is for everyone—for all "the nations"—including, even *with priority,* the Jewish people. While today the debate is over whether Jews are to be included within the universal Christian mission, originally the issue was whether anyone other than Jews was to be included. Initially Jesus saw himself as "sent only to . . . the house of Israel" (Mt. 15:24) and he forbade his disciples from going among the Gentiles or even entering a Samaritan town (Mt. 10:5-6). For Paul the pattern of mission was "first the Jew *and also* the Gentile" (Rom. 1:16; 2:9-10). Thus we can say that the mission to the Jews is the oldest Christian mission; that's where it all began.

My larger concern here is that if the Jewish people—who were the original focus of Jesus' mission—do not need Christ, then a similar theological case can easily be projected (as Baum and others are doing) to apply to other faiths until ultimately it becomes a rejection of the Christian mission to people of all other faiths (one of my critics calls this Anderson's religious domino theory). It is my position that Christians have no special mission to the Jews, but neither is there any special exemption of the Jews from the universal Christian mission. I am not calling for a crusade against the Jewish people, but I do want to establish a fundamental theological point, namely, that either all people need Christ or none do! This evaluation of Jesus Christ is inherent and central in the Christian faith.

Having said this, however, let me also say that as Christians, we cannot determine—or even adequately discuss—the means and limits of Christ's redemptive activity. A measure of humility, tentativeness, trust, risk, and occasional silence will not hurt our witness. We should always be prepared to listen and learn, as well as to talk and teach. In the spirit of the first letter of Peter, a Christian should "always be prepared to give an account of the hope that is in you, but do it with courtesy, respect, and reverence." It is also good to remember, after giving our account, that "only God gives the growth" (1 Cor. 3:7).

I want to close my remarks with the prayer that is quoted by Pope John Paul II in *Redemptor Hominis*:

> Come, Holy Spirit, Come! Come!
> Heal our wounds, our strength renew;
> On our dryness pour your dew;
> Wash the stains of guilt away;
> Bend the stubborn heart and will;
> Melt the frozen, warm the chill;
> Guide the steps that go astray.
>
> Amen

NOTES

1. Gregory Baum, "The First Papal Encyclical," *The Ecumenist*, May–June 1979, p. 55.
2. Roger Hazelton, "Redeeming Humanity: The Pope's Theological Vision," *The Christian Century*, October 3, 1979, p. 945.

3. Cf. J. Peter Schineller, S. J., "Christ and Church: A Spectrum of Views," *Theological Studies* 37, no. 4 (December 1976): 545; and Paul Knitter, "Christianity as Religion: True and Absolute? A Roman Catholic Perspective," in a forthcoming volume of *Concilium*, ed. David Tracy and Mircea Eliade.

4. Roger D. Haight, S.J. "Mission: The Symbol for Understanding the Church Today," *Theological Studies* 37, no. 4 (December 1976): 629.

5. Ibid., p. 630.

6. Quoted by Eugene Hillman, *The Wider Ecumenism* (New York: Herder and Herder, 1968), pp. 34, 52.

7. This terminology was suggested by Edmund Davison Soper, *The Philosophy of the Christian World Mission* (Nashville: Abingdon-Cokesbury Press, 1943), pp. 225–27.

8. Editorial, "Christian Mission and Jewish Witness," *Face to Face: An Interreligious Bulletin* (Anti-Defamation League of B'nai B'rith, New York City), 3–4 (Fall/Winter 1977): 1.

9. Ibid., p. 24.

10. The revised and authorized English translation of the study paper by Professor Federici, which is quoted here, was published in the English edition of *SIDIC*: Journal of the Service International de Documentation Judéo-Chrétienne (Rome), 11, no. 3 (1978).

11. Leon Klenicki, "Comments and Notes" (on the Federici document), *Face to Face* 3–4 (Fall/Winter 1977): 30, n.8.

12. John T. Pawlikowski, "The Contemporary Jewish-Christian Theological Dialogue Agenda," *Journal of Ecumenical Studies* 11, no. 4 (Fall 1974): 603–4.

13. Gregory Baum, "Rethinking the Church's Mission after Auschwitz," *Auschwitz: Beginning of a New Era? Reflections on the Holocaust*, ed. Eva Fleischner (New York: KTAV Publishing House, 1977), p. 113.

14. Ibid., pp. 124, 126.

15. Rosemary R. Ruether, "An Invitation to Jewish-Christian Dialogue. In What Sense Can We Say That Jesus Was 'The Christ'?" *The Ecumenist* 10, no. 2: 17.

16. Ibid., p. 22.

17. Ibid., p. 23.

2

Response

Kofi Appiah-Kubi

I want to register my sincere thanks to Monsignor Rossano for his helpful approach to this crucial subject, which is the pivot of present-day ecumenical thinking and an ardent task for the mission of the church. Much as I would like to respond in general to several aspects of his presentation, I would fail my duty if the emphasis of my brief comments were not focused on African religious heritage and life in relation to the Lordship of Christ. What I hear Monsignor Rossano saying is that Jesus Christ is the Lord of all religions and cultures including African religions and cultures. These various religions and cultures share in common the existential questions about humankind, about the meaning and source of life, the source and meaning of pain and joy, happiness, suffering, disease and health, and finally, death and life after death. Where does humankind come from; and where is it going? In an attempt to answer these questions it would seem to me that each and every group of people within their culture and religion may have different methods, but the ultimate goal should be the same; that is, fuller realization of the meaning of life, and God as the ultimate source and reality of life. Thus it can be argued that each religion and culture may represent the traditional way of response of the people to the gift and illumination of God. This, in fact, happens within a particular cultural and linguistic milieu or context.

The story of the evangelization of Africa is too well known to be repeated here, except to say that many of the early missionaries behaved as though they were the source rather than the channel of the gospel. From either ignorance or pure pride of ethnocentrism, they saw Africa as a blank slate on which anything could be written. Africa and its people were seen as living in a religious void. They were therefore denied any religious heritage at worst, and at best the religious heritage they were credited with was rendered pagan, devilish, primitive, and altogether dangerous. The evangelizers thus felt that they were bringing Christ to Africa in their luggage. They really forgot that God through Christ was already at work in Africa before the advent of the white missionary. Hence the use of such terms as "Bringing Christ to the heathens," "Planting Christianity in Africa," and so forth.

In this particular instance it would seem to me that the church in Africa has failed in its duty to translate divine revelation into every language, to bring it within the range of all cultures, so that all creatures of God can gain contact with their Redeemer in a manner suitable to the mentality and feelings of each one.[1]

At one with culture, religion is inextricably linked to the whole of life whose personal and communal activities it animates. The feeling of wholeness is an important aspect of African life.[2] The celebrations of ritual ceremonies take place in common and for common good. The spirit of solidarity plays a cardinal part in this and the existence of the individual cannot be conceived outside the framework of one's integration in society. Religion therefore acts as a unifying factor in African culture. It is like the soul, which keeps the whole body healthy. The Lordship of Christ over all religions and cultures is understood by Africans through their concept of God. To the African, there is no watertight distinction between God and Christ. God and Jesus are linked together. Jesus is, because God is. Hence most of the attributes of Christ are indeed attributes of God. Thus such attributes of Christ as Mediator, Savior, Power, Redeemer, Liberator, and finally *Healer par excellence* are all understood by Africans, be they Christian or otherwise, as attributes of God.

The church's duty therefore in dialogue with African religion and culture should not be one of condemnation but of understanding and fulfillment. The church should learn to understand Africa; and learn to address Africans as Africans—by always bearing in mind that God's self-disclosure is, in the first instance, to the whole world and that each race has grasped something of this primary revelation according to its capability.[3] This is not to create gods for every race but to emphasize the all-embracing power and quality of God (and therefore of Christ) as the Creator, Father, King and Judge of all possible religions, cultures, and indeed the whole world.

Furthermore, it must be noted that, in the African concept of humanity, a person is truly and fully human in community with others. This could be rendered in the words of John Mbiti thus: "I am because we are and because we are therefore I am." This idea strikes the great chord of African solidarity and the sacredness of the human community. Kinship therefore plays an important role in the African concept of God and the universality of humankind.[4]

Religion permeates every aspect of the African life, especially the crucial aspects of life, namely, marriage, birth, naming ceremony, initiation, puberty rites, illness, healing, and death (burial or funeral ceremony). In fact, one has to go through the various "rites of passage" to be accepted as a perfect man or woman in several African societies. The true community, in the African mind, embraces the dead (past), the living (the present), and the yet-unborn (the future). Thus the past, present, and future generations form one community. There is a very strong sense of respect for the ancestors, who are said to be the custodians of our moral, ethical, religious, and social life. Ancestor veneration is therefore at the core of our religion—God the universal Father and Creator of all the world and humankind is acknowledged, but the ancestors and the elderly people who are the manifestations of God the Father are very much revered. For, to many, the God to whom they perform their religious rites and pour their prayer of libation has a face like their fathers. Africans view their world as a spiritual arena, with spirits interacting with humans for good or evil. Good is rewarded and evil is punished.

Generally speaking, the African can be said to know no problem of evil or problem of suffering as such; the vital or the most important question is, however, the source of the evil and the cause of the suffering. For there are evil forces sufficient to account for the wickedness, tragedies, and misfortunes of life. It may result in illness, calamity, disaster, sorrow, or death.[5]

To the African, religion must be functional and indeed practical. It must have the qualities of solving, and be ready to solve most if not all human problems, from disease to want. Complete failure is not envisaged and when it does occur it might be attributed to some evil power at work, or divine punishment for an omission of religious rite, or just simply one's own destiny determined by God the Maker. Religion is therefore called upon to answer all life problems.

Religion, to be worthy of its name, should be powerful and able to provide all one's needs and answer all questions in human situations. It could generally be argued that African religious thought has no room for "God of the Gaps." God is accepted as the Source, Fountain, and Author of both good and evil. He is the Healer par excellence; hence the Akans of Ghana say that "Se Onyame ma wo yare a na woma wo ano aduru," which is literally rendered: "If God gives you a particular disease, he provides the cure."

Religion and healing have been bed- or soul-mates in human history. In African communities most healing ceremonials have religious overtones. In the early part of the church's work in Africa there was a firm recognition of this fact. Most mission stations had hospitals attached to them, especially to protect the life of the missionaries and in several cases to provide for the health needs of the converts. It is not an exaggeration to say that several of these hospitals became recruiting grounds for new converts to the church. With increased secularization, the hospitals that started in medieval European monasteries as hospices are now increasingly over-technologized, and the priest-healer ends with his Bible as the physician or doctor starts with his prescriptions.

Healing thus has become devoid of its religious elements. In proclaiming the Lordship of Christ to the African, therefore, the church in Africa has tended to overemphasize the *second* commission—"Go ye therefore and teach all nations, baptizing them in the name of the Father and of the Son and of the Holy Ghost, teaching them to observe all things whatsoever I have commanded you and lo I am with you always, even unto the end of the world. Amen" (Mt. 28:19-20)—to a total or near complete neglect of the *first* commission—"Heal the sick, cleanse the lepers, raise the dead, cast out demons. Freely you have received, freely give" (Mt. 10:8). Africans seek life and seek it more abundantly. They will therefore do anything to fortify and give fullness of life. Christ said: "I have come that you might have life and have it more abundantly." The African challenge to the church in Africa and the universal Christ is: Where is this abundant life?— when all around them Africans see anguish, pain, suffering, war, hunger, discrimination, oppression, and illness. The church's attempt to bring total health to the African convert did not take into serious consideration the *African's understanding of health and disease and also the African's world-view.* The condemnation by the church of things African as pagan, evil, and heathen has weakened the logic and therefore the force of the statement of the "Lordship of Christ over all religions and cultures," including, of course, African religion and culture. The church in Africa has failed to proclaim to the African convert the Christ portrayed by the New Testament as the Liberator and Healer par excellence.

Therefore the critical African observer is left to ask with Jeremiah: "Is there no balm in Gilead? Is there no physician there? Why then has the health of the daughter of my people not been restored?" (Jer. 8:22).[6] In fact, the African rendering of the foregoing should be something like this: Are there no priest-healers (the so-called witch doctors)? Are there no potent herbal remedies in Africa? Why then have the people of my forebears not been healed? These and many such questions and concerns make evangelism questionable and difficult in our context.

According to the African, disease is an attack by a spirit upon one's spirit and it can be overcome by medicine whose spirit is stronger than the spirit of the disease.

An illness which does not yield to medicine must be attributed to another baneful force. For the ordinary person, religion is largely the means of reinforcing life, of proper precautions against the destructive powers. When straightforward remedies fail, as in the case of illness not responding to normal treatment, a recourse to the priest-healer is necessary. Belief in witchcraft involves the idea that the African thinks it singular that he or she alone should be sick while all the people around enjoy good health. The belief in witchcraft therefore explains not how a misfortune happens but why a particular person suffers that particular misfortune. Witchcraft as a theory of causation does not necessarily deny that people fall ill from eating bad food or from certain unhygienic behavior or practices, but it explains why some of them fall ill at certain times and not at other times.

Thus the African believes that every misfortune, like every piece of good fortune, involves two questions: the first is *how* it happened, and the second is *why* it happened at all. The *how* is answered by common-sense empirical observation; it is the "Why me?" question that the African asks and to which he or she seeks the answer through divination by the help of the priest-healer or diviner. Belief in witchcraft therefore explains why a particular person at a particular place suffers a particular misfortune at a particular time. Belief in witchcraft is concerned with the singularity of misfortune.

For the African, health is symptomatic of correct relationship between one and one's environment, the supernatural environment, the world around one and one's fellow men and women.

Health is therefore associated with good, blessing, and beauty—all that is positively valued in life. Illness, on the other hand, shows that one has fallen out of this delicate balance, and this is normally attributed to the breaking of a taboo. Illness may also be due to the malevolence of an evil spirit. Health and disease among Africans are inextricably linked to socially approved norms, behavior, and moral conduct. To enjoy maximum health one must have good thoughts about one's neighbors. Sometimes disease is caused by failure to perform the right religious act at the right time. Generally speaking, Africans consider disease as a disequilibrium in the body as well as the society.

The African view of the focus of disease is cosmic—thus the individual illness is derived from a sick or broken society. Society becomes the point of departure for individual diagnosis. In order to gain total health, the emphasis is on participation rather than achievement. The African further believes that the whole person, and not only a part, is ill: body, soul, mind and spirit; and healing, therefore, must embrace the totality of the person. Disease and health to the African can be seen as psychosomatic. Healing ceremonials involve confession, atonement, and forgiveness. The healing ritual elicits confession of specific personal transgression based on detailed reviews of the patient's past history with special reference to the events surrounding one's illness. Healing also involves sacrifice.

The risk benefits of modern technological medicine are well known. The impersonality, prohibitive cost, alienation, and over-secularization of modern medical services are commonplace. The question is: What is the future of modern technological medical service, which is constantly alienating Africans from their past, their kinfolk, in its insistence on quantifiable evidence, which requires X-rays, blood-sugar counts, laboratory tests, and so on. Throughout the West today, anxious persons are looking for new ways of meeting the health needs of modern people without turning them into guinea pigs or things. African methods and approaches to healing that were once condemned are being seen as more humanitarian and realistic ways of meeting people's health needs. For the traditional healer has the time, the patience, and a deeper understanding of those seeking help. The approach is holistic.

For the mission of the church in Africa, this raises deep social, religious, ethical, and moral issues, especially for church leaders in Africa and for missionary agencies working in Africa. What really is your mission? What is the content of your evangelization? What is the goal? In the field of health, just to take one example, what is the focus of your message? Could the African pastor who has been thoroughly brainwashed into believing that the priest-healers are pagans or heathens advise parishioners to benefit by the services of priest-healers?

"How can one spit on the floor and put it back on one's tongue?" The Akans of Ghana say: "One does not spit and put it on the tongue." How can we preach the Lordship of Christ over all diseases and proclaim him as the Healer par excellence in our missionary-founded churches? For the church to be meaningful, to enter the depths of African religiosity and life and really dialogue with that life, it must learn to empty itself of its past glory, false arrogance, and sincere ignorance and weakness through sincerity (the church's history in Africa) and seek to understand Africa and learn to address Africans as Africans who also share in the economy of the Lordship of God (Christ).

I must confess that I have an uncomfortable feeling at ecumenical meetings where, on the one hand, we seem to say that other religions share in the Lordship of Christ and must therefore be accorded due respect, but on the other hand, we emphasize that Christianity has the pure truth which must be proclaimed to all peoples, at all times, and in all places. This is what my people call "Selling the dog and still holding its tail." Church statisticians tell us that by the turn of the century Africa will be the most "Christian continent" in the world, with about 85 percent of the population baptized. What does this mean to us? What is the function of African theology in the church's evangelistic thrust?

In conclusion, what I have tried to do in response to Monsignor Rossano is, first, to strike some chords of agreement with him by restating some of the common concerns of African traditional religions with other religions, especially Christianity. Namely, we all share the common human quest for the meaning of humankind, its life and its future; the deep quest for the life-force and the reality of God as the source of life and the Creator of the universe and humankind; the solidarity that Africans share in the economy of the covenant with all humanity; and the common understanding of the attributes of Christ as seen through the African attributes of God.

I reject the traditional affirmation that Christianity alone holds the ultimate truth. By so doing, Western evangelists have arrogated unto themselves the sense of having the truth, being the advocates of the truth, and of having the pure culture and therefore the true religion, to near denial of any moral, ethical, or religious values of African religion. The question for me is: Can the gospel be stripped of its cultural wrappings? How do we distinguish the will of God from that of the missionary, or for that matter, the local pastor? Can the Universal Christ whom Africans perceive through God be freed from the imprisonment of arid Western intellectual and narrow evangelical theological affirmations?

Furthermore, I have tried, by using the illustrations of healing practices in Africa, to test some of the concepts of Monsignor Rossano, in terms of concrete African life. I have tried to show that the church throughout its missionary effort to evangelize Africa has been asking the wrong question when it asks the African, "Are you saved, Brother?" The individualistic overtone implied in this question does not touch the African heart. Rather, the church should ask, as Jesus did, "Do you want to be healed?"

If the church could be humble enough to listen to others and at the same time share in the God-given life of others, perhaps its evangelism would be more meaningful to Africans in their common quest for the truth. The question is: "What is the role of the Holy Spirit in our missionary encounter in Africa today?" Can Africans be allowed to proclaim the Lordship of Christ in their own religious culture and life experience without adopting Western missionary styles, strategies, attitudes, and assumptions?

NOTES

1. See Kofi Appiah-Kubi, "Why African Theology?" *AACC Bulletin* (Nairobi), 1974.

2. See Kofi Appiah-Kubi, "Jesus Christ—Some Christological Aspects from African Perspectives," *African and Asian Contributions to Contemporary Theology,* ed. John S. Mbiti (Celigny/Bossey, Switzerland: Ecumenical Institute/ WCC, 1977).

3. See "Why African Theology?"

4. See "Jesus Christ—Some Christological Aspects."

5. See Kofi Appiah-Kubi, *Psychology, Religion and Healing: A Sociological Survey of Healing Practices among the Akans of Ghana* (Kumasi, Ghana: University of Science and Technology, 1979).

6. See Bishop Paul Gregorios, address at the Fifth Assembly of the World Council of Churches, Nairobi, Kenya, 1975.

3
Reply

Pietro Rossano

i

I am deeply thankful to Dr. Anderson for his response. He enlarges our horizon and gives me the opportunity to complete and clarify some points.

1. I note his observation that "Roman Catholic mission theology has undergone more radical change in those fifteen years [1964—79] than in the previous century." This is substantially true—and normal—because theology is a science which rethinks faith and revelation under the pressure of historical circumstances. It has been always so, from the beginning of the church. But the timespan indicated by Dr. Anderson is too short. For instance, I am thinking of books that deeply influenced my theological education, when I was a student, such as O. Karrer, *Das Religiöse in der Menschheit und das Christentum* (Freiburg i. B., 1934); H. De Lubac, *Catholicisme* Paris, 1938); J. Gross, *La divinisation du chrétien d'après les Pères Grecs* (Paris, 1938); J. V. Bainvel, *Nature et Surnaturel* (Paris, 1920); A. Verriele, *Le Surnaturel en nous et le péché originel* (Paris, 1932); and last but not least, M. J. Scheeben, *Die Mysterien des Christentums* (Freiburg i. B., 1865). Please take note of the dates and consider that these books were mainly concerned with anthropology and were part of that movement of return to medieval and patristic sources that

has characterized Catholic theology in this century. None of them deals specifically with the theology of mission. Until Vatican II there was a dangerous lacuna on this matter in the Catholic church. Finally, the gap has now been filled. But in addition to these mentioned books, I look at history and I see that my affirmations largely correspond to positions held by Nicholas of Cusa, Saint Thomas, Saint Bonaventure, Pseudo-Dionysius, Saint Augustine (cf. *Ep.* 102 *ad sacerdotem Deogratias*), Saint Irenaeus (cf. *Adv. Haer.* IV, 6, 7), Saint Justin, and even Saint Paul and Saint John. I think that what I have affirmed is rooted in the history of the Catholic church. Both innovation and fidelity are the duty and the law of theology. For this reason I am not sure that by A.D. 2000 Catholic mission theology will be radically different from the theology of today. On the contrary, I am sure that new aspects will be developed under the pressure of historical experience, but this does not mean a "radical change."

I am pleased with the assertion of Dr. Anderson that the affirmations of Pope John Paul II in his encyclical letter *Redemptor Hominis* about the relationship of every person with Christ, without exception, "is the single most significant doctrinal statement of the Catholic church for mission theology since Vatican Council II." I agree. I hope that right conclusions will be drawn from it. However, let me say that the papal affirmation itself is not only grounded in biblical and patristic testimony, but has been gloriously illustrated in the last century by the Catholic theologian M. J. Scheeben, in the work mentioned above.

2. At this point Dr. Anderson asks the pope the all-important question: "Since you have said that everyone is already redeemed by Christ and united with Christ, why mission? Why the church itself?" It is impossible for me to answer for the pope to such an enormous question. However, let me say that the church fulfills the obligation of evangelization in obedience to the Great Commission of Christ, and in doing this is "constrained by Jesus' love." The church gives witness to the *mirabilia Dei* which God has accomplished in our history through Jesus Christ, and calls all men and women to know them, to rejoice in them, and to share their fruits. This is the very *raison d'être* of the church itself, which has been described by Vatican II as "the sacrament of universal salvation," the sign and instrument of salvation for every-

one. However, it is known from the time of Cornelius (Acts 10) that God can use other means to call people to Christ and to pour his Spirit upon them.

3. So we are approaching the major question and the real focus of our topic. The Logos is already present in the world as spiritual light and life for everyone, but came nevertheless in Jesus of Nazareth and comes through the church. According to the prologue of St. John's Gospel and a part of the New Testament literature centered in the Ephesus area (Ephesians, Colossians, Revelation, etc.), Christ was at the beginning, is at the basis of everything, manifested himself in history, and is announced in the world by the church until his glorious manifestation. What is the relationship of Christ to human history? Dr. Anderson maintains that there are two traditions or two lines of thought, which can be found in Scripture and in the history of Christian doctrine—one of continuity and one of discontinuity. I am not at all certain that this is true. In any case, I am not at ease with this approach, even less with the conclusion that "it is imperative that both of these traditions in Christian thought be maintained in balanced tension." My reaction depends perhaps only on different sensitivity or language. But let me say that instead of two traditions, I prefer to see different aspects, various accents, different degrees of deepening, sundry explications in accordance with the circumstances and the existential needs and duties. My reason is that in one and the same author, for instance in Saint Paul and in Saint John, not to mention Irenaeus and Pseudo-Dionysius, Saint Augustine and Saint Thomas Aquinas, we see the coexistence of these "two different traditions." Consider for instance the case of the philosopher-martyr Saint Justin. In the *Acta* of his martyrdom (we have three texts of these *Acta* and the oldest is considered historical), we read Justin's confession of faith in "Jesus Christ, Son of God, announced through the prophets," and in his *Apologies* he describes Christ to the emperors as the Logos who enlightened the Greek philosophers so that "those who lived according to the Logos are Christians even if they were considered as atheists . . ." (1 *Apol.* 46). Could we say that Justin followed one tradition in his confession of faith before the Proconsul Rusticus and another one in his *Apologies?*

4. Just a brief word concerning the messianic witness to be

given by the church to the Jews. I am aware that the Federici document received some wrong interpretations; I regret this mishandling of such an important document. As a consequence, I appreciate and share Dr. Anderson's perplexities and reactions. I fully agree with him. He is quite right to affirm that the text, read in its context, does not say at all what some commentators pretend to see between the lines. The church cannot deny itself the duty of proclaiming Jesus of Nazareth as the Savior of all, including the Jewish people, with whom the church is linked through a "spiritual tie," and to whom a special place is due in the history of salvation and in the *mysterion* of God.

ii

I am thankful also to Dr. Appiah-Kubi for his lively and fascinating intervention. He did not give a direct response to my speech but chose to inform us about some urgent challenges that face the church and mission in Africa today. He reminds us that the Lordship of Christ does not mean the lordship of Western culture, of secularistic science, of a colonial power, but does mean attention to, and assumption of what is already present in African tradition, in which culture, religion, science, and medicine are closely related. As a consequence, Dr. Appiah-Kubi has good reason to criticize some practices of Christian missionaries in Africa. In so doing he helps us to rediscover the very core of the Christian message, to discern it from the Western forms in which it is embedded, to elicit from it some aspects in the light of the African *Weltanschauung,* aspects that could not emerge in the context of Western culture. So as a person of dialogue I cannot but listen to what he is saying. I am "ready to be taught."

V

A Radical Evangelical
Contribution from Latin America

Orlando E. Costas

The Christian faith stands or falls with the confession "Jesus Christ is Lord." This, the earliest Christian confession of faith (1 Cor. 12:3; Rom. 10:9), is also the most central. To be a Christian is to affirm from the depth of one's being that Jesus Christ is *the* Lord of history, of the world, and of one's personal life. What does this really *mean?* In a world of many lords, how does one distinguish Jesus Christ from them? How can one validate this affirmation in a religiously pluralistic world? Ultimately, the issue boils down to this: Does the Lordship of Jesus Christ mean anything outside one's personal faith?

The purpose of this essay is to render an account of one person's approach to the question above. Since human beings are not islands unto themselves but are part and parcel of a given social reality, and inasmuch as theological reflection in general and Christology in particular is always situated in a particular context, it is natural that the exposition that follows will reflect the author's reality and commitment. Accordingly, this paper has been written from a Latin American christological perspective[1] and a radical evangelical theological commitment.[2]

The latter statement has two implications. On the one hand, it implies a look at the Lordship of Christ from within the world of the oppressed and disfranchised; concretely, the struggle that is taking place therein against social and cultural oppression (racism and elitism), economic exploitation (capitalism), and political

133

domination (imperialism and hegemonism), in order to build a radically new order characterized by social equality and integral cultural development, an economy grounded on cooperation and social well-being (and not on competition and selfish profit-making), and an authentic participatory democracy. On the other hand, it implies an understanding of the Lordship of Christ from the specific angle of radical evangelical Christianity, which seeks to derive its knowledge of Christ from the witness of the canonical Scriptures, through the hermeneutical mediation of exegesis, historical studies, and the social sciences, motivated by a personal encounter with him and verified in a life of radical discipleship amid the struggles of history.

Thus my approach is unashamedly particularistic. I shall seek to interpret the Lordship of Christ from the "underside" of history[3] (the world of the disfranchised) and the witness of the biblical tradition. This double focus (from "below"[4] and from "before"[5]) will enable me, nevertheless, to get inside the problem of the universal significance of Christ in a religiously pluralistic world. Such an approach will make possible a meaningful dialogue with people of other faiths (and secular ideologies) by pushing the discussion outside the traditional boundaries of interreligious dialogue (from concepts to praxis) and by stressing the significance of Jesus Christ for the future of the world, namely, the possibility of overcoming the contradictions of history through the anticipation of the christological hope of a new earth in the human struggle for justice and liberation.

I propose, therefore, to begin with the fundamental presupposition of faith in Christ: the historicity of Jesus of Nazareth. I shall then consider the meaning of his Lordship in the light of his suffering death and the call to discipleship, considering in conclusion the implications of his uniqueness and universality for the role of religions as mediating signs and instruments of God's coming reign.

THE LORDSHIP OF CHRIST AND
THE HISTORICITY OF JESUS

To understand the meaning of Christ's Lordship we need to take account of the life and ministry of Jesus of Nazareth.[6] To be sure, the confession of Jesus as Christ and Lord (Acts 2:36) is grounded on the Easter experience: the encounter of the disciples with the risen body of the crucified Jesus and the new relationship that emerged as a consequence of that encounter. This experience witnesses to an eschatological event that has no parallel in history. In the words of Wolfhart Pannenberg, it is a "proleptic" event, an anticipation of that which is to come, the emergence of something radically new.[7] In this respect, its significance lies outside the control of historiography and needs to be verified "eschatologically."[8]

But since for early Christians the risen Lord was none other than the earthly Jesus, we can say that the Easter faith presupposes a historical fact: the life and ministry of Jesus of Nazareth. The empty grave that the disciples claimed to have discovered was the place where Jesus had been buried. Therefore, the one who appeared to the disciples could not have been a "superman" fabricated by the imagination of his followers. What they claim to have seen was not a ghost but a real man who talked and walked with them (Mk. 16:12; Lk. 24:13ff.). Some of them even claimed to have touched his wounded hands and to have eaten with him (Lk. 24:40–43; John 20:27; 21:13). Paul, in fact, enumerates a list of people to whom the risen Jesus had appeared (1 Cor. 15:1–11), some of whom were still alive and were presumably subject to interrogation. Hence the resurrection is a historical event that cannot be denied without putting into question the integrity of the early Christian community and the witness of the New Testament.[9] It not only presupposes the facticity of Jesus' life and ministry, but confirms its significance for the confession of faith in him as Lord and Christ.

What does the life and ministry of Jesus have to say about his Lordship as the Christ of God? Without pretending in any way to be exhaustive, allow me to note several items.

First, the life of Jesus of Nazareth tells us that the universality of Christ has meaning only in a particular sociohistorical context. Jesus was a Jew, the son of a modest family, who grew up in an insignificant town in the furthest province from the capital and the most culturally backward. He spoke with a Galilean accent, had a limited formal education, and was a carpenter by trade. He was aware of his cultural and religious tradition. He was aware that he belonged to a "unique people although one humiliated for centuries by foreigners."[10] Yet he was misunderstood by his family, his friends, his disciples, and the religious leaders of his country. Ever since he left his home to become an itinerant preacher, he lived a poor and lonely life, with no permanent abode. He so identified himself with the poor and the oppressed that he dedicated himself to a suffering service in their behalf. It is this poor, humble, enigmatic, lonely Jewish preacher who fearlessly defended the cause of the hurt of his society whom the Christian faith confesses as Lord.

It is a fact, nevertheless, that this confession has been often so abstracted from the life and ministry of Jesus that it has made his face unrecognizable. Christ's Lordship has been so universalized that it has lost all contact with concrete reality. Consequently, he has not only been left without historical content, but has been emptied of all historic significance. When christological universality is divorced from the particularity of Jesus, then the confessing community is unable to find christological images that correspond to its particular reality and Christ's universality ends up lost in a reservoir of vagueness. In such cases, Christ becomes a puppet in the hands of vested interests, as has happened in European, North American, Australasian, Philippine, South African, Eastern Orthodox, and Latin American culture-Christianity.

Second, the life and ministry of Jesus tells us that socio-historical particularity has universal significance when it points beyond itself to a future and transcendent reality. One of the outstanding features of Jesus was his preaching ministry.The Gospel of Mark tells us that he "came . . . preaching the gospel of God, . . . saying, 'The time is fulfilled, and the kingdom of God is at hand . . .' " (1:14b). Jon Sobrino, among others, says that this is the "most certain historical datum" about the life of Jesus and the theme that "dominated his public ministry."[11] The source of this message was not Jesus himself but God, and its content was not God himself but God's kingdom. Jesus saw himself as God's special envoy, sent to announce the nearness of his reign. Such a message had several implications.

For one thing, it anticipated an eschatological reality: the manifestation of God's rule in the form of a new order of life and on the basis of his unconditional free grace. This new order included reconciliation between God and humankind, between people, nations, sexes, generations, and races, and between humankind and nature. It involved, in short, participation in a new creation. To accentuate the radical nature of this message, Jesus gave a privileged place in his ministry to the weak and outcast, the poor, the oppressed, the sick, children, women, and tax collectors. Since in their social condition they were the most obvious victims of human sin, they became the recipients of Jesus' message. To them in particular, but to everyone in general, Jesus announced the imminent arrival of the year of Jubilee and anticipated it in his healing and teaching ministry.

Therefore, Jesus' proclamation of the kingdom was an indication of God's transforming presence in history, or of the presence of his coming kingdom. For Jesus, God not only ruled over history, he was engaged in the course of history; he was not only the Judge of history, he was its Redeemer; he had not only created the world, he was making it anew. This reality became evident in the authority that was manifested in Jesus' ministry.

The Synoptic Gospels tell us that Jesus came proclaiming the dawning of God's reign in the power of the Spirit (Mk. 1:13-14; Mt. 4:12-17; Lk. 4:14-15). Mark tells us that those who heard him were astonished with his message, perceiving in him an authority which the teachers of the law, the scribes, did not have (Mk. 1:22). Even the unclean spirits recognize his authority, fearing their destruction. They recognize him as "the Holy One of God" (Mk. 1:24), the same one who at the Jordan had been anointed by the Spirit and of whom the heavenly voice said: "Thou art my beloved Son, in thee I am well pleased" (Mk. 1:11). His message was not only authoritative to the ears, but to the eyes. He cast out a demon at the synagogue of Capernaum by the power of his word. All that were at the synagogue were amazed and questioned themselves: "What is this? A new teaching! With authority he commands even the unclean spirits, and they obey him" (Mk. 1:27).

The word "authority" *(exousia)* is used in this passage (vv. 22, 27) in regard to his (oral) discourse and his (mighty) deed. There was in Jesus' message a vibrance and freshness that the traditional expositors of the Scriptures did not have. His witness carried credibility, demanded attention, made people think, stirred the conscience, made the Scriptures come alive. The key to his authority was not in his words but in the fact that these words were *embodied in his presence*. His words were an extension of himself and he was filled with the presence of the Spirit of God. It was this Spirit-filled presence that scared the demon and set the man loose from its control. The words and the deed were, thus, vehicles of God's transforming power and signs of his coming kingdom.

Words and deeds do not appear here as opposites, nor as complements, but as instruments of the gospel. We have here words *in* the deed and a deed *in* the words. They both convey the "teaching" of Jesus. The words enlighten and rebuke, they open the eyes and unplug the ears, they instruct and correct because they disclose reality. The deed transmits the message of good news: the demon, who represents the power of darkness, of evil and decay, not only trembles before him, but obeys him. The good tidings are both in the words and in the deed. They are channels through which the new order is anticipated and God's transforming presence is disclosed.

Jesus' proclamation of the kingdom also implied a call to faith and repentance. Since God's rule had come within the reach of everyone, Jesus summoned his audiences to a decision. God's coming kingdom marked his graceful offer to women and men to come to terms with him and participate in his eschatological project of reconciliation. No neutrality was allowed. One had to choose whether to accept or not God's graceful offer. On the other hand, acceptance of God's grace involved a change of values and attitudes: a turning from a self-oriented existence to an others-oriented life, the abandonment of the anxieties of the present for the anticipation of God's coming kingdom and, above all, the disposition to put everything at the service of God's rule. No half way was possible. One had to repent, change his or her mind, turn his or her back on the existing order, accept the perspective of God's kingdom, and adopt a correspondingly new style of life. And one had to trust in the gift of the kingdom: open oneself like a little child to the One who was already revealing his transforming power. No area of life could be left out. The whole of it had to come under the rule of God.

Thus the particularity of Jesus' preaching ministry had a peculiar universal thrust. For it was neither concentrated on itself nor on the present. Rather, it focused on the future and summoned everyone to anticipate it in the present. It was not propaganda to join a private religious club that Jesus came proclaiming but, rather, the coming kingdom. This message issued an invitation to participation in the transformation of the world, which God was now graciously making possible. Hence Jesus' preaching ministry had a universal significance.

Third, the life and ministry of Jesus tells us that the Lordship of Christ becomes particularly meaningful and universally significant in the formation of community and the praxis of liberation. This proceeds from the special relationship that Jesus had with God.

On the one hand, through prayer (which, as recent New Testament scholars have taught us, constituted one of the most important characteristics of his life) Jesus came to know God as Father. His use of the word *Abba* in his prayers points to a distinctive relationship with God characterized by intimacy and childlike trust. Out of this relationship Jesus developed his consciousness of sonship. In the words of James Dunn: "*Jesus experienced an intimate relation of sonship in prayer:* he found God characteristically to be 'Father'; and this sense of God was so real, so loving, so compelling, that whenever he turned to God it was the cry 'Abba' that most naturally came to his lips."[12]

On the other hand, Jesus demonstrates in his ministry an awareness of being possessed by the Spirit of God. In the Old Testament prophetic tradition the Spirit was associated with God's power or God-in-action.[13] The Spirit was also linked with the messianic age (Joel 2:28; Isa. 32:15; 44:3; Ezek. 39:29). It was the awareness of God's Spirit in his ministry that constituted the basis of Jesus' eschatological proclamation of God's coming kingdom and of the authority reflected in his mighty deeds. As Jesus "found God in prayer as Father, so he found God in mission as power,"[14] or Spirit. By the same token, just as his prayer life reflected his complete trust in the Father, so his preaching and mighty deeds reflected his total obedience to the mission the Spirit had entrusted to him.

This double consciousness of God as Father and Spirit and this twofold relationship as trusting Son and faithful messenger, gives a communal and liberating foundation to Jesus' life and ministry. The intimate relation with the Father and the unconditional submission to the Spirit was the theological basis for the calling of the disciples and the formation of the messianic community. Jesus called a band of men and women to follow him. He taught them to pray to his Father and sent them forth (witness the case of the Seventy) in the power of the Spirit to participate in his mission. By the same token, Jesus was driven by the Spirit to proclaim the kingdom of God among the poor and the disfranchised and to teach thereby his fellow human beings the way to the Father. Thus Jesus' particular experience of God was universalized in his mission, and his mission was particularized in the formation of a concrete community, as a paradigm of the new age that was soon to be inaugurated, and in his liberating word and deeds on behalf of the poor and the oppressed, as signs of the cosmic transformation that was to take place in the *eschaton*.

THE LORDSHIP OF CHRIST AND THE DEATH OF JESUS

We turn now to an event of utmost importance for the interpretation of the Lordship of Christ in a pluralistic world: Jesus' death on the cross. If, as Jurgen Moltmann has suggested, the cross represents "the foundation and criticism of Christian theology," then we need to give special attention to its significance for the Lordship of Christ and to its meaning in the light of Jesus' death.

First of all, the cross of Jesus historicizes the Lordship of Christ. The New Testament traditions converge not only in the identification of the risen Lord with the man Jesus who was crucified, but also in the description of his suffering and death as that of a poor and oppressed man. Jesus died among two thieves. He was unjustly condemned. He was betrayed by a friend and was sold for thirty pieces of silver. He had no one to defend him; his friends left him. He did not even have a grave of his own.

These facts were no mere accident as far as early Christians were concerned. They saw in them God's hand. Therefore they did not hesitate to link Jesus' suffering with the Suffering Servant of Isaiah who "was taken away . . . by oppression and judgment," had to share "his grave with the wicked," and was "numbered with the transgressors" (Isa. 53:8–9,12). Apparently they saw Jesus accepting the role of the Suffering Servant once he became conscious of the inevitability of his death (Mk. 8:31; 9:31; 10:32–34; Mt. 20:17–19; Lk. 18: 31–34). Peter, especially, saw in Jesus God's servant (Acts 3:13, 26; 4:27, 30) who "bore our sins in his body on the tree" (cf. 1 Pet. 2:22–24). According to Luke, Philip's conversation with the Ethiopian eunuch revolved around the interpretation of Isaiah's fourth Servant Song in the light of Jesus' death (Acts 8: 26ff.). Paul, for his part, takes the servant motif to develop his own theology of the cross (1 Cor. 1:25, 27; Phil. 2:8).

The interpretation of Jesus' suffering in the light of Isaiah's Suffering Servant situates the cross on the side of the poor and the afflicted, the sick and the oppressed. Such contextualization is carried even further in Paul's linkage of the cross with the incarnation. According to Paul, Jesus takes the form of a slave in his incarnation, becoming totally identified with humanity in its lowest form. The cross is the ultimate test of this identification: Jesus became obedient unto death (Phil. 2:8). The fact that Paul makes this affirmation in the same passage where he affirms Jesus' exaltation by God as Lord is indicative of the fact that, for Paul, Christ's Lordship is associated with the same people with whom he was identified in his death.

This is carried a step further in Hebrews 13:13 where Jesus' death is located "outside" the Holy City—the place where the leftovers of the cultic sacrifices were thrown. Interestingly enough, however, Jesus' death appears in this passage in connection with his exalted role and future history. The fact that the community of faith is to go to him "outside the camp" and "bear the abuse he endured" indicates that for the writer of Hebrews Jesus' Lordship is to be located in the battles and heat of history, among the nonpersons of society.

Second, the cross of Jesus underscores the dissimilarity between the Lordship of Christ and the lords of this world. This is evident in what the New Testament calls the scandal of the cross. This scandal lies in the fact that the man Jesus, who came proclaiming the nearness of the kingdom of God "with mighty works and wonders and signs" (Acts 2:22), ended his life condemned as a blasphemer and a political rebel. But the scandal of the death of

Jesus is not so profound as that of Easter faith, which affirms that the so-called blasphemous and rebellious preacher who was forsaken and abandoned by his God and Father had indeed risen from the grave by the power of God's Spirit, and that he had been enthroned as the Lord of heaven and earth. This identity between the risen Lord and the crucified Jesus led early Christians to formulate the doctrine of the incarnation: the affirmation that the poor and oppressed preacher who died on Calvary was none other than God himself; he had become history in Jesus of Nazareth. Hence writers like Luke saw Jesus' entire life, from his annunciation to his death, from the perspective of the poor. The announcement of his birth is linked with the hope of the poor and disfranchised (Lk. 1:51ff.). He is born in a stable (Lk. 2:8) and his parents can only afford to fulfill the requirement of the law with the offering assigned to the poor (Lk. 2:24; Lev. 12:8). He locates his own mission among the poor, the captives, the sick, and the oppressed (Lk. 4:18). He calls the poor the heirs of the kingdom (Lk. 6:20). He seems to insinuate an identification with both the wounded man in the parable of the Good Samaritan (Lk. 10:30ff.; cf. 21–28, 38–41) and poor Lazarus in the story of the rich man who went to hell (Lk. 16:19ff.). He praises Zacchaeus for returning fourfold what he had stolen from the poor (Lk. 19:1–10), and points to his healing and heralding ministry as signs of the messianic age (Lk. 7: 22–23).

The point behind Luke's theology (substantiated by the other Gospels and the epistles of Paul) is that Jesus is not a Lord like Caesar, Herod, or the religious rulers of Israel. He does not rule as a despot or oppressor, but as a liberating servant. He says, "I am among you as one who serves" (Lk. 22:27).

Just as the Gospels and the epistles look backward to the theological life and work of Jesus in the light of the Easter experience and arrive at the conclusion that the one who came and died had to be the incarnation of God himself, so the book of Revelation looks forward to the eschatological revelation of the risen Lord and anticipates his sovereign presence in the course of history. Nevertheless, it maintains Jesus' identity as the one who was crucified.

In one of the most important visions of the book, John of Patmos is told that the only one who "is worthy to open the scroll" in the hands of the Father (which contains the secrets of history) is the Lion of the Tribe of Judah. This is a messianic title, which the author applies to the risen Lord. It is linked to his universal authority. Through his resurrection Jesus prevailed over sin and death. This means that he also conquered the evil one, Satan, and all earthly powers. The vision is one of royal power: Jesus is the conquering Lord; there is no other Lord who can match his authority in and over history. It is, therefore, very significant that following the announcement of the conquering Lion of Judah, John sees a totally different image: "a Lamb standing, as though it had been slain" (Rev. 5:6). To be sure, it has "seven horns" and "seven eyes," implying that it has absolute universal authority. Even so, its fundamental characteristic is the fact that it was *slain*. Hence the new song, which the representatives of earth ("the four living creatures") and heaven ("the twenty-four elders") sing:

> Worthy art thou to take the scroll
>   and to open its seals,
> for thou wast slain and by thy
>   blood didst ransom men for God
> from every tribe and tongue and people and nation,
> and hast made them a kingdom
>   and priests to our God,
> and they shall reign on earth [Rev. 5:9-10].

This apocalyptic vision and Christological doxology is meant to be a definite contrast between the Lordship of Christ and that of the political and economic lords of this world, specifically between him and Caesar. The Lordship of Christ is not grounded on military might, but on sacrificial love. It is not oppressive and emasculating, but creative and liberating. It is not totalitarian, but communal and fraternal. Hence it facilitates the formation of a new world community on the basis of love and service.

Christ's authority has been earned through suffering and death. It has been invested upon him by the Father who raised him from the dead. The redeemed community shares in his reign on earth, but it does so by intercession and service to the Father ("a kingdom and priests," Rev. 5:10). The Father remains the ultimate mystery. Jesus reigns in his behalf and is forming the new world community for the Father's praise and service.

Third, the cross of Jesus qualifies his role as the Christ of God and Lord of the world. It tells us why one man could be the anointed of God or be "God's faithful covenant partner," in the words of Berkhof. Moreover, it explains how it is that he could be given authority on heaven and earth and have sovereignty over all of life.

Throughout the New Testament we find multiple references to the suffering death of Jesus as having its root in the action of God himself. Paul says that God "did not spare" his own Son, giving him up for all of humanity (Rom. 8:32) and putting him forward as an expiation for its sins (Rom. 3:25). Elsewhere Paul states that God made Jesus "to be sin for us" (2 Cor. 5:21). John's Gospel refers to him as the Lamb of God, implying that he is God's sin-offering for the world (1:29). At Pentecost Peter states that Jesus' death was not an accident; he died in accordance with God's plan and foreknowledge (Acts 2:22).

Why would God offer his own Son as a sin-offering? The answer to this question lies in Paul's assertion that "God was in Christ reconciling the world unto himself" (2 Cor. 4:17). Jesus was made to be sin in order to take upon himself the death that belonged to every human being (2 Cor. 5:14; Rom. 5, passim). Death, in this context, is the consequence of sin (Rom. 6:23). Sin is ungodliness and unrighteousness; death is separation from God's fellowship (Rom. 1:18–3:23). Since all have sinned, all are subject to death (Rom. 5:12). Accordingly, Jesus died not just as the righteous and innocent Jew wrongly accused of being a blasphemer (Mk. 14:64; Mt. 26:65; John 19:7). He died, especially, as the innocent *man* who took upon himself the *universal blasphemy* of humankind (Rom. 2:12ff.). Therefore, he died the death of every human being (Rom. 5:6ff.). In the words of Wolfhart Pannenberg:

> Jesus died the death all have incurred, the death of the blasphemer. In this sense he died for us, for our sins. Of course, this does not mean that we no longer have to die. But it does mean that no one else has to die in the complete rejection in which Jesus died. Jesus' death meant his exclusion from community with the God whose coming kingship he had proclaimed. He died as one expelled by the entire weight of the legitimate authority of the divine law, excluded from the nearness of the God in whose nearness he had known himself to be in a unique

way the messenger of the imminent Kingdom of God. No one else must die the death of eternal damnation, to the extent that he has community with Jesus. Whoever is bound up with Jesus no longer dies alone, excluded from all community, above all no longer as one who is divorced from community with God and his future salvation.[15]

Paradoxically, in Jesus' death as the forsaken Son, God is revealed as passionately affected by suffering. God becomes accessible to humankind through the suffering of Jesus. In the words of Kazoh Kitamori, the cross reveals "the pain of God."[16] This leads Jon Sobrino to conclude that suffering is "a mode of being belonging to God."[17] We must not forget, however, Jürgen Moltmann's qualification that "the Father suffers with [the Son], but not in the same way."[18] At the cross we see the Father suffering the death of the Son even as we see the Son suffering his forsakenness by the Father. Therefore, we can appreciate the fact that the distress and trouble of Jesus on the cross (Mk. 14:33), the "loud cries and tears," which according to the espistle to the Hebrews (Heb. 5:7) accompanied his death, and his desperate quotation of Ps. 22:2, "My God, my God, why has thou forsaken me?" (Mk. 15:34), were not simply expressions of Jesus' passion, but also of the Father's own suffering over the forsakenness of the Son.

The Pauline expression "God was in Christ" refers not just to the fact that God delivered the Son and became thereby personally accessible to humankind, but also to the fact that God participated in the passion and suffering of the Son for the world. God refused to be identified at the cross by his power and glory. Rather, God was revealed in the helplessness and weakness of Jesus. The cross was both the culmination and test of the incarnation. It was the point where the self-emptiness of the Son was revealed in its crudest form. Therefore, the experience of the cross must be seen as the foundation upon which the criterion for the judgment of the nations at the *eschaton* is established (Mt. 25:31ff.). Jesus Christ not only suffered on his own cross, but continues to suffer the millions of human crosses around the world. These crosses are represented in the images of the orphan, the hungry, the naked, and the prisoner in the parable of the Judgment of the Nations. Thus the Father suffers with Jesus the pain of sinners and outcast. The nations will be judged at the end of history on whether they acknowledged the crucified Lord hidden in the suffering of their oppressed members and saw them as the Father's suffering ones. Seen in this perspective, is it any wonder that in the New Testament many Greeks and Jews would consider the cross a "foolish" and "scandalous" event? Is it any wonder that in our day many continue to consider it a "foolish" and "scandalous" sign? It not only challenges all human strategies of salvation, but especially the traditional concepts of God (as power and impassive). Because of this God cannot be manipulated by human reason or religious tradition, and the salvation of humanity cannot be bought or earned: it is given by grace alone and can be appropriated only by faith.

Jesus' death and suffering not only *opens the way to God* and *makes God accessible to humanity. It also opens the way to humankind* and *makes men and women available to the kingdom of God.* The Easter community confessed Jesus not only as the Son of God, but also as the Son of Man. This title, which has its origin in the Old Testament prophecy of Daniel, is not meant to portray Jesus as "an ideal superman."[19] Rather, it speaks of him as the true human because, like the Son of Man of Daniel, he does not proceed from the chaos and the deformity of human history. He has not been defiled and overtaken by the "beasts," which have dehumanized history (Dan. 7:1ff.). The Son of Man is the symbol of humanity in its fullest potentiality. Therefore, he proceeds from God (Dan. 7:13), the only one who can restore humanity to its creative potential. The Son of Man is the revealer of a new humanity. He is not only the One from heaven but the Person of the future. He is the bearer of justice and liberation.

The fact that the New Testament Gospels refer to Jesus as the Son of Man (either as a self-designation or as a title) is indicative of the intimate connection between the role that the Son of Man is called to fulfill in Daniel and the role that Jesus fulfilled. He is seen as the embodiment of the Son of Man: in his proclamation of the imminent manifestation of God's kingdom, in his commitment to justice and liberation, in his challenge to the powers of this world (represented in the Jewish religious structure and the Roman empire), and in his dedication to the liberation of history from its bondage and deformity.

However, unlike Daniel's Son of Man, Jesus does not reveal his unique identity first and foremost in a cataclysmic event (coming with power in the clouds), but on the cross. He reveals his triumph in his weakness, his righteousness in his blasphemous death, his authentic humanity in his inhuman suffering, and his liberating power in his total surrender. He does not transcend the predicament of human history by avoiding its perils, but rather, by taking upon himself the infirmities and corruption of deformed humanity. He reveals and restores true humanity by dying as the representative of the nonhumans. As the crucified Son of Man, says Moltmann, Jesus reveals his power

> in the impotence of his grace, in the reconciling force of his passion, and the sovereignty of his self-emptying love. His kingdom lies in the inelegant fraternity with the poor, the prisoners, the hungry and the guilty. Those who have been exiled by the kingdoms of this world are transformed in his community into the bearers of the human kingdom of the Son of Man.[20]

The cross reveals Jesus as the man for others and in so doing locates authentic humanity in being at the service of others. This is why, in the New Testament, humanization is possible only through self-denial, obedience, and death. One must deny oneself, take up the cross, and follow Jesus through the wilderness of life (Mt. 16:24; Heb. 13:13). Men and women discover and recover their true humanity in the process of discipleship. In the same process, they become aware of the fact that God has given Jesus sovereignty over the world (Mt. 28:18), that in his presence the lords of this world lose their dominion, and that those who are in communion with him not only participate in the hope of God's coming kingdom (cf. Mt. 16:25ff.; Heb. 13:14), but are already its first fruits (Rom. 8:23; Eph. 1:11–14, 22). In discipleship, the crucified Son of Man's eschatological identity is made apparent. Just as the crucified Son of Man is the sign of authentic humanity, so his eschatological identity is a sign of the final redemption (and therefore of the absolute humanization) of humankind. This soteriological and eschatological reality is confirmed by the resurrection. The event of the resurrection is the authentication of the cross as the central sign of the Christian faith. Hence the experience of the resurrection involves sharing the sufferings of Jesus (Phil. 3:10), and suffering with him implies anticipating in life God's coming kingdom (1 Pet. 4:13–14).

THE UNIVERSAL LORDSHIP OF CHRIST,
THE UNIQUENESS OF JESUS,
AND THE PARTICULARITY OF RELIGION

Where does this leave the Lordship of Christ in a pluralistic world? What are the implications of his uniqueness and universality in a world of many religions? What role, if any, do they play in his universal mission?

It has been asserted here that the uniqueness of Jesus lies not in his conquering power and might but in his love and service. This is uniquely expressed in his suffering death. Jesus Christ is a unique Lord because he has identified himself forever with suffering humanity, standing in solidarity with men and women at the lowest form of their existence: poverty and oppression. He is a unique Lord because he has revealed God's righteousness in history by taking upon himself the unrighteousness of the world, assuming their condition of death and thereby experiencing the forsakenness of his God and Father. And he is a unique Lord because in such a contradictory experience he can show himself as the true Christ of God: in his suffering God reveals himself in a new way; suffering appears "as a mode of being belonging to God." This challenges the Greek notion of God as apathetic and abstract and puts him in the center of the suffering and struggle of the world. It also makes it impossible for God to be manipulated by the economic and political lords of this world. The cross makes it impossible for Jesus to be confused with any other lord. It proclaims his uniqueness by underscoring his unconditional solidarity with the hurt of the world, his absolute surrender to the God of love who suffers with his Son the pain of the unloved of the world, and his righteousness in dying for the unrighteous in order to set them free from the power of sin and death.

This unique experience is given universal validity in the resurrection. The Easter event confirmed the triumph of God in the cross, the righteousness of Jesus' death and its saving significance for the whole world. Conversely, it denied that the cross had signified the end of Jesus' mission, that it had meant the triumph of unbelief, unrighteousness, and hopelessness, and that it had implied the defeat of the God whom Jesus came proclaiming. "The new and scandalous element in the Christian message of Easter," says Jürgen Moltmann,

> was not that some man or other was raised before anyone else, but that the one who was raised was this condemned, executed and forsaken man. This was the unexpected element in the kerygma of the resurrection which created the new righteous of faith. . . . If God raised this dishonoured man in his coming righteousness, it follows that in this crucified figure he manifests his true righteousness, the right of the unconditioned grace which makes righteousness the unrighteous and those without rights.[21]

If the uniqueness of Jesus lies in the fact that he is the crucified Lord, his universality rests on the saving significance of his resurrection. The crucified Lord is the risen Savior. Because of this, those who trust in his vicarious death are not disappointed; the resurrection is the confirmation of the fact that the way of the cross is neither intellectual "foolishness" nor a religious "scandal," but obedience to the God who is greater than science and above religion. Moreover, those who confess him need not be threatened by the principalities and powers of this world, for Jesus defeated them at the cross and through his resurrection has set free from the kingdom of this world and the threat of future death those who have trusted in him and have committed their lives to the kingdom of God. Finally, those who, through Jesus, trust the God who raises the dead and liberates from the oppressive powers of this world do not become part of an exclusive private club, but are immediately sent to incarnate God's love in the service of the unloved.

My argument thus far may have given the impression that I am advocating a position that leaves no room for other religious traditions to mediate God's presence in history. This certainly has not been my intention. On the contrary, by locating the Lordship of Christ in the cross of the risen Jesus, I have tried to set forth a christological structure upon which to construct an open, though qualified, concept of the role of religions as mediators of God's presence in history. I want, therefore, to outline in conclusion the way I see the relationship between the Lordship of Christ and the religions.

It is a well-accepted fact that all religions stem from a particular cultural situation. Simply stated, they represent cultural mediations of faith in that mysterious reality we refer to as God. This applies to all religions, including Christianity. Even though faith in this mysterious One transcends religion (understood as a body of beliefs expressed in cultural symbols, images, signs and concepts), it cannot be expressed without a religious structure. Hence, faith is always expressed in religious language.

It has been asserted in the course of this essay that for Christians this mysterious One, "the Great Other" in the words of Boff, has been revealed in the concrete history of Jesus of Nazareth. The center of that revelation is the cross of the risen Christ and the resurrection of the crucified Jesus. This faith, however, did not emerge *tabula rasa*. It is the offspring of Jewish religious culture: it derives its source of inspiration and orientation from Hebraic faith and religion as it is witnessed to in the Old Testament and as it is expressed in the language of first-century Judaism. The Jewish religion became, thus, the primary mediator of early Christian faith.

But when Christians began to spread their message throughout the Roman empire, they had to borrow new concepts and categories to communicate and express the meaning of their faith in a religiously pluralistic world. Hellenistic culture, in all its complexity, rose to the occasion, providing the new mediational tools for the Christian faith, since it represented the dominant cultural influence of the Roman world. So great was the influence of Greek culture upon the Christian faith that the latter became Christianity, a basically *Western* (Greek) religion. The Lordship of Christ was so interpreted in Greek categories that within a few hundred years its central mystery came to be formulated exclusively in Greek philosophical language. The "name of Jesus," which in the New Testament stands in direct continuity with the Old Testament name of Yahweh (Acts 4:12; Phil. 2:8), came to be interpreted not in the light of its Old Testament heritage but, rather in the metaphysical language of the Hellenistic world. This is best expressed, of course, in the christological formulas of the first five centuries. Jesus became a *Western* God-human. With the advance of Western civilization and its technological concentration of the Northern Euro-American sector of the West, the name of Jesus became a projection of North/Western culture. With the economic and technological expansion of the North/West came also the extension of its Christ: the overpowering Lord whose kingdom coincided with the North/Western historical project in all of its forms and varieties.

In recent decades Christians within and outside the Western world have begun to reassess Western Christology. With the stimulus received from the social sciences, historical and phenomenological studies of religion, and the various liberation movements, these Christians have become uneasy with the cultural triumphalism behind traditional Western Christologies and have sought to find a way out of what cannot but be described as the cultural (ideological), social (racist and classist), economic (capitalistic), and political (imperialistic) captivity of Jesus Christ. At the same time, biblical scholars have begun to rediscover the Jewish roots and Hebraic background of early Christian faith. These simultaneous processes have made it possible for Christians to consider the possibility of other religious mediations for the "name of Jesus."

In the opening chapter of *Christian Faith in a Religiously Plural World*, Donald G. Dawe suggested the concept of the "translatability of the name of Jesus" as a way beyond the traditional triumphalism of Christianity. He argues that

> the "name of Jesus" is the disclosure of the pattern of God's action in human salvation. As such, it is open to translation. The "name" may be translated or given fresh expression in differing times and places. It is not in the continuity of a verbalism but in faithfulness to its meaning that the saving power revealed in Jesus is actualized. This is true because the "name of Jesus" is the disclosure of the structure of new being. It is the pattern of salvation. So the universality of Christianity is grounded in the translatability of the "name of Jesus," not in the imposition of particular formularies on others. This power

of new being operates throughout the world under the names of many religious traditions. It is recognized and celebrated by Christians because they know its pattern or meaning through Jesus of Nazareth.[22]

I can appreciate Dawe's intention, but question his proposal on biblical, theological, and historical grounds. For one thing, in the New Testament the meaning of the "name of Jesus" is indissolubly linked to the history of Jesus of Nazareth, as I have argued here. For another, the Christian concept of salvation is grounded on the cross of the risen Jesus. Thus it cannot be signified without a reference to that *concrete* event. In fact, when this has happened (as it has occurred in the history of *Christendom*) the result has been an emptying of the saving significance of the "name of Jesus" and its cooptation into a religious ideology.

In my opinion, the *historical* "name of Jesus" is a criticism of all religions. (The first religion that it criticizes is Christianity, in all its forms and varieties; the second is Judaism; and the third is Islam. All of these have some form of reference to his name, for he refuses to be incorporated into any *one* world-view.) The crucified Jesus as God's pattern of salvation refuses to become the private possession of any one culture and religion. Rather, he calls them all to accountability in terms of the establishment of the new order of life that he proclaimed in his ministry and embodied in his life, death, and resurrection.

If in the name of Jesus, God has disclosed his coming kingdom, if this name cannot be translated without a reference to the concrete history of Jesus of Nazareth and if it is true that this name represents a continuous critique of all religions (insofar as they represent absolutistic systems or world-views), then it follows that the religions (including Christianity) can mediate God's presence in history only insofar as they are signs and instruments of God's coming kingdom. In my opinion this can occur only under three conditions.

First, the religions may be signs and instruments of God's kingdom if they can accept the scandal of the cross of Jesus amid the human crosses of the world. Since the poor, the powerless, and the oppressed (those whose historical destiny has been marked by the crosses of exploitation, injustice, and oppression) have been given a privileged place in the kingdom, it follows that no religious structure can be an adequate sign of its reality if it is not identified with the dispossessed in their misery and suffering. To be able to be such a sign, however, religious structures need to accept the representative par excellence of the poor and the oppressed: the crucified Jesus. He is the standard and measuring stick for the identification with the disfranchised. If the scandal of his cross is not accepted, neither will the scandal of human crosses be accepted. By the same token, when the latter are *really* accepted, the cross of Jesus ceases to be a scandal and is accepted as a sign of justice, freedom, and hope.

Second, religions may be signs and instruments of God's kingdom if they lead their adherents to come "outside" the enclosed circle of their "religious" interests to the battlefields of life and join the crucified Lord in the struggle for the liberation of the poor and oppressed of the world. Since the kingdom of God is an eschatological reality, only those religious structures that are open and committed to its future can be instrumentalities of its fulfillment. Likewise, inasmuch as the locus of God's kingdom lies in the emergence of a new world characterized by justice, freedom, and peace, it follows that a religious structure can serve the kingdom if it is working *against* injustice, alienation, and war and *for* a new righteous, fraternal, and peaceful world community.

Third, the religions may be signs and instruments of God's kingdom if they are anticipating it in their inner life. This means that their inner structure must be a paradigm of justice, freedom, and hope. Conversely, it implies that they forfeit their mediating role if they allow injustice to take place in their midst, if they alienate their adherents from the struggles of history, if they do not promote social peace, and if they close the horizon of hope.

In Karl Marx's 11th thesis against Feuerbach we read: "Heretofore philosophers have interpreted the world in different ways; the point is to change it." Paraphrasing this statement, I would say that heretofore religions have explained God's relationship to the world in different ways; the point is to become God's instruments in its transformation. And this is precisely the challenge that the Lord Jesus Christ poses to the religions of the world: to become signs and instruments of God's new order of life by joining forces with him in his solidarity with the dispossessed, in his struggle against the principalities and powers that keep two-thirds of humankind in infrahuman conditions, and in his active participation in the liberating transformations that may be witnessed already in many parts of the world. For ". . . the kingdom of God does not consist in talk but in power" (1 Cor. 4:20).

The challenge before Christians in a religiously plural world is, therefore, not one of accommodation to a pluralism that reinforces the traditional "superstructural" (ideological) role of religion. Rather, it is a challenge to commitment and engagement in the liberating mission of the crucified and risen Lord who is to be found among the disfranchised of society. To the extent that they are influential in enabling religions to follow this path, they will help religions to fulfill an "infrastructural" (praxial) role that will turn them into signs of a new humanity.[23] Religion will thus cease to be a social, economic, and political opium as Marx saw it, and will become instead a powerful historical force that will contribute to breaking down the chains of oppression and bringing forth a qualitatively different type of human society. In a word, religion will become a "midwife" of the new earth that has been promised in God's coming kingdom. This alone justifies the mandate to proclaim the "name of Jesus" in *all* the nations.

NOTES

1. See, especially, Jon Sobrino, *Christology at the Crossroads: A Latin American Approach*, trans. from the Spanish original by John Drury (Maryknoll, N.Y.: Orbis Books, 1978); Leonardo Boff, *Jesus Christ Liberator*, trans. from the Portuguese original by Patrick Hughes (Maryknoll, N.Y.: Orbis Books, 1978); "Jesucristo liberador: una visión cristológica desde latinoamérica oprimida," in *Jesucristo en la historia y en la fe*, ed. A. Vargas-Machuca (Salamanca: Ediciones Sígueme; Madrid: Fundación Juan March, 1977); José Míguez Bonino and others, *Jesús: Ni vencido ni monárca celestial* (Buenos Aires: La Aurora, 1977).

2. See, especially, Jim Wallis, *Agenda for Biblical People* (New York: Harper & Row, 1976); John Howard Yoder, *The Politics of Jesus* (Grand Rapids, Mich.: Wm. B. Eerdmans, 1973); Andrés Kirk, *Jesucristo revolucionario* (Buenos Aires: La Aurora, 1974); C. René Padilla, *El evangelio hoy* (Buenos Aires: Ediciones Certeza, 1975); Samuel Escobar and John Driver, *Christian Mission and Social Justice* (Scottdale, Pa.: Herald Press, 1978); Orlando E. Costas, *The Church and Its Mission: A Shattering Critique from the Third World* (Wheaton, Ill.: Tyndale House, 1974); *The Integrity of Mission: The Inner Life and Outreach of the Church* (New York: Harper & Row, 1979); Alfred Krass, *Five Lanterns at Sundown: Evangelism in a Chastened Mood* (Grand Rapids, Mich.: Wm. B. Eerdman, 1978).

3. Cf. Gustavo Gutierrez, *Teología desde el reverso de la historia* (Lima: CEP, 1977).

4. This phrase is not limited to those Christologies that proceed "from the investigation of the historical Jesus" (Wolfhart Pannenberg, *Jesus: God and Man* [London: SCM Press, 1968], p. 53), but includes those that arise "out of the concrete experience and praxis of faith within a lived commitment to liberation . . ." (Sobrino, *Christology*, p. 10), or as Raúl Vidales has put it: out of the concrete encounter with the poor, "which is the privileged place where Christ reveals the mystery of his person" (*Desde la tradición de los pobres* [Mexico City: Centro de Reflexión Teológica, 1978], p. 124.). James Cone takes a similar christological approach in *God of the Oppressed* (New York: Seabury Press, 1975), pp. 108ff.

5. Cone uses a similar approach when he locates the meaning of Jesus Christ not only in the social existence of black people in the United States but also in the witness of Scripture as it has been handed down in the church's tradition (*God of the Oppressed*, pp. 110–112).

6. We need not debate the issue raised by Martin Kahler and Rudolph Bultmann as to the futility of trying to get back to the historical Jesus. It will suffice to point to the works of E. Käsemann and J. Jeremias, who argue that it is indeed possible to gather from the New Testament documents the basic traits of Jesus' life and ministry with at least moral certainty. See Martin Kahler, *The So-Called Historical Jesus and the Historic Biblical Christ* (Philadelphia: Fortress Press, 1964); Rudolf Bultmann, *Primitive Christianity in Its Contemporary Setting* (Cleveland: World Publishing Co., 1956); *Jesus and the World* (New York: Scribners, 1934); E. Kasemann, *Essays on New Testament Themes* (London: SCM Press, 1964); and J. Jeremias, *The Problem of the Historical Jesus* (Philadelphia: Fortress Press, 1964).

7. See Pannenberg, *Jesus*, pp. 53ff.

8. See Jürgen Moltmann, *The Crucified God* (London: SCM Press, 1974), pp. 172–73.

9. On the historicity of the resurrection, see the ample discussion in Pannenberg, *Jesus*, pp. 88–106.

10. José Comblin, *Jesus of Nazareth: Meditations on His Humanity* (Maryknoll, N.Y.: Orbis Books, 1976), p. 15.

11. Sobrino, *Christology*, p. 41. See also Pannenberg, *Jesus*, pp. 226ff.

12. James D. G. Dunn, *Jesus and the Spirit* (London: SCM Press, 1975), p. 26.

13. Ibid., pp. 47, 89; H. Berkhof, *La doctrina del Espíritu Santo*(Buenos Aires: La Aurora, 1964), pp. 13–14.

14. Dunn, *Jesus*, p. 90.

15. Pannenberg, *Jesus*, p. 263.

16. Kazoh Kitamori, *Teología del dolor de Dios*, translated into Spanish by Juan José Coy from *Theology of the Pain of God*, 5th English edition of the Japanese original (Salamanca: Ediciones Sígueme, 1974), passim.

17. Sobrino, *Christology*, p. 195.

18. Moltmann, *God*, p. 203.

19. Jürgen Moltmann, *El hombre: antropología cristiana en los conflictos del presente*, translated from the German by José M. Mauleón (Salamanca: Ediciones Sígueme), p. 153. Quotation translated from the Spanish version by O.E.C.; Eng. trans.: *Man: Christian Anthropology in the Conflicts of the Present* (Philadelphia: Fortress Press, 1974). According to Joachim Jeremias the title "Son of Man" belongs to the tradition of the sayings of Jesus and can be traced back to Jesus himself. Cf. *Teología del Nuevo Testamento*, vol. 1, p. 310.

20. Moltmann, *El hombre*, p. 153.

21. Moltmann, *God*, p. 176.

22. Donald G. Dawe, "Christian Faith in a Religiously Plural World," in *Christian Faith in a Religiously Plural World*, ed. Donald G. Dawe and John B. Carman (Maryknoll, N.Y.: Orbis Books, 1978), p. 30.

23. For an analysis of religion as superstructure and as infrastructure, see Enrique Dussel, *Religión* (Mexico City: Editorial Edicol S.A., 1977).

1

Response

Mary Carroll Smith

"To accentuate the radical nature of this message [i.e., participation in a new creation], Jesus gave a privileged place in his ministry to the weak and outcast, the poor, the oppressed, the sick, children, women, and tax collectors." So says Orlando Costas in his essay on the Lordship of Christ, as he focuses on the social condition of the "most obvious victims of human sin." Elsewhere in the essay Costas speaks about Jesus' exaltation by God as Lord based on Philippians 2:8. He notes, with Paul, that Jesus "totally identified with humanity in its lowest form," which is undoubtedly the poor, oppressed, women, and tax collectors. The fact that women are singled out as victims of human sin could lead to the conclusion that only men are human sinners. Costas' use of the Pauline texts also suggests an equation of women with some type of deformity as human beings. Costas is not intentionally setting up such an equation, but a brief survey of the language of Lordship and kingdom shows some of the undeniable consequences inherent in the language he uses to align Jesus with the cause of the poor and the oppressed.

The history of lordship, or the kingly servant, goes back to the fourth millennium. The Egyptian pharaoh around 3100 B.C. achieved a political union of two feuding kingdoms, and as an external sign of the coming of the new kingdom, the pharaoh became the son of god and his true servant. Meanwhile, even earlier, but with only the testimony of destruction to mark their appearance, a group of people designating themselves Aryan, or "the noble ones who obey the law," began to spread their new religion of lordship and domination over the face of the known world. The Aryans, or Indo-Europeans, developed their notion of lordship on both spiritual and earthly planes through the use of rigorous ascetical disciplines which resulted in obtaining the favor of the god, attracted by the ascetical or sacrificial practice; the kingdom was extended and the lord was the incarnation of the peace and justice under law or *dharma*. But what of the social condition of those who were not practitioners of the stern discipline, namely, the sick and the lame, children and women? Clearly the god of power and might was not interested in such outcasts. Moreover, the actual extension of the kingdom by warfare resulted in the destruction of the enemy and often in the forced rape of the nubile women.

Orlando Costas says that Jesus' proclamation of the kingdom was an indication of God's transforming presence in history, or of the presence of his coming kingdom. Jesus, he tells us, joined forces with the sick and the lame, children and women. Since the language is relatively unchanged from Aryan usage, my question is concerned with the hidden agenda in the semantic load. What assurance does such language offer for a radical change in expectations? My study of the history of religions would indicate that there is none. Since it turns out that Jesus became a victor in the end, the very radical nature of the transposition is actually denied. There is nothing revolutionary about the final results if they are victory and success, triumph and conquering. If Jesus conquers sin and death, so the poor and outcast will conquer injustice by following Jesus. Once they have conquered, who will be the victims?

By picturing Jesus as ministering to the outcasts, including the half of the human race that is female, Costas actually reinforces the old Indo-European ideology of racism and sexism. I would hold that there can never be a radical change of meaning possible while kingdom imagery is used. Kingdom imagery results from a mythic structure of conquering and defeat in order to produce the ultimate victory. In Christian contexts the enemy is "Death," but death need not be considered as an enemy at all if Indo-European ideology is set aside. The old European religion, whose cult shrines were often dedicated to divinities with female attributes, used the cross for thousands of years as a symbol of the life-and-death cycle. These non-Aryans recognized the theme of resurrection and exemplified it with decorated eggs.[1] In these signs there is room for creativity and new life. Jesus is associated with these signs, but the kingdom and Lordship designations radically change their intent and meaning.

The silent evidence of the Old European peoples may stimulate new language possibilities for relating Jesus' life and his teachings. When Jesus put the emphasis on his servant position he was specifically trying to move his disciples' thinking away from the triumphal consciousness that would cause them to aggrandize spiritual power for their own glory. Jesus was aware of social conditions and he was aware of the power of languages. As Costas says, when consciousness "contradicts the established sense of reality reflected in prevailing social and linguistic structures," it is time to change not only the social structures, but the language structures as well. Kingdom and Lordship images are offensive to the poor, the sick, outcasts, and women. By its inbuilt triumphalism, on whatever physical or spiritual plane, it is offensive to other religious views of the world, whether those views are Christian or non-Christian. Costas says faith is always expressed in religious language. It is not language that is religious but the faith. Language is culture-bound. It is time now to examine the language of triumphalism implied in Lordship. Kingdom language owes its source to both Semitic and Indo-European sources with dualistic views of good and evil in the world. It is insufficient to allegorize the interpretation of that language if the historical reality of that language has not changed. Lordship language is not what Jesus came to save.

NOTE

1. See Marija Gimbutas, *Gods and Goddesses of Old Europe 7000–3500 B.C.* (Berkeley: University of California Press, 1974), pp. 89–150.

2
Response

Donald G. Dawe

With typical forthrightness, Orlando Costas drives to the heart of the matter in his reflections on the Lordship of Christ. "Ultimately, the issue boils down to this: Does the Lordship of Jesus Christ mean anything outside of one's personal faith?" One of the most frequent responses to religious pluralism is retreat into religious privatism. Its devotees say: "Whatever may be said of other times and places, Jesus Christ is Lord of my life, my Savior, and the guarantor of my spiritual serenity." Costas rightly asserts that this is a denial of all the Christian faith sums for us in its confession of Christ. Lordship is a universal category and implies necessarily that Jesus is Lord of history, nature, and society in all their dimensions. Hence he rejects privatism and interprets the Lordship of Christ in its most universal terms.

Still further to sharpen the focus, Costas says he approaches his analysis of Christ's Lordship from a very particular standpoint, that of "a Latin American christological perspective" and "a radical evangelical theological commitment." From the perspective of the disfranchised of the world, from the "'underside' of history," the universality of Christ's Lordship is to be investigated. With this liberationist theological perspective as his formal principle, Professor Costas turns to the Bible as his material principle to create his own unique blend of liberation theology with an evangelical twist.

As intriguing as this methodology may be, does it not undercut the very task he was assigned? How is it possible to explicate the universality of the Lordship of Christ from the particularity of his Latin American liberation perspective, to which is added the even greater constriction of the picture of Jesus given by biblical scholarship? What can be more particular, if not downright private, than an approach to the historical Jesus via the route of Marxist-based social theories? Yet this is precisely the route, Costas argues, that holds promise of interpreting Lordship adequately where traditional methods have failed. The logic by which he is able to move from the particularity of the life, death, and resurrection of Jesus to the universality of his Lordship is at the heart of the issues before us in this study. He rejects all attempts at ensuring the universality of Christ by stripping away Jesus' historicity. In this he is right. His zeal in this matter is so great that it leads him to misunderstand my own position. The difference between his position and mine, at this point, is over just how and where we encounter the elements in Jesus' life and ministry that allow us to confess him as universal Lord. But the vital point here is the logic of his move from particularity to universality.

THE UNIVERSALITY OF THE PARTICULAR

Costas' logic for linking the particularity of Jesus to his universal Lordship has three steps: (1) The universality of Christ's Lordship is grounded in Jesus being poor and oppressed, a fact given its final expression in his death on the cross. Paradoxically it is this death that historicizes his Lordship. (2) Jesus' death has a universalizing power because it is more than the death of yet another victim of oppression. He is the bearer, in the power of the Spirit, of the kingdom of God. In him, the time of waiting is fulfilled, and the redemptive power of the kingdom has broken into history. (3) Jesus' life, death, and resurrection are proleptic events that point beyond themselves "to a future and transcendent reality." As proleptic *eschaton*, Jesus is the disclosure and empowerment of the "end" of history—the kingdom of God—before the "end" is actually reached. The kingdom of God is universal; Jesus, in his historical uniqueness, is the key to the kingdom.

In making this move in logic from the historical Jesus to "the future and transcendent reality," Costas is following a pattern common in contemporary theology. The universal importance of Jesus is not grounded in an ontological doctrine, as in patristic theology, nor in a universal ethic, as in liberalism, but in the futurity and transcendence of the kingdom of God. To assert that Jesus is universal because he is eschatological Lord is to solve a number of theological problems at one fell swoop. Since it implies no specific theory of being, it pacifies all those who say it is impossible to talk about ontology any more. Because it rejects the ethical idealism of liberalism as being hopelessly bourgeois, it makes glad the heart of the social, political radical. And it overcomes the reductionism that eschews the social, political, economic, and ecological as legitimate spheres of God's activity. But the question is: What does it do for us who live short of the fulfillment of the kingdom in history?

The problem for Christian faith today is not that Jesus promised a golden future but that that future has not come. The nexus of the Christian struggle for faith and for social justice is not in some "future and transcendent reality" but in the proximate challenges of the here and now. The universality of Christ will be vindicated in a future and transcendent reality, but what faith and obedience look for are some evidence of this universality in the present.

Ostensibly during this interim we are to look for the kingdom to where liberation is now occurring. This is where we would be looking, according to Costas, if our vision had not been obstructed by the idols of bourgeois, Western civilization that remade Jesus into its own image. The difficulty in Costas' proposal lies in the ambiguity of liberation as the basic metaphor for salvation. It is here that his combination of liberationist social theory with neo-evangelical biblical theology fails to give us the guidance he promises.

DEFINING LIBERATION

Liberation theory has developed out of the humanistic Marxist tradition, which does not see religion in the wholly negative fashion of classical Marxism. Rather, à la Ernst Bloch, religion, with its millennial dreams and myths, points to new possibilities for human consciousness that transcend those amid which we now live. Religion serves as the rejection of a view of human nature as limited by its present state. Religion rejects what Bloch calls "an inelastic conception of human being as it now exists." But religion does not transform the conditions of consciousness to create this new being. Rather, changes in the social/economic/political order transform the conditions of consciousness and usher in the new age.

Liberation theory is based upon the Marxist conception of superstructure and substructure. While religion has a positive role, it remains part of the superstructure of culture and ideology. Basic reality is found in the substructure formed by the dialectical unfolding of the changing means of production. The religious vision may point to new possibilities for human existence but, as part of superstructure, it does not create these new forms of life. This power of change resides in the social/economic/technological processes of the substructure.

By contrast, biblical theology sets transformation in the context of the divine initiative. God acts, and the response of faith makes human action obedient to the divine will. Through the triumph of grace over the perversions of sin and death, limited but real transformations of society are accomplished. The transformations in the social/economic/political sphere are a reflexive, derivative action from the divine initiative apprehended by personal faith. In this, it is the opposite of the model for transformation given by liberation social theory. For liberation theory, faith is derivative and indicative; while for biblical theology, faith is primary and imperative.

This irresolvable conflict between the basic models of salvation in liberation perspective and neo-evangelical biblical theology renders Professor Costas' position ambiguous. At some points, he calls us to join in movements to overthrow the present means of production and so be propelled into the new age. At other points, he calls us to bear the "pain of God" in faith, believing in a liberation into which we will not enter. His biblicism finally saves him from sanctifying the moral ambiguities of revolutionary movements. For Costas we are justified by Christ and not by revolutionary acts. So why does he paraphrase Marx to prophesy a golden age for theology, if realigned by Latin American perspectives?

What does not emerge is a hermeneutic that can clarify either our present existence or the biblical witness. The hermeneutic of

Rome, or even that of Geneva, is but an imperfect light dimmed by its own imperialisms, to be sure. But the hermeneutic of Latin America is not the victory over this ambiguity. Rather, it threatens to bury the faith response under the dialectic of material process.

3
Reply

Orlando E. Costas

True to the role assigned to them, Mary Carroll Smith and Donald G. Dawe have offered two different but complementary responses to my position paper. They reflect their own ideological commitment and professional interests.

i

Let me begin my response to Professor Smith's critique with a categorical denial. I simply refuse to accept the equation she has made between my language and that of Aryan/Indo-European ideology. I reject this contention on the ground that I have argued that the Lordship of Christ is tied up with a radically new order of life whose focus is the *reconciliation* of all things (God and humankind, humankind and nature, people, nations, sexes, generations, and races) and, consequently, the total *abrogation* of evil and alienation and the syndrome of victor and victim. The message of this new order is for *everyone in general* and especially for those who are the most obvious victims of the distortion of life (evil and alienation). In my opinion, biblical eschatological faith gives a different content to the language of Lordship and kingdom than Aryan/Indo-European religion. This is why I consider it very strange that Professor Smith's bold assertion hardly had any reference to the way the Old and New Testaments use the concepts of Lordship and kingdom. One cannot make an external criticism of a thought structure without first interacting internally with its content. First we have to hear what it actually says, and then look for its parallels elsewhere. Professor Smith has accentuated the ("seeming") parallels of the biblical language of Lordship and kingdom with Aryan/Indo-European religious beliefs and on that basis claims for it a content which, I insist, is neither in the biblical text nor in my exposition of it.

That Mary Carroll Smith has not been clearly listening to my exposition of biblical eschatological faith is evident in the negative response that she gives to the question she has raised, namely, "What assurance does such language offer for a radical change in expectations?" In my paper I outline three such assurances.

The first and most foundational is that of *Christology.* New Testament christological faith affirms that Christ is not a Lord like Caesar (or the Aryan/Indo-European lords). His uniqueness lies not in his *conquering* power and might but in his love and service. Such a christological image is not simply a movement away from the language of Lordship but a fundamental qualification of its meaning along the line of Old Testament messianic hope. By so doing, Jesus breaks the basis of the old world order (hatred, injustice, enslavement, and destruction) and gives a new one (love, justice, freedom, and well-being). Such qualification makes it impossible for Jesus Christ to be manipulated by the political and economic lords of this world or by any ideology. Hence faith in the Lordship of Christ is a categorical negation of any historical determinism (whether Aryan or Marxist) and a categorical affirmation of a new world order that cannot be compared to any human project (though it is certainly anticipated in history), since it is both a gift of the Creator/Redeemer God and an eschatological reality. As both the apostle Paul and the prophet Isaiah said, what "God has prepared for those who love him" is that which "no eye has seen, nor ear heard, nor the heart of man conceived . . ." (1 Cor. 3:9; Isa. 64:4).

The second assurance is that of the life and mission of the *messianic community.* New Testament Christian faith speaks of the new age as being witnessed to and anticipated in the formation of a distinctly different community, one that in its inner structure is an authentic paradigm of love, as expressed in freedom, justice, and peace. As such, there is to be in the ecclesial community "neither Jew nor Greek, slave nor free, male nor female" (Gal. 3:28). That this has not always been the case does not abrogate the fact that this is the identity that the foundational source of Christian knowledge has given the community of faith and that this has been actualized in not too few instances in Christian history. In other words, the fact that the Christian church may have failed to live up to its nature does not abrogate the ecclesiological assertion that the new order of life is to be vividly anticipated in the life and mission of the Christian community. In fact, today we can point to a growing number of situations (especially in the Third World) where the Christian community is authenticating its calling, witnessing in word and deed, in its life and mission, to the future that is promised and proclaimed in the gospel.

The third guarantee is that of *contemporary liberation movements and experiments*. In spite of all the shortcomings of many of these movements (it is usually easier to point out shortcomings than achievements!), I at least see many signs that point to the creation of the conditions that are making possible new ways of organizing a more fraternal, just, and peace-loving society. Not that these movements and experiments will necessarily fulfill the goal of the kingdom. No society is or will ever be perfect. The kingdom of God will always lie beyond history, yet within it. Therefore no revolution can ever expect to be an absolute anticipation of the kingdom. Even so, situations like Nicaragua (to mention one specific experiment from my own context) give us reason to hope for the breaking of the syndrome of domination embedded in Professor Smith's argumentation. Our task as Christians (and members of the messianic community) is to discern the Lordship of Christ and of God's kingdom at work in such situations.

This is not to belittle Professor Smith's implicit warning, namely, that the notion of Lordship and kingdom can be an ideological arm at the service of oppression. The memory of the Crusades, Western Constantinianism, the conquest of the Americas, the liberal-capitalist movement, and the ideology of Manifest Destiny are too fresh in our collective Christian memory to take lightly the warning of a neo-Christendom hiding beneath a resurgent Lordship and kingdom imagery among contemporary Christians. But in the contexts of Latin America and of radical-evangelical Christianity this is a matter that we are aware of and (think) we try to guard ourselves against.

By the same token, Professor Smith's own proposal (the image of death-and-resurrection cycle in old European religions) offers no real guarantee for a dynamic and radically new order for at least two reasons. First, it seems to leave out the crucial principle of judgment without which there cannot be any significant reordering of society and reconciliation of the world. As I have argued, the early Christian community did not discover the hope of the resurrection in the trauma of the cross but, on the contrary, it discovered the necessity of the cross (which stands for God's judgment on sin and evil) in the experience of the resurrection. The only theological guarantee that we have for a radically new future is that of a decisive overcoming of the problem of sin and death through suffering. Put in other terms, there is no new life without suffering and death. Unfortunately, the death-and-resurrection cycle is based on a naturalistic process and not on a decisive historical event that overcomes the fundamental distortion of human life: alienation. I have the suspicion that in adapting Professor Smith's suggested imagery, early medieval European Christians (identifying the resurrection with Easter eggs) did not clarify the meaning of faith in the risen Christ but, rather, distorted it by substituting for the historical-eschatological image a naturalistic-cyclical one (which had a lot to contribute to Christian faith and living, but *not as a substitute* for eschatological faith). This eliminated the fundamental goal of Christian hope: the eradication of sin and evil and the creation of a totally new world order by God's direct intervention.

Second, Professor Smith's proposal also raises in me a suspicion of a new sophisticated form of "Western liberalism" with the death-and-resurrection cycle as its new evolutionary utopianism and comparative religious history as its new source of authority. Her apparent rejection of Christian radical discipleship on the ground that it is based upon a triumphalistic Christology and that it offends the dignity and religious views of other people, her seeming commitment to reconciliation without costly suffering, and her apparent vision of an enlightened and harmonious world without conflict makes me "smell" the traditional odor of liberalism. It is valid, therefore, to warn Professor Smith of the theological, ethical, and historical bankruptcy of Western liberalism. The theological indictment against this current of thought was given many years ago by H. Richard Niebuhr. Paraphrasing and updating his classical dictum, I would say that liberal theology simply robbed Christian eschatology of its dialectic and ended up with a God without wrath, who brings men and women without sin into a new creation without judgment, through the ministration of a Christ without a historical cross. I prefer to take the risk of being accused of an offensive triumphalism (especially if it's in the "spirit" of 1 Cor. 1:18) than to fall into the vagueness and relativism of such a theology. But the moral and historical indictment against liberalism is even worse because, for all the talk about love of neighbor and a better society, liberalism ended (and ends up) siding politically and economically with the established order; ultimately it revealed itself to be an ideology of the status quo. Liberalism has yet to prove that its more enlightened, nonconflictive way offers any effective hope for a new, fraternal, just, and peaceful social order.

Hence *if* that is the direction that Mary Carroll Smith is proposing, I simply have to say, No, *muchas gracias*, we've been through that route before and it leads nowhere—at least for Third World women, children, *and* men, and their poor and oppressed nations.

ii

For his part, Donald G. Dawe's critique reflects several assumptions that I must immediately call into question. The most obvious is that my understanding of liberation is not only informed but shaped by neo-Marxist social theory. Then there are the assumptions that a Latin American theological perspective is automatically that of Latin American liberation theology and that a personal biblical commitment must necessarily stand in opposition to the struggle for human, political liberation. These assumptions lead Professor Dawe to make a Neo-Orthodox idealistic stew of my position and to serve it on the platter of a Reinhold Niebuhrian reactionary realism. And since I have a taste for neither Neo-Orthodox idealism nor Niebuhrian realism, I have no other choice than to pass up Dawe's meal!

The notion of liberation in Latin American theology (which is far wider and more complex than liberation theology) has longer and deeper roots than Ernst Bloch and any of the European neo-Marxists. The Mexican evangelical missiologist Pablo Pérez has, for example, traced the concept to Pre-Columbian aborigines, and the Roman Catholic historian-theologian Enrique Dussel has traced it to the sixteenth century missionary episcopacy symbolized in the figure of Bartholomé de las Casas. Moreover, such Latin American theologians as Leonardo Boff (*Los sacramentos de la vida y la vida de sacramentos*), José Míguez Bonino (*Christians and Marxists*), and Enrique Dussel (*Religión*) have argued that Christian faith is *not* a superstructural religion, but an *infrastructural faith*, because it is praxial and labors in love, faith, and hope for the transformation of history as the proper response to God's grace.

To say that Latin American liberation theology is based on an opposite model from that of biblical theology is simply to distort its position. As far back as 1966, Rubem Alves pointed out in his doctoral dissertation (later published, in 1969, as *Theology of Human Hope*) a fundamental difference between humanistic messianism (Marxist) and messianic humanism (biblical): whereas for the former, liberation is a task to be achieved, for the latter it is a gift to be received. This gift offered in the gospel is appropriated in the obedience which is faith (Rom. 1:5). The question then is not whether faith is derivative or primary, indicative or imperative (I would say that it is *both* indicative and imperative, primary and derivative), but whether faith is to be an abstract assent and a theoretical commitment, or an active, obedient response to the liberation that God has revealed in the death and resurrection of Jesus Christ.

While I do not deny that there are differences between evangelical soteriology and Christology and that of most Latin American liberation theologians, the supposedly "irresolvable conflict" that Dawe is so eager to point out between a Latin American liberation perspective and a *radical* evangelical commitment is not one of them. There is, however, a real conflict between Dawe's idealistic epistemology and my historical-eschatological approach to theological inquiry, between Dawe's abstract academic theology and my practical radical-evangelical theology, between his North American pragmatism and my Latin American praxeology.

For Dawe my hermeneutic ends up in ambiguity. To prove his point he roams through my essay selecting what fits into his scheme and leaving out what does not. Dawe's implicit ideological commitment inhibits him from seeing what is to me a clear correspondence between personal faith in a liberating God whose coming kingdom is anticipated in and mediated by his suffering for the world, and a political engagement with and in behalf of "the wretched of the earth" that passionately anticipates and suffers the abrogation of the structures that keep them bound to infrahuman conditions. He rejects the assertion that God's liberating action in history, grounded as it is in Christ's sacrificial death, is nevertheless hidden in the struggles to bring about a new social order, and that Christians are called to discern that action under the guidance of the Spirit and the judgment of the Word *in* the obedience of faith. Apparently he also has difficulty with the claim that the community of faith is a paradigm of the future of God's kingdom and thus anticipates in its koinonia, worship, witness, and service the love, justice, and peace of the kingdom. He shows an insensitivity to the dialectics of Christian faith, love, and hope, which express themselves in the enablement of Christians to love even in the midst of conflict, to go on believing in the God of life, even when religious leaders have sold out to the gods of consumerism, technology, and capitalism, which continuously threaten the world with death, and to go on hoping for the new heavens and the righteous new earth that God has promised— even though all they hear from cautious, pragmatic theologians is a message of hopeless resignation to the status quo!

It doesn't surprise me, therefore, that Donald Dawe, who as a theologian has been so eager to listen to the challenges of other religions, shows himself unwilling to hear the challenge of a secular prophet of the past century against an alienated and alienating religion. It isn't even ironical to see him make his way to biblical (covenant) theology in order to give a proper response to the question of the Lordship of Christ in a religiously pluralistic world and bypass the fact that as far back as the apostle Paul (1 Cor. 4:20) and John (1 John 3:7, 10) and the Prophets of Israel (see, e.g., Jer.

22:16; Mic. 6:8), biblical faith had already given a positive response to the Marxian critique of religion. And it isn't any surprise because, at the bottom, Dawe's problem with my hermeneutic is not theological but *ideological.*

In my opinion, when theology is so ingrown on itself that it is not able to hear the historical challenges that come from the outside (the world) or the innerside of faith (the Word), then it is time to throw it out the window, because it has forfeited its place as a servant of Christian faith and mission. In this case, theology has become an ideological arm at the service of an alienating religion; in a word, an opiate—and not just to society, but especially to Christian faith and mission.

VI

Models for Christian Discipleship amid Religious Pluralism: A Panel Discussion

1
An African/Afro-American Perspective

J. Deotis Roberts

In order to focus our discussion, I would like to recall two incidents: first, during the middle 1960s, I was sent to Asia to study various religions. This was a period of retooling for several younger scholars who had earned doctorates in religion, but who were called upon to teach non-Western religions in colleges and universities. The advice of the sponsoring group was blunt: "Stay away from the missionaries!" Being an ordained minister, I thought this counsel ill-advised and hard to follow. After meeting several conservative, culturally biased missionaries, I understood the wisdom of this admonition. *It was necessary for me to find my own basis for this dialogue.* I shall say more about this later.

Now I wish to relate a second incident. A banker from a midwestern American city sat with me on the board of an ecumenical organization recently. He was puzzled by a comment offered by his son, who is studying for the ministry. He related that his son observed that the ministry opens up for him a great opportunity to be of service to many people *if the church doesn't get in his way.*

These two brief illustrations provide a perspective for viewing Christian discipleship in the next decade. We shall need to find a way to have meaningful dialogue with many cultures and religions. And, furthermore, we shall need to rethink the purpose of the church and its ministry in a climate of religious pluralism.

A LIBERATIONIST PERSPECTIVE

Existentialism has made a lasting impression upon my mind and spirit. It has informed my life and ministry. For years I researched in this area of thought, majoring in Pascal and Kierkegaard. What I discovered was the fact that many black religious thinkers were moved by the existential mood. A people who are oppressed and who try to make sense out of life are attracted to experiential and introspective reflection upon religious experience.

More recently theologies of liberation have attracted Third World theologians. The search for identity, freedom, dignity, and the contextualization of theology among black and Third World theologians has made the *political* perspective of theology attractive. In my judgment, the *existential* and *political* dimensions of theology are complementary; they are not in conflict. Unfortunately, some Euro-American theologians find it necessary to discredit Kierkegaard totally in order to make room for the Marxist analysis of the human condition. A holistic perspective requires a search for meaning as part of the quest for liberation. I hold to a world-view and to thought-structures that are *holistic.* Humans are persons-in-community. This is echoed in Third World religious traditions, but it is also biblical.

Schubert M. Ogden is a typical white-Western-straight-male theologian as he writes his critique of liberation theology in *Faith and Freedom: Toward a Liberation Theology* (Nashville: Abingdon, 1979). He criticizes liberation theologies (including black and feminist theologies) for being too concerned about liberation and not sufficiently concerned with redemption. It needs to be said that he juxtaposes personal redemption to social.

Another way of stating his objection is to assert that liberation theologians are concerned with God's *liberation* acts at the neglect of a proper focus upon the *being* of God. God the Emancipator is exalted, while God the Redeemer is neglected. In sum, liberation theologians are too political and are inadequately metaphysical in their understanding of God.

Evangelical theologians do not share this metaphysical longing in Ogden. We understand that Ogden is trying to be true to Bultmann and Whitehead at the same time—a noble and yet an impossible task, perhaps. This is not, however, the basis upon which evangelical theologians question the authenticity of liberation theologies. This latter group notes a lack of interest in personal sin and salvation in liberation theology. Personal piety and spirituality are all but dismissed, they assert. Liberation theologians should not brush this criticism aside, for it is crucial. When black theologians are true to the holistic character of black religious experience, they *must* include personal piety and spirituality without losing the social outreach dimension.

On the other side of the account, evangelical theologians need to become more aware of "immoral society" and the "crimes of history." World hunger, racism, sexism, economic exploitation, and numerous collective evils run amuck, destroying classes, races, and whole nations of human beings, while evangelicals major in personalizing, spiritualizing, and eschatologizing the gospel. Recently, on Phil Donahue's television show, Billy Graham was asked why he did not provide a forceful message against the systemic evils. His answer was that he did not want these concerns to get in the way of the Gospel. It is interesting that "full" gospel often turns out to be "one-sided" or "half" gospel. In this debate, black theology and much African theology take the liberationist stance. In no way are we tied to Latin American liberation theology, which is heavily Roman Catholic and Marxist. Most black as well as African theologians are neither, and yet they advocate a gospel of liberation.

CHRIST'S LORDSHIP AND RELIGIOUS PLURALISM

It seems almost a contradiction to attempt to relate these concepts with their usual connotations. The Lordship of Christ and religious pluralism would appear to neutralize each other. Is it possible to have both? The task is simple if no dialogue is intended. And yet dialogue is of central concern in this discussion. I understand dialogue to be possible where there are equal partners and mutual exchange. If this is not the case, we have monologue. What I understood of Pope John Paul II's speech on the Washington Mall, during his visit to the United States in 1979, came through as a monologue. Several Roman Catholics had the same feeling. The pope came to "tell" and not to "listen." The pope is not alone. Western religionists have desired to "tell" but not "listen" to other cultures and religions. It can easily happen to any of us.

It is difficult for theologians to suspend their faith-claims or for philosophers to hold their judgments. But real dialogue requires the ability to *hear* what others have to say before making an honest response. I know this to be a painful process. Some years ago I spent one month in South India in the city of Mysore. My project was to study the doctrine of grace, comparatively, in Christianity and Hinduism. Two Hindu philosopher-theologians acquainted me with their understanding of "grace" for two weeks. I read, discussed, and worshiped with them. We went on pilgrimages to Hindu temples together. They were my gurus, my spiritual directors for the first two weeks. This was a time for listening. As a theologian I went armed with a Christian theological understanding of grace. During the final two weeks, therefore, I invited my learned and saintly friends to dialogue. It was then that I was able to agree and disagree on substantive matters like creation, evil, and salvation. It needs to be said that during my early exchange, my Hindu friends learned much about my culture and my religion. Dialogue requires that we "listen" as well as "tell" and that we "tell" as well as "listen." There must be a free exchange of ideas and beliefs between equal partners.

It seems to me that this is a point where the work of Mircea Eliade and the Chicago School of the History of Religions opens up some possibilities. The descriptive, nonevaluative approach to religious phenomena provides an entré into the nativistic religious experiences everywhere. It is important to let the sacred "show itself" before we impose traditional Western interpretations upon it—many of which are culture-bound. East-West religious conversation is easier than North-South conversation. In East-West discussion there is often Scripture, language affinity, and ideological and psychological similarities. When we turn to Africa or to Amerindians, we encounter a new set of problems. We meet tribal and oral religious systems that require different perspectives and investigative methods to unpack their richness of meanings. An evolutionary perspective, which rates religions by Euro-American standards of progress, is no longer tenable. We cannot, however, ignore the vast numbers of people in the southern hemisphere. We are *condemned by history* to begin a dialogue with those on the *underside of history.*

"Lordship" plays into the hands of Christian triumphalism. It expresses the resurrection without the cross, victory without suffering, and kingly rule or regal splendor without humility and servanthood. In liberation theology, Christ is often referred to as Liberator. He sets the captives free. He does so not so much as king, but as priest and prophet. He rediscovers the humanity of God through an encounter with a "crucified God." God is no longer so transcendent that he is the "alone" removed from human suffering.

And then there is the need felt for a link between the particular and the universal. This is the basis of a contextualization that makes religious and cultural pluralism a reality to be understood. Christ is Savior of *each* people as well as Lord of *all.* We no longer leap to an abstract universal. We move from the *concrete* particular to the religious experiences of the entire human family. God's creation, providence, and redemptive action are inseparable. The Author of nature is the Giver of grace. God reveals himself in creation and history, even though he does so uniquely and supremely in the incarnation as far as Christians are concerned.

This outlook has implications for human rights. We need to discover a principle of humanity similar to the Stoic Logos. The Stoics believed that there is a divine spark in every human, which is part of the Divine Fire. They went on to claim that there is a Logos in each person based upon the Divine Reason in the universe. This was the Stoic foundation for a cosmopolitanism as the anchor for human equality and universal law and justice among humans. It is absolutely imperative that Christians together with other religionists seek a common basis for human rights for the cause of human well-being and survival. As Christians we must find the path to liberty, dignity, and humanity for all peoples, whether or not they read the Bible, go to church, or name the Name of God through Jesus Christ.

A FINAL WORD: THE AFRICAN/AFRO-AMERICAN/ THIRD WORLD CONNECTION

Economists are talking about the relation between the First and Third worlds in such matters as trade, consumer goods, and production. This is closely allied to religio-ethical interests in overpopulation, nutrition, and hunger. There is an obvious need for religionists to join humanitarian secular movements seeking some of the answers to the this-worldly concerns of the global human family. An escape into spiritual piety will not suffice.

Black Americans share the human misery and ancestry with most Third World peoples. The roots of their heritage are in Africa, but the experience of deprivation is similar to that found in most Third World societies. Black Americans live in the First World under Third World conditions, and are, therefore, a vital link between America and the peoples of the southern hemisphere. A great challenge faces black theologians and churches at this time in history. The objective of this discussion has been to provide some perspectives on dialogue and ministry toward the fulfillment of this mission.

I believe that one of the important roles we must assume in discussions like this one is to make sure that the African/Afro-American cultural and religious experience is included in interreligious dialogue. East-West conversation must continue, but North-South dialogue must now be actively promoted. This cause is assigned to black theologians. I do not find that other theologians *care enough*. We black theologians must wage a persistent protest against racism in the churches and among religious leaders as well as scholars. And, finally, we shall insist that all religions of the human family enter fully into any conversation on religious pluralism. To this task many are called, but few are chosen.

2
A Southern Baptist Perspective

William R. O'Brien

I approach this discussion with the knowledge that what we share together is heard and responded to in the larger interest of sharpening our mutual understanding and our common commitments. Having said that, I do feel that in fairness to the listening process, since I am a newcomer to this arena, you should note the context from which these remarks will be made. In this whole process I can be nothing more than transparent, for that which I want to probe with you is simply a reflection of my own current struggles and pilgrimage of becoming. It is not simply a personal or individualistic pilgrimage, but one that I am studying from within the context of covenant community, which may be an aspect of understanding that Baptists have lost—especially when we emphasize autonomy of the local congregation and a democracy that implies 51 percent are right, whether God believes it or not.

My family and I served in Indonesia under appointment by the Southern Baptist Foreign Mission Board from 1962 until 1974. Since 1976 I have been in Richmond, Virginia, at the headquarters offices of our Foreign Mission Board in a team effort to help sensitize Southern Baptists to their mission responsibilities through the churches. It is too bad that missions became institutionalized so quickly; we have reaped several hundred years now of the consequences of that institutionalization. Somebody said that the sad fate of an idea is that it becomes an ideology. And once having done so, it quickly gets institutionalized; then we spend the rest of our days defending the "sacred" institution and too often are always taking the backward look from a defensive posture, rather than being open to the dynamic leadership of the Spirit of God, who is still up to something in this world. I think the model for discipleship that I am struggling with is one that at this point will have biblical integrity, while still being cast within a denominational framework, since I have willfully chosen to work within that framework because of what I believe and what I have committed myself to. Also this is the way we, as 35,000 local congregations within Southern Baptist life, have chosen to work together.

The Foreign Mission Board of Southern Baptists is not an initiator either of missions from the local church or of centralized strategy beyond the local church. Rather, we try to serve as an enabling agent for persons coming out of these various covenant communities going throughout the world where they feel God is leading them to affirm a pilgrimage shared in the life of other covenant communities. We also try to serve as equippers for them, as well as a bridge for the extension of obedience and discipleship for their local churches. Our commitment to the model I shall be talking about lies in the fact that mission comes out of the heart of God, and in its churchly dimension it is expressed through the local church. All of this must be understood from a certain context. We live in a world of configurations. In those configurations, the whole is more than the sum of the parts. Spiritually speaking, discipleship and missions are but a component of the larger purpose of God and the kingdom. Dr. Stendahl was indeed stimulating at this point in the Bible study he led concerning the kingdom (see Chapter I, above). God is up to something. And if we can determine what it is, all that is left for us to do is cooperate with him. If God is like Jesus, we then who are his disciples submit to his Lordship, believing that out of creative purposiveness he will enable us to engage continually in a maturing pilgrimage within kingdom purposes and intent. We must not, therefore, start with just a perceived condition of humankind, and project some mission onto him. Rather, we must try to understand the authority of the Lord Christ and respond to that. For, wherever we find ourselves in the world, it is not the prerogative of the church or mission to assume its Lord's rank; rather, it should assume his model and his lifestyle.

One further word concerning the model for discipleship that we are struggling with: it must be one that has been shaped, so far as I am concerned, with more positive dynamics than simply reacting to the caricatured models of the past. I, too, am aware of history, and particularly our own Baptist history, where we have tended to be "exclusivist." While desperately wanting to learn from the past, and not repeat mistakes, I am choosing not to waste emotional energy in reactionary processes. The challenge of today and tomorrow demands better than that from all of us.

In 1954 I first heard of a Christian musical drama presented by Union Theological Seminary in New York entitled *For Heaven's Sake*. It was a combination of song and monologue, and one of the monologues I have never forgotten was about teaching a baby how to walk. You want your child to walk sooner than any other child on the block. At about six months you jerk him up and put your arms down behind the child's back, putting one hand on each thigh and whispering into the ear of the child, as you lift one leg after the other, "This is the way you walk." And walking is shaped in the mind by the word. And the Word became flesh, and dwelt among us. He said, "I am the way," and this is the way you walk. And walking for us is shaped in the mind by the Word. How did he walk? In what context did he teach and model?—certainly not in an isolation booth, but in the context of community, and as an extension of his body and therefore of his purpose and of his mind. A convenant community was left behind. The model for the future must take into account the presence of believers within such communities all over the world. The question is not moratorium, but relationships. From our persuasion, we feel that the Christian can never work himself out of a job in the world, but he continually works himself out of roles. If the only biblical calling is that to followship, at what point can we quit following? The real question is not: Should we disciple? Rather, it should be: In the light of kingdom purposes, how can we effectively engage in the witness of covenant communities all over the world, in mutual sharing activities that not only strengthen and edify the believers, but also enable that sharing process to be enhanced at all levels of creation, be it personal, corporate, or natural?

Therefore the model for discipleship must be a two-way street. One we are struggling with, and perhaps can come to, is one in which we engage in a global mosaic of multilateral missions. I could envision a model for us in which there might be regional sending agencies where the shared gifts of covenant communities all over the world begin to integrate themselves and flow across all kinds of lines. For us in North America it could come as a tangible symbol much more quickly if countries all over the world would start sending missionaries to us. This is not the bastion of the faith, and the day of unilateral sending is over. For us, then, in this kind of model, the word "missionary" has meaning only for the sending body, not for the receiving body. Once having crossed a cultural or linguistic line, the missionary should be known as a servant of the local convenant community, integrating oneself into the culture, the language, and expressions of that area. While one will always remain alien in terms of looks and accent, through a humble submission of gifts and life to Christ's presence in that covenant community, the gifts can be blended for the continued sharing in life at its deepest levels. Therefore, we don't go so much in a teaching posture, as we do in a learner-sharer-learner posture, total reciprocity. We are most anxious that the two-way flow of mission education be accelerated. It must come. We have much to learn, as people from all over the world begin to flow into the processes of our church life, and teach us, whether it be in warm bodies through their presence, or through the written word, or video technique, or whatever. But we must quickly speed up the two-way flow of the sharing, integrated process so that all the gifts within the body of Christ can be brought to bear in missions and discipleship. This is the age of reciprocity, the age of multilateral mission. It is from this holistic, multilateral approach that integrity of relationship is maintained, witness is shared, and issues are confronted.

I shall conclude by saying that maybe someday, and I hope before some cataclysmic event forces us to it, we who celebrate life around the centrality of Jesus Christ as our Lord will engage in what might be termed whole church/whole world mission. Not out of a spirit of triumphalism; rather, in humble obedience to our Lord, serving our fellow humans not for hope of gain, recognition, or churchly conquest—even risking misunderstanding for our presence, to the point of death, that all of God's creation might continue to move toward that fulfillment for which it was made.

3
An Orthodox Perspective

Demetrios J. Constantelos

i

The character of our theme is such that it cannot be examined outside of historical empiricism. We cannot anticipate any forms or models of Christian discipleship of the future without an understanding of what occurred in the past. Even those who emphasize the here and now, the need for a departure from creeds, attitudes, customs, and traditions—those who are impatient with ecclesiastical history—must realize that without an understanding of the forces that shaped the past, we cannot change the present or determine the course of the future.

A model, of course, is a standard for imitation, a prototype. And the prototype in the history of Christianity has been the person of Christ. But whereas for Christians there is one model, in their efforts to emulate the example of their model or to practice his teachings, Christians have expressed themselves in such a variety of ways and experience that the archetype became the subject of many interpretations resulting in the creation of many versions.

Christianity has never been monochromatic. Within the context of Greco-Roman and Oriental religious pluralism, Christianity, too, assumed the character of a diversified phenomenon. Long before the first major Christian schism, following the Council of Chalcedon (451), there were many different styles of Christian discipleship. A model presupposes a faith, and to every faith corresponds a dogma.[1] In the early Christian community emphasis was placed on one faith—faith in the God incarnate, who "became what we are that we may become what He is."[2] But the "one faith . . . in one Lord . . . God and Father of us all" (Eph. 4:4–6) resulted in a diversity and multiplicity of creeds and eventually in many models of discipleship.

The prayer of Christ "that they may be one" (John 17:11) and Paul's many appeals for unity (Rom. 12:4; 1 Cor. 10:17; 12:12; 14:62; Phil. 1:27–29) were never realized. The first major disagreements arose among the apostles and their disciples (Acts 11:2–3; 15:1–12, 39; 1 Cor. 1:10–13; Gal. 2:11–15). Christianity and Greco-Roman religious pluralism engaged in several vital and mutual interactions. The result was that Christianity consciously adopted the religious and philosophical mind of the times and became an organic part of the whole society. However, Christianity's adjustment to the culture and the mind in which it developed diminished neither its power nor its influence, though it contributed to its fragmentation. Faith in Christ and the efforts of his followers to place him more accurately in the context of the Scriptures or in the Christian community's experience gave rise to several movements and many models of discipleship within and without the mainstream of the Christian *ecclesia*.

Epiphanios of Cyprus relates that when he wrote in 377 there were eighty heresies in the Roman empire, of which sixty were Christian (the first twenty belonged to the pre-Christian period and were of Scythian, Jewish, and Hellenic origins).[3] Shall we call them heresies, schisms, or models of Christian discipleship? To be sure, the mainstream of the Christian movement expressed through church synods deep concern over the disunity and fragmentation of Christ's disciples. And Christian emperors, whether for political or religious reasons, were eager to establish unity, law, and order. "Such is the regard I pay to the lawful Catholic church that I desire . . . no schism or division of any kind anywhere," said Constantine.[4] But was church unity meant to follow the principle of the *Pax Romana* or the principle "where Christ is, there is His Church"?[5] The fact is that law and order and unity of faith and custom never prevailed in Christianity as absolute virtues. The fourth-century phenomenon of Christian diversity was present in the eighth century and beyond.

The eighth-century Armenian historian Leontios (Ghevond) has preserved an interesting letter that the Byzantine emperor Leo III wrote to the caliph of Bagdad, Omar II.[6] Omar had written a letter to Leo inviting him to denounce Christianity and embrace Islam. Leo's reply is an extensive and well-written defense of the major tenets of his faith as opposed to Islam, and in turn he invited Omar to accept the Christian faith.

In his reply to Leo in 718, Omar questioned the validity of Christianity because it had been divided into seventy-two versions. A divided Christianity was considered a scandal and an impediment to a more effective witness. Present-day Christian churches, denominations, sects, schisms, heresies, or models of Christian discipleship if you prefer, are in the thousands. All use biblical passages to justify their creed and their existence. Thus the first lesson of history is that not only the world but also Christendom itself has always been religiously plural. The early and medieval church of the Greek East achieved a unity in diversity. In fact the Orthodox church has achieved a unity in doctrine, worship, and major ethical issues with a great deal of diversity in polity, custom, and tradition. Is there any basis that would justify an anticipation of changes in the remaining years of the twentieth century?

Admittedly, in the past twenty years the Christian world has seen several ecumenical advances. Many dialogues between Protestant and Roman Catholic, Eastern Orthodox and Roman Catholic, Protestant and Eastern Orthodox, and Eastern Orthodox and Oriental churches have been held. On the local level we have seen numerous regional, state, and city ecumenical meetings, including prayer services and conciliar fellowships.

In spite of ecumenical dialogues we have also seen forms of divisiveness, a renewed consciousness of denominationalism that has led certain denominations to proselytize and expand in the name of evangelism. Several years ago I attended a huge revival in New York's Madison Square Garden. In the back room of the arena, I was invited to leave my church because "it does not teach the Bible," an invitation based on total ignorance of the Orthodox Church. Recently, the *New York Times* carried a story about a major American denomination which sent missionaries to evangelize Greek Orthodox Christians in the Boston area. And a few years ago, when my wife and I were traveling to Greece, we met a young American college graduate who told us that she was going to Greece as a missionary. Apparently she did not know that Paul

of Tarsus had been there first! Nine years ago, when I lived in the
Boston area, I was invited to speak to the laity of an enlightened
congregation in Lexington, Massachusetts. Before I was introduced by the local pastor, I was approached by a group of middle-
aged women who very seriously asked me, "Do you still believe in
Zeus?" Yes, indeed, I said, except that we have baptized him unto
Jesus Christ! Why do I relate these experiences? Simply to indicate that the grassroots of present-day Christians have not been
much affected by ecumenical activities. Thus, before the Christian churches face a religiously pluralistic world in the days
ahead, they must first face each other's theology and reconsider
their theological stance, for what they call genuine Christianity
may be self-righteousness, arrogance, or egoism. Several American denominations and religious movements are not distinguished for any self-criticism or sense of humility.

ii

How does one anticipate the relations of the Orthodox with
other faiths in the context of religious pluralism? Is there any
basis to expect institutional realignments in the coming years? In
order to answer these questions, we need, once again, to see the
Orthodox Church in history, within the Christian *ecumene* as well
as within a religiously pluralistic world.

The Orthodox have always emphasized the continuity of God's
revealing truth before as well as after the incarnation of the Logos. The living God "in past generations allowed all the nations to
walk in their own ways; yet he did not leave himself without witness" (Acts 14:16-17), and "what can be known about God was
known to them, because God revealed it to them. Ever since the
creation of the world his invisible nature, namely, his external
power and deity, has been clearly perceived in the things that
have been made" (Rom. 1:18-19). On the other hand, Pentecost
is an ongoing event. The Holy Spirit continues to live in the
church, to guide it to new interpretations and to new revelations.
It is the same Spirit who created, who spoke through the
prophets, who guided the apostles, and in whom we live, move,
and have our existence (Acts 17:28).

Christianity's claim to be inherently exclusive of other religions was an inheritance from its Hebraic roots. But as early as the apostolic age Christianity became rooted in the Hellenic tradition as well. The tensions between the Hebraic and the Hellenic elements were constant in early Christianity. There is little doubt, however, that the future of Christianity was shaped not by people like Tatian and Tertullian, who rejected what the Orthodox call natural revelation, the truth of God outside the Old Testament, but by Justin, Clement, and Origen of Alexandria, Synesios of Cyrene, Basil the Great and the other Cappadocians, who achieved a synthesis between indirect, or natural, revelation, and direct—the self-disclosure of God in Christ. For the early church, Christ was the point of convergence between the Jewish Messiah and the Logos of the Greeks.

As Hellenistic-Jewish writers of the pre-Christian era made significant compromises with Hellenism in their theology, likewise early Christian writers adjusted their theology to Hellenic thought and philosophical categories, which they perceived as another form of God's revelation.[7] Recent research has shown that a great degree of syncretism occurred at the beginning of the Christian era. By the fifth-century Christianity had developed into a very syncretic religion. And if we don't like syncretism, why blame it on human beings and not on God, who created human beings, who allowed this syncretism? Is Old Testament religion less syncretic?

The Hebraic and Hellenic tensions in early Christianity gave rise to two different attitudes toward the religious truths of the outside world, as evidenced in the Bible itself, as well as in early Christian literature. In his Areopagus speech, Saint Paul implied that the Athenians who worshiped the unknown God were actually crypto-Christians, Christians without knowing it. The opening words of John's Gospel, that in the beginning was the beloved Logos of the Greeks, prepared the way for the early church to take a positive attitude toward nonbiblical truth. Many acknowledged that there was more divine truth in Socrates' teachings than in some Old Testament books. For example, it is more humane and godly to assert that "it is evil to return evil for evil,"[8] as Socrates advised, than to follow Deuteronomy's bellicose teaching that "your eye shall not pity; it shall be life for life, eye for eye, tooth for tooth, hand for hand, foot for foot" (19:21).

Apologists, ecclesiastical writers, and church fathers of the Christian East adopted Saint Paul's attitude toward nonbiblical truth as expressed in the seventeenth chapter of Acts as well as in his epistle to the Romans to such an extent that Orthodox Christianity developed a more positive attitude toward non-Christian religions. With very few exceptions, among them Augustine, the Christian West was more influenced by Old Testament attitudes and by people like Tertullian and developed not only an exclusiveness like that of the Old Testament but also a militancy against dissenters and non-Christians. The re-Judaization efforts after the sixteenth century made Western Christianity even more exclusive. Whereas the Greek influence tended to make Christianity a universal philosophy of belief and life, the Old Testament inspired religious enthusiasm, which led to particularism, to fanaticism, inquisitions, persecution, crusades, religious wars.

It was under the influence of Greek thought that Justin proclaimed that all who had lived according to the Logos, the Reason of God, were Christians before the coming of Christ. Clement of Alexandria, after Justin, stressed that it was to the whole of humankind that "God spoke in former times in fragmentary and varied fashion." And Origen, one of the great theologians of all times, emphasized that there is no truth independent of the direct action of God, whether in Judaism or in Hellenism. Gregory of Nazianzus, Gregory of Nyssa, Basil the Great, and Augustine, notwithstanding their condemnation of idolatry, saw in history the presence of God guiding all to the truth. As Irenaeus wrote: "There is only one God who, from beginning to end, through various economies comes to the help of mankind."[9] The Greek fathers achieved a marvelous synthesis between biblical truth and Greek thought, for they were students both of the Scriptures and of Greek literature; they cared much more about universal than individual salvation. In their efforts to universalize Christianity and break away from the particularism of Old Testament religion, they embraced the totality of God's creation. It was for this reason that Orthodox, or patristic, Christianity did not destroy the past but, instead, absorbed and consecrated what it considered good and profitable, for "the good is part and parcel of the truth wherever found," as the ecclesiastical historian Socrates wrote in the fourth century.[10]

There has always been in the Christian church a plurality of theological elaborations and opinions, and theological opinion has always had a cultural or intellectual background. Indeed the Holy Spirit does not destroy the individuality of the theologian or his mind and cultural background; the Holy Spirit elevates and inspires, but each theological mind works under its own predisposition and training. Biblical authority, the nature of Scripture, should be viewed in the light of ecclesial authority, for it was the *ecclesia,* the Christian community, that formulated the canon of the Scripture.

A doctrine, a belief, or a custom is not necessarily unchristian because it is Greek, Roman, or of Oriental origin. Many historians and theologians acknowledge that the translation of many ideas, concepts, and cultural tools into Christianity proved salutary. Anything in Greek thought and even mythology that would help the cause of Christianity was used by the early church. To be sure, Christianity took a risk but a risk worth taking: "Otherwise Gentile Christianity would have perished as Jewish Christianity did," to quote the words of an evangelical theologian.[11] The incarnation of Christ invites all to become participants in the very life of God.

In the history of Christianity much emphasis has been placed on the partial Abrahamic covenant, whereas the universal or cosmic covenant that God made with Noah has been overlooked. It is on the basis of this covenant that a fruitful dialogue can be conducted between Christians and non-Christians.[12] The Greek Fathers recognized that God was revealing his truth outside biblical revelation. But God is the same yesterday, today, and tomorrow, and one cannot limit God's presence and God's revealing self. Now we see as in a mirror darkly, and it is not given to Jews or Christians to judge where God is not. As Saint Peter confessed: "I now see how true it is that God has no favorites, but that in every nation the person who is god-fearing and does what is right is acceptable to him" (Acts 10:34–35). Why cannot God speak even today in various ways and diverse manners? Who shall confine his energy and his will? Indeed we may know where God is, but it is not given to us to know where God is not. Faith in the reality of the Holy Spirit, pneumatology with its implications, provides valid ground for an understanding of religious pluralism.

If it is true that no two people encounter God in the same manner or have the same religious experience, why should we preclude the work of the Holy Spirit outside Christianity? Religious pluralism does not contradict the unity of humankind. The Orthodox emphasize their sense of divine presence, of individual saintliness within the world, the communion of God's people across both space and time, of koinonia, or community, in God's bosom. This in no way denies Christ's claim that he is "the Way, the Truth, and the Life." But Christ is not limited by space or time; his Spirit lives, speaks, and acts in human history everywhere, often through mysterious and humanly unintelligible ways. What human being or organization can limit the Spirit's involvement in history? As Clement of Alexandria writes: "Nothing exists unless God gives it the cause of its being, so there is nothing which is hated by God nor indeed by the Logos, for both are God. . . . If he hates nothing of the things he made, he must love them. . . . He who loves something wishes to be of service to it."[13]

The gospel is the good news that shows how people can be brought back to God's presence, but it is not a guide for all earthly issues or a blueprint of God's working in history. The Holy Spirit acts on specific occasions—the New Testament speaks of his "outpouring" (Acts 2:1–4, Rom. 5:5, Tit. 3:6)—yet he has never stopped hovering over the earth (Gen. 1:2). The Spirit of God is a spirit of action over all humankind (cf. Joel 2:28); he meets people everywhere. He lifts up, inspires, and unites all in whom he dwells and bonds all humankind into the People of God. The People of God cannot be one branch of humanity as one part of the body cannot be separated from the other. The particularism of ancient Israel, or of its successor "New Israel (the church)," was not God's work but the result of a self-reflective history, of a deductive self-serving system. It is on the basis of pneumatology that Christianity can improve its relations with other faiths.

iii

How do the Orthodox face the future and what do they foresee in their relationships with non-Christians and Christians alike?

They will face the future in the same manner that they faced the world before. For many centuries millions of Orthodox Christians have lived amid Muslims. And now, many more live among atheists, Marxists, and people of other creeds. Even though Orthodox Christians have been persecuted and there are hundreds of neo-martyrs who died rather than convert to Islam, Orthodox Christianity and Islam have coexisted for many centuries. If there has ever been a "suffering servant" second to Christ, that suffering servant is the Orthodox Church, which has been preyed upon by both the Islamic East and the Christian West. Historical events have exposed Orthodox Christians to religious pluralism. Either because of historical circumstances or because of philosophical and pyschological disposition, the Orthodox have viewed religion as the right *doxa*, and *doxa* means glory, glorification. Thus Orthodoxy is not so much right creed as right doxology-worship of God the Creator.[14] As in the case of Christ, prayer is not religion, a tie, a legalistic bond, but an unceasing quest and awareness of God's presence in humankind. The Orthodox cherish personal belief and conduct, kindness and humane personal and societal morality more than religious zeal or aggressive proselytizing. For this reason Orthodox Christianity cannot sympathize with religious sentiment that leads to emotional movements such as the Crusades, religious wars, coercive or subversive and divisive missions.

The theological objective of the Orthodox Church continues to be the divination of humanity and of life itself, the absorption of the human being into God as the ultimate source of existence. The pedagogy that ultimately leads persons to seek rewards or receive punishments on their way to God and which views God as a stern Jehovah rather than as *Philanthropos Theos*, a God in love with his creation, is antithetical to the notion of *theosis*. *Theosis*, ultimate life in God, is the fruit of God's love for the human being.[15] Christ is never mere man or god but always the *theanthropos* (God-man), seeking to elevate human beings to *theosis*. As long as other religions have the same goal, the elevation of humanity to divine life, they are perceived by the Orthodox as instruments of God in God's world.

Concerning the relationship of the Orthodox with other Christian churches, I expect no change in the fundamental principles of Orthodox faith. Though fully committed to the ecumenical cause, the Orthodox are reluctant to compromise dogmas defined in ecumenical synods, unless a new ecumenical council redefines or changes the dogma. They have no difficulty in accepting differences in liturgical usage, or local variations of religious customs, for these are not impediments or obstacles to reconciliation. For the Orthodox, the boundaries of Christ's church and the organic unity of the church are ontologically related, but they are two different theological concerns. The boundaries reflect the horizontal dimensions of the church. Ecclesial elements are uniting all those who bear the Christian name. But the unity of the church is the vertical dimension that is present where the faithful gather in prayer around the Eucharist, to receive from the same cup in union with their presbyters and their bishops; to hear the word of the Scriptures and receive inspiration from the Holy Spirit.

Searching for unity among fellow Christians for a better understanding with non-Christians, the Orthodox emphasize their belief that this is God's world and that his revelations cannot be limited by human beings, for "the Spirit moves where it wills" (John 3:8). As the churches intensify their efforts in ecumenical dialogue and are exposed to each other's point of view, a new ecclesial syncretism will emerge. The Holy Spirit expects the synergy of human beings. This is the lesson of history. After all, it was a syncretic approach that won Christianity its followers in the first five centuries. There was diversity of opinion among Christians of different countries and of different cities in the same geographical area; there were different rules and different customs, but the church assumed "that those who agreed on the essentials of worship ought not to separate from one another on account of customs," as the fourth-century historian Sozomenos writes.[16] Worship in the early church meant, as it does in modern Orthodoxy, the centrality of Christ in the Eucharist, in faith, life, and action. In the Eucharist the faithful express their unity in faith and spirituality, in theological and religious discourse, in love and care for each other in a manner that encompasses the totality of humanity's needs of soul, mind, and body.

Thus, models of Christian discipleship will continue to be many and varied. We hope, however, that they will not be antagonistic to each other, that instead, they will draw closer. And as long as they accord Christ, the Christ of Scripture and history, the primacy of worship and commitment they will be legitimate models. For "anyone who is not against us is for us" (Mk. 9:40), as the chief model of all Christians has said.

NOTES

1. See the pertinent comments of Stefan Zankow, "The Church's Common Confession of Faith," in *The Orthodox Church in the Ecumenical Movement*, ed. Constantin G. Patelos (Geneva: World Council of Churches, 1978), pp. 161-62).

2. Ireneus, *Adversus omnes Haereses,* III. 14.1; iv.38.1.

3. Epiphanios of Cyprus, *Panarion*; Karl Hall, ed., *Epiphanius (Ancoratus und Panarion)*, Die Griechischen christlichen Schrifsteller der ersten drei Jahrhunderte, vols. 1-3 (Leipzig, 1915, 1922, 1933). Epiphanios enumerates all eighty heresies, including schisms, Greek schools of philosophy such as the Pythagorians and Stoics, and Jewish parties and sects such as the Pharisees, the Sadducees, and others, in the *Ancoratus*, 12 and 13. He writes that of the eighty "sixty falsely bear the name of Christ."

4. Eusebius, *Ecclesiastical History*, X.5, 15-22.

5. Ignatius, *To the Smyrneans*, 8.2.

6. Arthus Jeffery, "Ghevond's Text of the Correspondence between Omar II and Leo III," *Harvard Theological Review* 37 (1944): 281-330; cf. J. Muyldermans, *La domination Arabe en Armenie extrait de l'Histoire Universelle de Vardan* (Louvain and Paris, 1927), p. 101.

7. Justin, *First Apology*, 5.4; Clement of Alexandria, *Paedagogos*, III, 98.1; Idem, *Stromateis*, VII. 7.7; Origen, *De Principiis*, I.2; idem, *Contra Celsum*, III. 62.79. The literature on the subject by scholars of the last seventy years is enormous. Excellent summaries are provided by H. Chadwick, *Early Christian Thought and the Classical Tradition* (New York: Oxford University Press, 1966), W. Jaeger, *Early Christianity and Greek Paideia* (Cambridge, Mass.: Harvard University Press, 1961), and S. Angus, *The Religious Quests of the Graeco-Roman World* (New York: Biblo and Tanner, 1967, a reprint of the 1929 edition), esp. pp. 60-65.

8. Plato, *Crito*, 47D-49B.

9. Ireneus, *Adversus omnes Haereses*, III, 12:13.

10. Socrates, *Ecclesiastical History*, bk. III, chap. 16.

11. Michael Green, *Evangelism in the Early Church* (Grand Rapids, Mich.: Wm. B. Eerdmans, 1975), pp. 141-42.

12. Georges Khodr, "Christianity in a Pluralistic World—The Economy of the Holy Spirit," in *The Orthodox Church in the Ecumenical Movement*, pp. 302-3.

13. Clement of Alexandria, *Paidagogos*, I.8.

14. Cf. Georges Florovsky, "The Elements of Liturgy," in *The Orthodox Church in the Ecumenical Movement*, p. 172.

15. See Demetrios J. Constantelos, "The Lover of Mankind," *The Way* 9, no. 2 (1969): 98-106.

16. Sozomenos, *Ecclesiastical History*, VII.19.

4
An Ecumenical Protestant Perspective

John B. Carman

Our panel topic shifts the focus from Christ as Teacher and Lord to his followers as disciples and servants. The New Testament has other metaphors to express Christ's relationship with us: foundation and building, vine and branches, head and body, bridegroom and bride.

The second and third metaphors make clear the communal character of Christian discipleship, while the third and fourth interpenetrate. It is not as separate individuals, female or male, that we can think of ourselves as "brides" of Christ; but, as members of the body, branches of the vine, or blocks in the building, we form part of the special people, the holy nation inexplicably chosen for this high honor and intimate service. We are disciples as distinct individuals—we are to present our bodies as living sacrifices—but our life in Christ and our service for Christ is as members of his body, the church. We share in the same mission, Christ's work of reconciliation. Fellowship, service, and witness are all part of the church's work in the world and at the same time part of the church's intimate service to the Lord.

At Saint Paul writes to the church in Rome, "For as in one body we have many members, and all the members do not have the same function, so we, though many, are one body in Christ, and individually members one of another" (Rom. 12: 4–5; cf. 1 Cor. 12).

We are set various tasks, for which we are equipped by a diversity of gifts. Not only are we dependent on one another within the body, but we share in one another's tasks; we share even when we disagree on how those tasks are to be performed.

In my opinion interreligious dialogue is a very distinct task for Christian discipleship, a task that is neither the same as nor a substitute for evangelism, any more than educational work or medical work is the same as or a substitute for evangelism. All of these tasks have a distinctively modern form; all carry more baggage than Jesus allowed his first disciples when he sent them out two by two. We need to remind ourselves of that fact, as well as of the spiritual outfitting of the disciples of which Saint Paul writes.

The expensive equipment of the modern world, such as the betatron in the cancer unit of a hospital, can be a great boon, but it has to remain a tool in our hands, as we have to remain tools in Our Lord's hands. Sometimes we must do without such tools because we cannot afford them, sometimes because we cannot control them, and sometimes because they are no longer what the situation requires. It may be that the increasing cost of oil and other natural resources will force us to trim our present equipment, as well as to forge new tools for the years ahead.

I say this as a word of criticism to myself and to my fellow scholars who are trying to provide this modern equipment for the task of interreligious dialogue. We utilize and grow dependent upon expensive modern libraries and expensive modern transportation—the airplanes that fly us from one continent to another to participate in conferences like this one.

Dialogue, I would suggest, needs to begin with modest expectations and a modest definition. In our present context it is very simply a deliberately planned conversation where conversation has previously not occurred or where such conversation has reached an impasse. It is needed precisely where there is disagreement, misunderstanding, and division. Undoubtedly it can have deeper and deeper levels, but it need not imply them and it should not be confused with the worship of God in the fellowship of the church.

The agreement it requires initially is whatever is necessary to get the conversation going: some agreed procedures, usually a common language, and certainly a common will to converse both in spite of and because of the differences between us. This discussion itself is such a dialogue among Christians with different backgrounds and different convictions. Here we should *worship*

together because we are united in Christ, but we need to *talk* together because we are divided, and we should not expect the division to disappear by the time our discussion ends.

Some sense of shared interests or value is needed to motivate
any dialogue, but I believe that common meeting point is much
clearer in a meeting of Christians, however widely separated, than
in interreligious dialogue. That does not mean that our discussions here are necessarily more amicable or more fruitful. The
courtesy of which Kenneth Cragg writes is not always in evidence
in meetings among Christians. Such courtesy is all the more necessary in interreligious dialogue where the different participants
bring not only different perspectives, but also different views of
the very basis for meeting, and often different expectations of the
results.

Mutual understanding may seem a modest goal for dialogue,
but that does not mean it is easy to achieve. The particular vocation to which I am called is to assist with the scholarly outfitting of
the pilgrimage caravan of dialogue.

There is a genuine and sometimes profound nonscholarly dialogue in which those of different religions communicate, in which
they open their hearts and minds to one another and share their
convictions and their aspirations. Scholarly dialogue, or the
scholarly assistance for dialogue, is not superior to nonscholarly
dialogue, but it is different. It tries to take seriously the tradition
that the living contemporary partner in dialogue holds sacred,
which means to be in dialogue with the great voices and also the
pervasive murmur of the lesser voices of that tradition. I am
speaking of what can be a lifetime vocation, though it can also be
a shorter-term and less-consuming endeavor. It is in any event a
constant back-and-forth between one's own faith with all its intellectual and emotional expressions, and at least one other religious
tradition.

To what extent it can be such an inner conversation with all
other religious traditions it is hard to say. There are some mental
and spiritual giants who may attempt such a task. I find it hard
myself to do more than keep in conversation with one strand of
the Hindu tradition, the devotion to the Lord Vishnu and His
Divine Consort Lakshmi. The negative view of that theistic tradition toward atheistic Jains and Buddhists, as well as toward the

monistic Hindu school of Sankara, has certainly made it harder for me to converse at the same time with these other traditions.

If I am over-personalizing our topic, I beg your indulgence. I must speak of the kind of discipleship I know best, but I do so in the knowledge that I share this particular vocation with many of you, and that since we are fellow members of Christ's body, you all share in my vocation as I share in yours. We are members one of another. The equipment needed for this vocation has to be frequently reassessed. It may be too bookish or too Western. And the vocation itself is not a primary one. It is a service to the servants of God.

There are many disciples and they play different roles. Some are lifted up but once in the pages of the Gospel. Others are never mentioned by name. I commend to your notice Saint Andrew, who did not share the glorious sight on the Mount of Transfiguration, who was almost but not quite part of the innermost circle of Jesus' disciples. In the Gospel of John, however, Andrew is mentioned twice. The second time is in a favorite story of my childhood. It was he who brought the little boy's loaves and fishes to Jesus for the feeding of the five thousand. But even earlier in the Gospel, when he met Jesus, he ran back and told his brother Simon, "We have found the Messiah," and he took Simon back to meet Jesus. Andrew stood with empty hands before Jesus. On neither occasion were the material or intellectual gifts that he had to offer what Jesus most needed. But on both occasions Andrew had the simplicity and the humility to bring to Jesus someone who did have those gifts: a boy with bread and fish to give the multitude a foretaste of the Messiah's great banquet, and before that, an impulsive young fisherman to lead these new "fishers of men," his own brother Simon to become the bedrock of the new community awaiting God's kingdom on earth.

Like Saint Andrew of old, we American Christians may have to face our Lord in the future with empty hands. God grant us both the wit and the humility to recognize in others the gifts we lack and to bring those people, not grudgingly but enthusiastically, to Our Lord. If we must decrease that others may increase, so be it. We are members of one family and we rejoice together when God uses all our gifts and all our lives to produce a new sign of the kingdom to come.

VII

An Attempt at Summation

Wilfred Cantwell Smith

My assignment has been one that—I think you may agree—is
just a trifle impossible: namely, to sum up our conference. Surely
you will forgive me when I do it inadequately. I especially ask
forgiveness from those of our speakers whom, or whose positions, I may in what follows have represented awry, or less than
they deserve, in inadequate proportion. Even more humbling is
my awareness of being unable to do justice not to the spokesmen
and -women of its various aspects so much as to our mighty theme
itself. I apologize ahead of time. Nonetheless, obediently I have
made the attempt.

First, since I am myself a historian, I begin by making two historical points. One is that this gathering itself marks something of
a milestone in historical development. You need hardly be my age
to remember a time not long ago when *this* sort of conference just
would not have happened. Instead, the topic would have drawn
together a few of us apparently eccentric types, a minority concerned, and even deeply concerned, about these very issues, but
peripheral; whereas here we have had before us weighty and central persons addressing in full seriousness what is manifestly recognized as, again, a central issue of the whole church. We have
had an official representative of the Vatican, and one of the World
Council of Churches; a leader of the World Evangelical Fellowship; major mission board officials of what are called mainline
Protestants; significant thinkers from such disparate sectors of
Christendom as the Latin American liberation movement, major
establishment seminaries, black theology, Greek Orthodoxy, and

196

so on—all not merely focusing on, but wrestling with, a theology for religious pluralism. This is new, important, exciting. The church is on the move.

My second historical observation is a counterpart of the same point. The dramatic change in church concern is a matter not simply of thinking, but of historical involvement. The issue, as we have seen, is not one on which Christians change their mind readily, so soon as they are presented with a new argument. Rather, thinking is compelled—to use Dr. Samartha's term proffered illustratively, but I apply it generically—by drastically new situations. The ramifying enmeshment in changed world and personal conditions it is, whose reflex we have witnessed here. And vice versa: a new outlook and awareness will in turn ramify into the whole world. Dr. Costas's political application—his appeal for participation in "the transformation of the world"—was the most conspicuous illustration, but only one. (It was striking that it was an evangelical who presented that plea for social justice! Yet Dr. Stendahl, on the other side, so to speak, also pled for our plunging into the movement for the kingdom.) The church's new conceptual awareness will increasingly be correlated with its increasingly inescapable and deep involvement in the novel, dynamic, planetary interconnectedness of humankind. The sense was expressed by several that the coming decade will more than ever and with new urgency entwine both Christians and others in mighty matters, perhaps mighty crises—and will do this, we may be sure, to Christians and others *jointly*. The problem of our consultation is not theoretical but every day more concrete.

We have talked of religious pluralism. More vividly, we have displayed it. The phrase may have been coined to name an awareness of multiplicity of alternatives other than the church, for men and women of faith. Let us recognize, however, at the end of this consultation if we did not at its beginning, that first of all Christians are becoming aware of a pluralist multiplicity of forms of faith internally, among Christians. Orthodox, Catholic, Protestant—those we have known (though as we take each other more seriously, it means that we learn to respect and to accept differences, pluralism: it is striking, how much in our stride). Yet also, what we did not recognize until recently, with seriousness: other pluralities. Evangelicals calling *themselves* (did you notice?) "approaches," "angles from which . . .," and so on. Black liberation theology, explicitly discriminating itself from Latin American liberation theology. African forms of Christian faith presenting themselves, and being recognized, as *particular* forms. Christian pluralism was manifest not as present-day only, but in history: Christian forms, Christian thought, Christian outlooks, as obviously different in different centuries. A pluralism of Bibles, even, was noted—certainly of translations; but over the dinner table, also of manuscripts, readings, texts. Certainly, of course, a pluralism of exegesis. A pluralism of Lordship of Christ, even, if one listened carefully—both within the Bible and within the church. A pluralism of men's and women's perception of things; and in the study group devoted to that, within the mere half-hour that I dropped in on it, a pluralism within women's perceptions.

Religious pluralism is a Christian fact; not merely a world comparativist one. Indeed, at times I was slightly disquieted lest I discern greater variety within the gamut of Christian positions than was genuinely appreciated outside them, almost as if matters so variegated as Hindu, Muslim, Buddhist, Chinese, African forms of faith could all be lumped together to make a mere dualism in God's eyes of Christian and non-Christian. (Admittedly, the issue of whether Jews are special was raised—as if every child of God were not?)

"Christ's Lordship and Religious Pluralism." Was the topic intended to ask whether we might legitimately recognize others' having other lords? Yet some were orthodox enough Christians to remind us that the Christian herself or himself has others: we worship God as Trinity, or should; and although it would be heretical to use the new word "pluralism" there, yet that would be not nearly so serious an aberration as is the unitarianism of the Son, of which some reminded us. Christomonism is un-Christian, surely. We were reminded that the hymn in Acts that sings most exultantly of Christ as—penultimately—Lord over all, culminates in his, in turn, turning over everything to God the Father. Even so, I heard much less of God himself these three days than my own theocentric faith would rejoice, and even expect, to hear. And of the Holy Spirit, to whom a serious consideration of the diversified religious life of humankind might be expected to give careful and lively discussion, we heard remarkably little.

Jesus Christ is Lord; yet there is clearly a pluralism of epithets and attributes and predicates ascribed to him. Speaker after speaker reminded us that if he is Lord, he is many other things as well—servant, especially, and reconciler, among others: terms that would have made our problem from the start more tractable. I was myself surprised, I will admit, at both the frequency and at times the vehemence with which the Lordship language was questioned. My own tendency was to wonder whether it was chosen for the title of our consultation perhaps with the precise purpose of being conciliatory (without realizing that it might not work out so). An aspiration of this conference was presumably to bring together on the religious pluralism issue—today, as I have said, a, and perhaps the, central Christian theological problem—all main Christian groups; and especially those—namely, the evangelicals—who might be expected to stand aloof from groups most actively concerned about this problem. To that extent one had to make clear that the basic issue was not going to be sidestepped. If we address pluralism in direct relation to the Lordship of Christ, I can imagine the organizers consciously or unconsciously saying, surely the evangelicals will come. And come they did. Others, however, turned out to be less delighted.

For pluralism showed up here, too! It turns out that "the Lordship of Christ" is evangelical phraseology—but not everybody's. I had not known that, because I was brought up an evangelical; and *of course* I think of Christ as Lord. Yet I was fascinated to sit at lunch and to overhear Dr. Stendahl and Mrs. Margarethe Brown asking each other how one would say "the Lordship of Christ" in Swedish or Danish, and their not finding an answer. They do not say it! Lutherans do not say it. It is not in the Bible. The Christian tradition is a religiously plural one!

"Lordship language is offensive to . . . women," said Dr. Mary Smith, in strong language. Others were less provocative, and some merely expressed a view that alternative images would be less triumphalist; or even that of course we say "Lord" but it is important how we interpret the concept. Yet this much became clear: there is a pluralism of language, and it will repay close attention.

On the verbal matter, is it not curious that no one reminded us that Christ himself said, "Not everyone that saith unto me, Lord, Lord, . . . but he who doeth the will of my Father . . ."?

Entrancing on this matter was Monsignor Rossano's pointing out to us that in the church in the early centuries also there were dialogue folk and anti-dialogue—with the former dying as martyrs (Justin, Origen), the latter (Tertullian and the like) dying in their beds, but alienated from the church. The Monsignor traced a strand from the early centuries through Nicholas of Cusa to the modern world situation, and set forth then the view of Christ as the Reconciler in whom everyone, in every age, finds salvation, even in the era B.C.; through him, cosmically, being forgiven is more primarily human than being a sinner. My note at that point was that evidently if one have a sufficiently high Christology, pluralism is not a problem.

That is slightly quippish, however, and this is too serious a matter to be glib. The fundamental problem seems to me to lie in a very subtle distinction between what might be called a formal and a substantial recognition of Christ as Lord. The dividing line is tenuous, even unstable; a given person might appear to fall on one side of it to him- or herself, on the other to those looking on. By "formal" I mean averring Christ as Lord as a proposition only, and by "substantial" I mean really living one's life in his service. The latter is transformed at once into discipleship, and the panel topic under that word seemed to many, one felt, among us a right and proper transition. This takes "Christ is Lord" as an existential rather than an ontological statement: he is my Lord, or what says the same thing, I am his disciple, or will be, will live as. True, I must not only be his disciple, but must witness to him; and yet the life that Christians live in discipleship is the truest, the most eloquent, witness.

This notion of service could fuse the Lordship language with the kingdom language. It also can obviate the dilemma of pluralism. I personally have no difficulty in saying that Christ is my Lord, and recognizing, at the same time, that the Buddha is Dr. Mahinda Palihawadana's Lord.

On pluralism, I wish to make another point, of increasing importance nowadays, that came up in our deliberations but not explicitly: namely, that religious pluralism in our modern world is dynamic in both directions. It is not simply a name for a situation out upon which Christians look, or toward which they formulate a one-way policy. Conversion was mentioned a few times; perhaps

I was not listening carefully enough, but I think that I heard it only in the sense of conversions to the church. Incipient but increasing in our day, however, are also conversions of Christians to Hindu, Buddhist, Muslim, Jewish forms of faith. A teasing question is: Does one thank God when a secular youth finds faith for the first time in such a form? Less pointedly: borrowing from other religious systems has begun, and may be expected to grow. Feminists, and some male thinkers, are beginning to wonder whether The Goddess in Hindu orientations may not help us as we think through our inherited but perplexing patriarchal conceptualizations of the divine. Dr. Mary Smith wondered if pre-Indo-European, pre-Semitic ideas on feminine divinity might not serve Christians well. Some thinkers are asking whether Sankara or Ramanuja may not be more apt philosophers than was Aristotle or than is Whitehead for articulating Christian theology. Muslim mystic thought, expressed in some of the most splendid poetry in the world, is helping some Christians to make sense of religious pluralism, of Christ and God, and of one's own life. Modern Western logic, I myself am pretty sure, though serviceable for computers, is in other ways inept and is particularly ill-suited, it seems, for thinking about human affairs and especially about spiritual matters. We may have to construct for our culture a different and better logic than that currently in vogue; but perhaps other cultures can help us out.

Dr. Stendahl made the point that from the positive affirmations of the confession, drawing negative conclusions might not be appropriate. I have wondered whether the powerful and winsome positions of the evangelicals among us may not be fully valid in themselves and spiritually more profound than various liberal ones, but be rendered unacceptable to many modern Christians because tied to logical inferences, especially of a negative kind, that seem to follow from them only because of the limitations of Western secular logic (such as the true-false dichotomy, the excluded middle, or the propositional locus of truth) with which for no good reason they are currently tied.

Dr. Glasser pled the importance of truth. For a moment I was tempted to respond by pleading for the moral injunctions, rather, of the Christian revelation. As we face Christ on the cross, and as teacher, we are made aware of imperatives toward reconciliation, brotherhood, the dignity of the neighbor, peace, concord, respect; matters with all of which denigration of others' forms of faith collides. Exclusivism strikes more and more Christians as immoral. If the head proves it true, while the heart sees it as wicked, un-Christian, then should Christians not follow the heart? Maybe this is the crux of our dilemma.

The temptation did not last long, however. I am an ordained minister who does not have a parish. I have chosen the academic path. I am a man of the head. On the matter of Lordship, must I not mention the important point that I both would and should resign my post as a university professor were it not that *my* lord, first and last, is truth? I differ from philosophers like Tarsky in that for me, as for Aquinas and others, truth is God. Since I am an intellectual, I seek God through intellectual truth. Yet I am not only an intellectual; and for me God is revealed also in other ways—in history and in nature, as one of our speakers said; and in the Lord Jesus Christ. I personally cannot fully imagine what it would mean to say that God is revealed only in Christ, since I see him almost everywhere. Yet perhaps this is an aside. Dr. Glasser is right: integral to, if not even ultimate for, religious life is the question, What is true?

Yet truth, surely today we know, is an incredibly complex and subtle and elusive and—I must add—a transcendent thing. Many of us are resolute to think about religious pluralism, rigorously and precisely. Yet what appears to any of us as true is a matter, in part, of where and how we live. There is the "sociology of knowledge," as Dr. Schreiter reminded us theoretically, and our black friends and Third World friends in more down-to-earth ways. The sociology of perception, I should prefer to call it. Our "knowledge" is a function of whether we are men or are women. And as others reminded us, there is a psychology, too, of knowledge: what we finitely know is a function of our unconscious hopes and fears and drives. We have become much more humble but also more sophisticated about claiming truths articulated in words; and about judging whether two statements made in differing circumstances contradict each other even though they seem to do so. Theologizing these days is a vastly more subtle undertaking than it has seemed. There is an interim pluralism of truths, also.

My colleague and friend Dr. Carman gave a moving reminder

of the church as a corporate body in which we are all members one of another, forbearing one another, serving one another, and corporately serving God by severally attending each to his or her appointed or chosen assignment. We have striven in this consultation to attain that concord, even though the divisions that divide us are sharp and deep. I wonder if he will allow me to say that not only do I personally feel and hold that the corporate body of which I am a member, of which all are members, interdependent, corporately serving God by severally attending each to our intertwining and mutually determinative roles, in final collaboration, is the whole human race. I further wonder whether perhaps the church can deal with the issue that it has addressed here, and can bridge its own divisions, only if it comes to recognize that in the new age now upon us, it lives within the whole community of religious pluralism, and serves God aright by serving all his creatures, in corporate loyalty to each other and to him.

There are, as a matter of clear fact, some Christians who have correlated and do correlate the Lordship of Christ with a recognition—as I understood Dr. Constantelos to put it, as Orthodox doctrine; yet going beyond him—of God's having been salvifically at work from the beginning of history among all communities. These Christians not only hold this, but feel that they (we) must hold it because of what from Christ they learn of God, humankind, and the world. This consultation has not attained an agreement among all of us on this point. There is, I repeat, religious pluralism within the church as well as across the globe. We do not (yet) agree in either *dharma* or *dristi,* morals or doctrine. Yet I submit that our gathering has demonstrated that the two pluralisms are of the same kind. This is so in God's eyes; and our task is to let it become so now also in ours.

Contributors

Gerald H. Anderson, director of the Overseas Ministries Study Center in Ventnor, New Jersey, and editor of the *International Bulletin of Missionary Research,* was formerly professor of church history and academic dean at Union Theological Seminary, Manila, Philippines, and president of Scarritt College, Nashville. He is the editor of *Asian Voices in Christian Theology* (Maryknoll, N.Y.: Orbis Books, 1976).

Kofi Appiah-Kubi, a lay theologian of the Ghana Presbyterian Church, is an advocate of African theology, the church's healing ministry, and African traditional healing practices. Former theology secretary of the All-Africa Conference of Churches, Nairobi, he is presently on study leave at Columbia University School of Public Health, New York City. He is co-editor of *African Theology en Route* (Maryknoll, N.Y.: Orbis Books, 1979).

Margrethe B. J. Brown was educated in Denmark, England, Scotland, and the United States, and holds degrees in theology from both Copenhagen University and Union Theological Seminary, New York. She is an ordained minister of the United Presbyterian Church and is presently the executive presbyter for Genesee Valley Presbytery, upstate New York. Her contribution at the Chiang Mai consultation on "Dialogue in Community" appeared in the symposium *Faith in the Midst of Faiths* (Geneva: World Council of Churches, 1977).

John B. Carman is professor of comparative religion and director of the Center for the Study of World Religions at Harvard University. Born in India of missionary parents, he himself served as an American Baptist missionary in India from 1957 to 1963, and has a continuing interest in the relation of Christian faith to Hindu culture. He is the author of *The Theology of Ramanuja* (New Haven: Yale University Press, 1974), and co-editor with Donald G. Dawe of *Christian Faith in a Religiously Plural World* (Maryknoll, N. Y.: Orbis Books, 1978).

Demetrios J. Constantelos, born in Greece and ordained as a priest of the Greek Orthodox Church, is professor of history and religious studies at Stockton State College, Pomona, New Jersey. A former president of the Orthodox Theological Society in America, he is the author of *The Greek Orthodox Church: History, Faith and Practice* (New York: Seabury Press, 1967).

Orlando E. Costas, born in Puerto Rico, has a doctorate in theology from the Free University of Amsterdam and has ministerial standing in both the American Baptist Churches and the United Church of Christ. From 1973 to 1980 he served as director of the Latin American Evangelical Center for Pastoral Studies (CELEP) in San José, Costa Rica, and is now the Thornley B. Wood professor of missiology and director of Hispanic studies at Eastern Baptist Theological Seminary in Philadelphia. His publications in English include *The Church and Its Mission* (Wheaton, Ill.: Tyndale House, 1974), *Theology of the Crossroads in Contemporary Latin America* (Amsterdam: Rodopi, 1976), and *The Integrity of Mission* (New York: Harper & Row, 1979).

Donald G. Dawe is professor of theology at Union Theological Seminary in Richmond, Virginia. A minister of the United Presbyterian Church, he has taught at Macalester College, Union Theological Seminary in New York, and the Punjabi University in Patiala, India. He has lectured in Korea, Japan, Spain, and England, as well as in the United States, on his work in Christology and the relation of Christian faith to other faiths with special emphasis on the devotional traditions of Hinduism and on the Buddhism of Tibet. He is the author of *Paul Interpreted for India* (Punjabi University Press, 1976), and co-editor with John B. Carman of *Christian Faith in a Religiously Plural World* (Maryknoll, N. Y.: Orbis Books, 1978).

Arthur F. Glasser is senior professor of mission theology and East Asian studies at Fuller Theological Seminary, School of World Mission, Pasadena, California. His missionary service was with China Inland Mission in southwest China 1946–51, in Singapore 1956–57, and then as home director of the China Inland Mission/Overseas Missionary Fellowship 1957–69. He is the editor of *Missiology: An International Review,* the quarterly journal of the American Society of Missiology, and has contributed to *God, Man and Church Growth* (Grand Rapids, Mich.: Wm. B. Eerdmans, 1973), and *The Gospel and Islam* (Monrovia, Calif.: MARC/World Vision, 1979).

William R. O'Brien was a Southern Baptist missionary in Indonesia from 1962 to 1974, working in the field of music and mass media. He is now executive vice-president of the Foreign Mission Board, Southern Baptist Convention, Richmond, Virginia. In 1980 Convention Press (Nashville, Tenn.) published his *Missions for Tomorrow.*

J. Deotis Roberts, a Baptist minister, is president and professor of philosophical theology, Interdenominational Theological Center, Atlanta, Georgia, and serves on the board of directors of the Black Theology Project of Theology in the Americas. He is the author of *Black Political Theology* (Philadelphia: Westminster Press, 1974), and *Roots of a Black Future: Family and Church* (Philadelphia: Westminster Press, 1980).

Pietro Rossano, a native of Alba, Italy, and a Roman Catholic priest, is secretary of the Vatican Secretariat for Non-Christian Religions, and lecturer on theology of religions both at Urban University and at Gregorian University in Rome. His publications include commentaries on *Thessalonians* (Torino: Marietti, 1964) and *Corinthians* (Rome: Ed. Paoline, 1970), and *Theologie der Mission* (Zurich: Benziger, 1972).

Stanley J. Samartha is director of the Program on Dialogue with People of Living Faiths and Ideologies, World Council of Churches, Geneva, Switzerland. An ordained presbyter of the Church of South India, he was formerly professor and principal of Serampore College, Serampore, West Bengal, India. He has written *The Hindu Response to the Unbound Christ* (Christian Literature Society of India, 1974), and edited *Living Faiths and Ultimate Goals: Salvation and World Religions* (Maryknoll, N. Y.: Orbis Books, 1975), and *Faith in the Midst of Faiths: Reflections on Dialogue in Community* (Geneva: World Council of Churches, 1977).

Robert J. Schreiter, C.PP.S., is dean of the Catholic Theological Union in Chicago, and co-director of the Chicago Institute of Theology and Culture. His doctorate in theology and history of religions is from the University of Nijmegen, The Netherlands. He is the author of *Constructing Local Theologies* (Maryknoll, N.Y.: Orbis Books, forthcoming).

Waldron Scott is general secretary of the World Evangelical Fellowship. His missionary experience includes service with the Evangelical Synod of Syria and Lebanon and the Navigators in the Middle East and Southeast Asia. He is the author of *Karl Barth's Theology of Mission* (Downers Grove, Ill.: Inter-Varsity Press, 1978), and *Bring Forth Justice* (Grand Rapids, Mich.: Wm. B. Eerdmans, 1980).

Mary Carroll Smith, third generation Irish-American Roman Catholic, is assistant professor of history of religions at Vassar College. Educated at Trinity College, Washington, D.C., and Harvard University, she was a member of the Sisters of Notre Dame de Namur from 1957 to 1967. Her articles have appeared in the *Journal of the American Oriental Society* and the *Journal of Ecumenical Studies*.

Wilfred Cantwell Smith is professor of the comparative history of religion at Harvard, and has been given the task of developing at that university a new program in Arts and Sciences in the Study of Religion. A Canadian, he is an ordained minister of the United Church of Canada. Formerly director of Harvard's multi-faith Center for the Study of World Religions, he has taught also in India and in Canada. His latest books are *Belief and History* (Charlottesville: University Press of Virginia, 1977), *Faith and Belief* (Princeton, N.J.: Princeton University

Press, 1979), and *Towards a World Theology* (Philadelphia: Westminster Press, 1980).

Krister Stendahl is professor of divinity at Harvard Divinity School where he teaches New Testament, preaching, and worship. He taught biblical studies at Uppsala University in Sweden 1951–54. Since then he has been at Harvard Divinity School and served as its dean 1968–79. An ordained priest of the Church of Sweden, he was president of the Student Christian Movement in Sweden in 1954. He is the author of *The Bible and the Role of Women* (Philadelphia: Fortress Press, 1966), *Paul among Jews and Gentiles* (Philadelphia: Fortress Press, 1976), and the essay "Biblical Theology" in *The Interpreter's Dictionary of the Bible* (Nashville, Tenn.: Abingdon Press, 1962).

Thomas F. Stransky, C.S.P., was president from 1970 to 1978 of the Paulist Fathers, the first missionary society of priests founded in the United States (1858). He is a member of the Joint Working Group between the World Council of Churches and the Roman Catholic Church, an official consultant to the Vatican Secretariat for Promoting Christian Unity, and a participant in the Scholars' Group sponsored by the Southern Baptist Convention and the U.S. Catholic Bishops' Ecumenical Commission. In 1979–80 he was visiting professor of missions and ecumenics at Princeton Theological Seminary in New Jersey, and at the Washington Theological Union in Washington, D.C. He is the editor of *Ecumenical Documents,* vol. I: *Vatican Statements 1964–1980* (New York: Paulist Press, forthcoming), and is co-editor with Gerald H. Anderson of the *Mission Trends* series, published jointly by Paulist Press and Wm. B. Eerdmans Publishing Co.

OTHER ORBIS TITLES

ANDERSON, Gerald H.
ASIAN VOICES IN CHRISTIAN THEOLOGY

"Anderson's book is one of the best resource books on the market that deals with the contemporary status of the Christian church in Asia. After an excellent introduction, nine scholars, all well-known Christian leaders, present original papers assessing the theological situation in (and from the viewpoint of) their individual countries. After presenting a brief historical survey of the development of the Christian church in his country, each author discusses 'what is being done by the theologians there to articulate the Christian message in terms that are faithful to the biblical revelation, meaningful to their cultural traditions, and informed concerning the secular movements and ideologies.' An appendix (over 50 pages) includes confessions, creeds, constitutions of the churches in Asia. Acquaintance with these original documents is imperative for anyone interested in contemporary Asian Christian theology." *Choice*

ISBN 0-88344-017-2   *Cloth $15.00*
ISBN 0-88344-016-4   *Paper $7.95*

APPIAH-KUBI, Kofi & Sergio Torres
AFRICAN THEOLOGY EN ROUTE

Papers from the Pan-African Conference of Third World Theologians, Accra, Ghana.

"If you want to know what 17 Africans are thinking theologically today, here is the book to check. ' *Evangelical Missions Quarterly*

"Gives us a wonderful insight into the religious problems of Africa and therefore is well worth reading." *Best Sellers*

"This collection of presentations made at the 1977 Conference of Third World Theologians reveals not a finished product but, as the title suggests, a process. . . .On the whole, the book is well written and, where necessary, well translated. It adds to a growing literature on the subject and is recommended for libraries seriously concerned with theology in Africa." *Choice*

ISBN 0-88344-010-5   *184pp. Paper $7.95*

BALASURIYA, Tissa
THE EUCHARIST AND HUMAN LIBERATION

"Balasuriya investigates. . .the problem of why people who share the Eucharist also deprive the poor of food, capital, and employment. . . .For inclusive collections." *Library Journal*

"I hope Christians—especially Western Christians—will read this book, despite its blind impatience with historical and ecclesial details and balance, because its central thesis is the gospel truth: eucharistic celebration, like the faith it expresses, has been so domesticated by feudalism, colonialism, capitalism, racism, sexism, that its symbolic action has to penetrate many layers of heavy camouflage before it is free, before it can be felt." *Robert W. Hovda, Editorial Director, The Liturgical Conference*

ISBN 0-88344-118-7 *184pp. Paper $6.95*

BURROWS, William R.
NEW MINISTRIES: THE GLOBAL CONTEXT

"This is an exciting, informed, thoughtful, and ground-breaking book on one of the most vital and threatening issues facing the contemporary church. Father Burrows seeks effectively to show that the older forms of church and clerical life, developed in the West, are both irrelevant and stultifying when transferred *in toto* to the Third World, and that as a consequence, new forms of church and clerical life, forms still within the Catholic heritage to which he belongs and which he affirms, must be developed if the church is long to survive in that new World. Burrows makes crystal clear the need for more open attitudes towards the forms of church and clergy if the newer churches are to become genuinely creative forces in the Third World rather than lingering embassies from the First World. I found the work exceedingly stimulating and the approach fresh and open." *Prof. Langdon Gilkey, University of Chicago Divinity School*
ISBN 0-88344-329-5 *192pp. Paper $7.95*

CABESTRERO, Teofilo
FAITH: CONVERSATIONS WITH CONTEMPORARY THEOLOGIANS

"This book shows what an informed and perceptive journalist can do to make theology understandable, inviting, and demanding. These records of taped interviews with fifteen European and Latin American theologians serve two major purposes: we are allowed to eavesdrop on well-known theologians in spontaneous theological conversation, and we are introduced to new and stimulating minds in the same way."*Prof. D. Campbell Wyckoff, Princeton Theological Seminary*
Conversations include Ladislaus Boros, Georges Casalis, Joseph (José) Comblin, Enrique Dussel, Segundo Galilea, Giulio Girardi, José Maria González Ruiz, Gustavo Gutiérrez, Hans Küng, Jürgen Moltmann, Karl Rahner, Joseph Ratzinger, Edward Schillebeeckx, Juan Luis Segundo, Jean-Marie Tillard.
ISBN 0-88344-126-8 *208pp. Paper $7.95*

CAMARA, Dom Helder
THE DESERT IS FERTILE

"Dom Helder Camara of Brazil, is a Roman Catholic archbishop whose sense of God's presence breathes through every page. But there is a difference. For Dom Helder has found God's presence in the lives of the poor, in the voices of the oppressed, and he communicates this sense of God's reality very powerfully. He takes us on a spiritual journey that can be utterly transforming if we will risk opening ourselves to him. He is no pessimist; in a world that seems devoid of God's presence, Dom Helder insists that *The Desert Is Fertile*. He does not minimize the 'desert' quality of modern existence: the increasing gap between rich and poor, the insanity of the arms race, and the 'marginalization' of human life, by which he means our tendency to treat the majority of the human family as nonpersons, those who are pushed over to the edges of life and ignored. 'The scandal of this century,' he writes, 'is marginalization.' He reminds us that if to have too little is a problem, so is having too much. 'Poverty makes people subhuman. Excess of wealth makes people inhuman.'" *Christianity and Crisis*

ISBN 0-88344-078-4   *75pp. Cloth $3.95*

CARDENAL, Ernesto
THE GOSPEL IN SOLENTINAME I

"Farmers and fishermen in a remote village in Nicaragua join their priest for dialogues on Bible verses. The dialogues discover Jesus as the liberator come to deliver *them* from oppression, inequality, and injustice imposed by a rich, exploitive class: they identify Herod as dictator Somoza. Their vision of the Kingdom of God on earth impels them toward political revolution. This is 'Marxian Christianity' not as abstract theory but gropingly, movingly articulated by poor people. Highly recommended to confront the complacent with the stark realities of religious and political consciousness in the Third World." *Library Journal*

ISBN 0-88344-170-5   *Paper $4.95*

THE GOSPEL IN SOLENTINAME II

"Volume 2 follows the pattern of the first volume: villagers in Nicaragua join their priest, Ernesto, in interpreting New Testament verses. These volumes offer a profound challenge to the Christian conscience, and insight into the recent uprisings in Nicaragua. Highly recommended." *Library Journal*

ISBN 0-88344-167-5   *Cloth $6.95*

THE GOSPEL IN SOLENTINAME III

"A continuation of guided discussions on Gospel passages by the peasant folks in the Central American village of Solentiname. Has a most refreshing outlook." *The Priest*

Fortunately, the manuscripts for this and the fourth volume were safely in Orbis' hands before Somoza's soldiers destroyed Solentiname.

ISBN 0-88344-172-1   *320pp. Cloth $7.95*

CARRETTO, Carlo

LETTERS FROM THE DESERT

"Carretto, a very active layman in Catholic Action in Italy for twenty-five years, gave it up at the age of forty-four to become a Little Brother of Jesus. He heard the call to prayer and went into the desert. After a while he began to jot down things. The book was an instant success in Italy where, since its appearance in 1964 it has gone through twenty-four editions. It has been translated into Spanish, French, German, Portugese, Arabic, Japanese, Czech, and now, gracefully enough, into English. I hope it goes into twenty-four more editions. It breathes with life, with fresh insights, with wisdom, with love." *The Thomist*
ISBN 0-88344-280-9   *146pp. Paper $4.95*

LOVE IS FOR LIVING

"This book is truly excellent. Because we are all, indeed, poor, weak and empty, this series of meditations aims right at the human heart and beautifully articulates what goes on there. Some of the chapters are simply brilliant!" *The Cord*
"This book is meant for slow, prayerful pondering—a page or two at a time. It would probably be of help to persons searching for a deeper meaning in daily life, as well as those seeking a better knowledge of the Bible." *Religious Media Today*
ISBN 0-88344-291-4   *158pp. Cloth $6.95*
ISBN 0-88344-293-0   *Paper $4.95*

SUMMONED BY LOVE

"Those of you who treasure Carlo Carretto's books will be pleased by his latest, *Summoned by Love*. The book is a sustained meditation based on a prayer of Charles de Foucauld known as the *Prayer of Abandonment to God*." *Sign*
"Disarmingly simple and direct, Carretto's reflections testify to his familiarity with Scripture, the Church Fathers, and the down-to-earth realities of daily living. For one who is so 'traditional' in his spirituality, many of Carlo Carretto's ideas could be labeled 'liberal.' His writings indicate that he is in the mainstream of what is, and has been, truly vital in the Church universal. This valuable and timely book offers encouragement and challenge for all seeking to live within the changing Church and to find hope and love therein." *Catholic Library World*
ISBN 0-88344-470-4   *143pp. Cloth $7.95*
ISBN 0-88344-472-0   *Paper $4.95*

IN SEARCH OF THE BEYOND

"This little book will spur the reader to find his Beloved in solitary prayer. Creating a desert place for yourself means learning to be self-sufficient, to remain undisturbed with one's own thoughts and prayers. It means shutting oneself up in one's room, remaining alone in an empty church, or setting up an oratory for oneself in an attic in which to localize one's personal contact with God." *Western Michigan Catholic*
" 'To lead others to contemplation is the heart of the apostolate,' according to Carretto. Here are excellent reflections on Scriptural themes, both old and new." *Spiritual Book News*
ISBN 0-88344-208-6   *175pp. Cloth $5.95*

CLAVER, Bishop Francisco F., S.J.

THE STONES WILL CRY OUT
Grassroots Pastorals

"Bishop Claver is the gadfly of the Philippine Catholic hierarchy who persistently buzzes in the ears of President Fernando Marcos and all his toadies. The bishop's book is a collection of fighting pastoral letters to his congregation after martial law closed the diocesan radio station and newspaper." *Occasional Bulletin*

"His gutsy strength has made him a prophet against the repressive regime. Some of his U.S. colleagues could learn from him." *National Catholic Reporter*

ISBN 0-88344-471-2   *196pp. Paper $7.95*

COMBLIN, José

THE CHURCH AND THE NATIONAL SECURITY STATE

"The value of this book is two-fold. It leads the readers to discover the testimony of those Latin American Christians who are striving to be faithful to the gospel in the midst of a most difficult situation characterized by the militarization of society, the consequent suppression of public freedom, and violation of basic human rights. It also invites the readers from other cultural and historical contexts to seek in their own situations the inspiration for a real theology of their own." *Theology Today*

ISBN 0-88344-082-2   *256pp. Paper $8.95*

JESUS OF NAZARETH
Meditations on His Humanity

"This book is not just another pious portrait of Christ. Its deeply religious insights relate the work of Jesus as modern scholarship understands it to the ills of our contemporary world." *Review of Books and Religion*

ISBN 0-88344-239-6   *Paper $4.95*

THE MEANING OF MISSION
Jesus, Christians and the Wayfaring Church

"This is a thoughtful and thought-provoking book by a Belgian theologian and social critic, who has lived and taught in Latin America for 20 years. His rich background in evangelization, both in theory and in practice, is evident throughout his book." *Worldmission*

ISBN 0-88344-305-8   *Paper $4.95*

SENT FROM THE FATHER
Meditations on the Fourth Gospel

"In a disarmingly simple and straightforward way that mirrors the Fourth Gospel itself, Comblin leads the reader back to biblical basics and in doing so provides valuable insights for personal and community reflection on what it means to be a disciple of the Lord, to be 'sent' by him." *Sisters Today*

ISBN 0-88344-453-4   *123pp. Paper $3.95*

FABELLA, Virginia, M.M. & Sergio Torres

THE EMERGENT GOSPEL

Theology from the Underside of History

"*The Emergent Gospel*, I believe, is an expression of a powerful and barely noticed movement. It is the report of an ecumenical conference of 22 theologians from Africa, Asia and Latin America, along with one representative of black North America, who met in Dar es Salaam, Tanzania, in August 1976. Their objective was to chart a new course in theology, one that would reflect the view 'from the underside of history,' that is, from the perspective of the poor and marginalized peoples of the world. Precisely this massive shift in Christian consciousness is the key to the historical importance of the meeting. The majority of the essays were written by Africans, a smaller number by Asians and, surprisingly, only three by Latin Americans, who thus far have provided the leadership in theology from the developing world." *America*

ISBN 0-88344-112-8   *Cloth $12.95*

FENTON, Thomas P.

EDUCATION FOR JUSTICE: A RESOURCE MANUAL

"The completeness of the source material on the topic and the adaptability of the methodology—stressing experiential education—to groups at the high school, college, or adult levels make this manual a time and energy saving boon for most anyone having to work up a syllabus on 'justice.' This manual would be a worthwhile addition to any religion and/or social studies curriculum library." *Review for Religious*

"The resource volume is rich in ideas for a methodology of teaching Christian justice, and in identifying the problems. It is also very rich in the quality of the background readings provided. The participant's volume is a catchy workbook with many illustrations. It encourages the student (young or adult) to look at the problems as they are experienced by real live persons." *The Priest*

"Replete with background essays, tested group exercises, course outlines and annotated bibliography, this manual should give any teacher or seminar leader plenty of material to launch a thorough study program—and plenty of strongly stated positions for students to react to." *America*

ISBN 0-88344-154-3   *Resource Manual $7.95*

ISBN 0-88344-120-9   *Participant Workbook $3.95*

GUTIERREZ, Gustavo

A THEOLOGY OF LIBERATION

Selected by the reviewers of *Christian Century* as one of the twelve religious books published in the 1970s which "most deserve to survive."

"Rarely does one find such a happy fusion of gospel content and contemporary relevance." *The Lutheran Standard*

ISBN 0-88344-477-1   *Cloth $7.95*

ISBN 0-88344-478-X   *Paper $4.95*